Enactments

EDITED BY RICHARD SCHECHNER

To perform is to imagine, represent, live and enact present circumstances, past events and future possibilities. Performance takes place across a very broad range of venues from city streets to the countryside, in theatres and in offices, on battlefields and in hospital operating rooms. The genres of performance are many, from the arts to the myriad performances of everyday life, from courtrooms to legislative chambers, from theatres to wars to circuses.

ENACTMENTS will encompass performance in as many of its aspects and realities as there are authors able to write about them.

ENACTMENTS will include active scholarship, readable thought and engaged analysis across the broad spectrum of performance studies.

Enacting Pleasure

ARTISTS AND SCHOLARS RESPOND TO
CAROL GILLIGAN'S NEW MAP OF LOVE

EDITED BY

PEGGY COOPER DAVIS AND LIZZY COOPER DAVIS

LONDON NEW YORK CALCUTTA

Seagull Books 2011

Individual essays © with the authors
This compilation © Seagull Books 2011

ISBN-13 978 1 9064 9 769 9
ISSN   1751 0864

British Library Cataloguing-in-Publication Data
A catalogue record for this book is available from the British Library

Typeset by Seagull Books, Calcutta, India
Printed and bound by Hyam Enterprises, Calcutta, India

For Margarett and Gordon

with special thanks to Richard Schechner, Quan Trinh, Laura Lewis, Stephen Rechner and Jeremy Heilman

Contents

ODES TO PLEASURE

An Invocation

An Invocation

PEGGY COOPER DAVIS

> *Psyche reclined, the pains coming now at shorter intervals, Eros timing them . . . "Are you curious?" he asks her and then smiles: of course. He too. The physical labor a relief after the long psychic labor that has brought them to this place where she can see and say what she knows and he is no longer hiding his love. And now the final mystery unraveling: the face and shape of the child . . . Head coming first, torso following, shoulders turned, . . . beauty, yes, and dark like her mother and like her mother, a girl, a daughter, and seeing her, delighting in her they call her by the name Pleasure.*

Carol Gilligan (2002)

With these words, Carol Gilligan reimagines the culmination of an ancient tale. The tale is familiar, although it changes from telling to telling:

> Psyche is a mortal of uncommon beauty. Eros is the god of love, born of the god of gods and the goddess of beauty. Eros is persuaded by his jealous mother to see that Psyche remains isolated and unmarried. He does his mother's bidding, but falls in love with Psyche himself. At the direction of an oracle, Psyche's parents take her to a mountain top to be surrendered to a monster, for no man will have her. Psyche is swept away to a palace where she is treated as a goddess and coupled with a lover who visits her gently every night but forbids her to look at him. Months later, lonely and with child, Psyche persuades her lover to permit her a visit from her sisters. The sisters, seized by jealousy at the sight of Psyche's accommodations, remind Psyche that her lover is a monster and persuade her that she must kill him in order to save herself and her unborn child. During one of the lover's darkened visits, Psyche attempts the murderous deed. She looks at her lover in order to kill him. She sees who he is and loves him at once. Eros is startled awake and flies away, shaking Psyche loose as she tries to cling to him. Enraged to learn of Eros's love for Psyche, Eros's mother assigns Psyche a series of apparently mortal tasks, the last of which is to bring a box of beauty unopened

from the underworld. With the help of gods and creatures of the earth, Psyche completes each task, save the last: she is unable to resist opening the box from hell, and its contents put her into a deep sleep. Eros comes to Psyche's rescue and then persuades his father to make Psyche immortal and to make her his bride. A daughter is born to the couple, and they name her Pleasure (ibid., 13–15).

In Gilligan's telling, Psyche and Eros's reunion in the light of day stands as (and for) their psychic accomplishments: *she can see and say what she knows, and he is no longer hiding his love.* The result is Pleasure.

Like the child of Psyche and Eros, this book was conceived in acts of pleasure—in what theorists Wendy Brown and Janet Halley once described as "the pleasure of connection in intellectual and political work" (2002, 32). Pleasure is a natural byproduct and proper reward of meaningful critical exchange. So, we write in part to share with one another and to share with our readers the great pleasure of engaging a set of challenging and politically significant ideas about the human psyche. But pleasure is more than the mood of our labors. It is our subject. Each of our essays responds to Gilligan's *The Birth of Pleasure: A New Map of Love.*

Gilligan's text is ranging and complex. It follows an "associative" rather than a linear logic, and following another's associations can mystify as easily as it can satisfy. Basic things are nonetheless clear. To the extent that *The Birth of Pleasure* can be said to have a central claim, it is the claim that relational pleasure is natural and healthy to the human condition. But the work is more an exhortation than a message—an exhortation to resist the moral that Gilligan sees embedded in Sigmund Freud's Oedipal story of human psychological development. Oedipus was wounded so that he would not love his mother and blinded himself because he loved her nonetheless. His tale cautions us to remain detached so as to avoid love. It leads us to think of love as something dangerous, something we might cripple ourselves to avoid and blind ourselves in order not to see. Gilligan uses Psyche and Eros's tale to lure us out of mother-fearing detachment. She tells us that detachment leads to tragedy, and invites us to follow Psyche's rebellious example—to open our eyes and enact love's pleasures.

Gilligan's call is pertinent to romantic love, but it has a much broader sweep. It is a call to resist detachment in every dimension of our lives, from the personal to the public and political. In the most personal dimension, she challenges us to fall hope*fully* and pleasurably in love—to surrender our defenses as poets know that lovers do:

your slightest look will easily unclose me
though I have closed myself as fingers,
you open always petal by petal myself as Spring opens
(touching, skillfully, mysteriously) her first rose.

e. e. cummings (1996)

In the political dimension, Gilligan challenges us to construct cultures of relationship rather than cultures of detached control. To embrace a community-based politics in the spirit of the Obama political movement in the United States. To enter something akin to the new South Africa's constitutional commitment to "a democratic and open society" with a government "based on the will of the people" and committed to "improv[ing] the quality of life of all citizens and free[ing] the potential of each person" (South African Constitution Preamble, 1996).

Reading *The Birth of Pleasure* as invocation rather than dogma, we offer this collection of essays in response. Some of us quarrel or quibble with Gilligan; others take her insights and attempt to run with them. What unifies our contributions is an effort to respond seriously to Gilligan's request that we conquer a culturally embedded fear of love and give play to the pursuit of relational pleasure.

Pleasure in love is controversial, and some contributors to this volume question whether Gilligan is right to urge as unhesitatingly as she does that we pursue it. Resignation to the fatalism of Greek tragedy seems more prudent. Freud's Oedipal story brings order to a dangerous world. Restraint is admirable, and we have been taught to believe that restraint in the matter of mother-love will build a foundation for restraint in all things. Beyond this, as Toni Morrison said clearly when a group of us met to open our conversation about *The Birth of Pleasure*, the self-affirming relational pleasures of which Gilligan speaks manifestly include sexual pleasure. And we have much evidence—from the violence of ritual clitoridectomy and infibulation to the violence within some quarters of the antiabortion movement to the persistent vehemence of antifeminism and the vehement persistence of sexual double standards—that exuberant female sexuality is an intensely provocative idea.

It should also be said that Gilligan is nearly as controversial as her subject. Her decidedly qualitative research methods have often been criticized. Her practice of drawing conclusions about human psychology from classical and postcolonial literature has raised eyebrows across an ideological spectrum from skeptics that "truth" can be found in the frozen words of the classics, to skeptics that "truth" can be found in the agitated stories of colonial subjects. And her (very Freudian) "associative" method of analysis—mirrored in an associative presentation style—can unnerve us, living as we do in a culture that prizes linear logic and distrusts *psycho*logical reasoning.

But despite controversy, misgivings, and worries, Gilligan's invocation pulls at us.

We have been drawn to her work since 1982, when she shook the worlds of academic, clinical, and popular psychology by pointing out in her first book, *In a Different Voice: Psychological Theory and Women's Developement*, that regnant theories of human development were based almost exclusively on studies of male subjects. She made the simple, profound observation that we cannot write a story of human psychological development by interpreting studies of only men and boys. She made women and girls the subjects of her research, and, considering what she knew about men, women, boys, and girls, she began to retheorize human psychology. The result was not, as the popular press is wont to claim, the creation of "Difference Feminism" and all of the often silly ideas floating under its banner. The result was an emerging theory of relational psychology, so named not because women are relational and men are not, but because inclusion of women subjects in psychological research allowed us to see that humankind is a relational species and that relational health is central to our survival and emotional well-being.

We must confess that we are drawn, too, by the inherent appeal of Gilligan's subject. However dangerous it may sometimes seem, and however much we have learned to deny it, the pleasure of relationship is something we have known and something we crave. Gilligan draws on neuroscience, infant research in developmental psychology, and her own systematic observations of preschool boys and preadolescent girls to argue that human beings are "wired" to take delight in relationship. Making the point that relational pleasure is something that once came easily to all of us, she describes the openness and empathy with which little boys and preadolescent girls are able (in the absence of extreme trauma or deprivation) to face the world. We remember when kisses and laughter and tears were soft accents in a comfortable life-rhythm, and we are pulled.

We are drawn, too, by the familiarity of Gilligan's account of the pall of tragedy that the Oedipal story casts over heterosexual marriage. Gilligan's analysis builds on her earlier descriptions of the differently paced psychosocial development of boys and girls, as well as on her newer theories of relational pleasure, to paint a discouraging picture: the male partner, living in an Oedipal story, has marshaled tremendous psychic energy to become a "man" by separating from The Mother and the stereotypically feminine qualities that she represents. He has internalized The

Father's legislative voice and bends to The Father's prohibitions against being intimate with The Mother or emulating her "childish" relational exuberance.[1] His rejection of "feminine" or maternal qualities is so strong that in addition to keeping them at bay, he is inclined to demean and stand above them. Falling in love with a woman other than his mother has pulled him to an intimacy that may be only modestly compromised by his allegiance to the law of The Father. But as the marriage matures into patterns of nurture (be it feminine or, in more equalitarian marriages, mutual), or as the wife becomes an actual (as well as a symbolic) mother, associations with the forbidden Mother are likely to cause the man to recoil and to leave the relationship—in spirit if not in body.

The female partner living in an Oedipal story is apt to have a less conflicted response to relational intimacy, for, on Gilligan's account, she has not been discouraged from identification with The Mother, nor taught in early childhood to fear the relational comfort of the nursery. But by the end of adolescence her culture has taught her that relational values are demeaned outside the nursery. And she has learned that when she interacts with men—and, more generally, when she interacts in traditionally male social, political, or professional spheres—relational candor may be unwelcome. She has adapted by losing her voice. To maintain her ability to interact in the world, she has learned to forgo genuine relationship. She has become complicit; she does not require that people relate meaningfully to her, that they voice their own feelings, or that they give resonance to hers. Sensing how ferociously he clings to it, she protects her partner's pose of contented detachment.

We have seen or experienced the gnawing discontent behind these detached poses and complicit silences. We know what it is like to be socialized or to socialize a child to detachment and silence. Gilligan reminds us that Oedipus's tragedy began with a trauma: a frightened father and a complicit mother expelled the infant Oedipus from the nursery, staked his feet, and left him alone in the wilderness. She argues that we can avoid the tragedy by understanding and refusing to repeat the trauma. We think of our loved ones, and we are pulled to hope.

Perhaps most importantly, we are drawn by the social and political implications of *The Birth of Pleasure*. Gilligan is not the first to observe that making separation from The Mother the goal of psychosocial development leads to denigration of the stereotypically feminine qualities associated with mothering. But *The Birth of Pleasure* breaks new ground. We—antipatriarchs all—are struck by Gilligan's demonstration of the fit between the Oedipal story and patriarchy. She argues that if we accept as the story of human psychological development a family story in which the maternal is demeaned and maturity is achieved by internalizing the father's voice, we accept and naturalize patriarchy. For what is patriarchy but subordination of women and children to the law of the father? From this insight about hierarchy's arguably most insidious form, Gilligan begins to chart a map that leads to a more democratic understanding of the state, as well as a more harmonious understanding of community and family. She helps us to see that the legal systems we construct and the policies we adopt will depend importantly on whether we take a detached or a relational stance in our political and public lives. We consider the state of our polity, and we are pulled to a more relational conception of justice.

Our essays are gathered in seven sections. "The Psychobiology of Pleasure" takes up the neuroscience and infant research on which Gilligan relies and the emerging principles of evolutionary biology that also bear on her premise that we are hard-wired for relational pleasure. It also addresses the Freudian theories that Gilligan builds on as well as those she resists. Gilligan's often controversial research methods are taken up in "Methods for Recovering Pleasure." In "The Places to Find Pleasure," you will find critiques of Gilligan's uses of classical and postcolonial literature. In "The Form of Pleasure," you will find literary analyses of *The Birth of Pleasure*. In "The Politics of Pleasure," you will find responses to Gilligan's claim that the patriarchal command to flee relationship has political as well as personal consequences. "The Fear of Reckless Pleasure" takes up the aforementioned worries that the quest for pleasure is dangerously irresponsible. And "Odes to Pleasure" makes room for those who wanted simply to sing of resonances between *The Birth of Pleasure* and the struggles and joys of their own lives and work.

The authors of this collection come from different disciplines and with different mixes of enthusiasm and skepticism. We speak from a variety of political, cultural, artistic, and scientific perspectives. But we are all engaged by Gilligan's evolving work and are pleased to invite you into our conversation about it.

Note

1   The initial capitalization signifies that in the son's psyche the idea of the primary nurturing figure (usually, but not always, the mother) has taken on idealized qualities and significance. Similarly, initial capitalization of The Father signifies that in the son's psyche the rival for the primary caregiver's affection has taken on idealized qualities and significance.

References

BROWN, Wendy, and Janet Halley (eds). 2002. *Left Legalism/Left Critique*. Durham, NC: Duke University Press.

cummings, e.e. 1996. "somewhere i have never traveled, gladly beyond." In *The Norton Anthology of Poetry, 1285–86*. Edited by Margaret Ferguson, Mary Jo Salter, and Jon Stallworthy. 4th edn. New York: W. W. Norton.

GILLIGAN, Carol. 1982. *In a Different Voice: Psychological Theory and Women's Developement*. Cambridge, MA: Harvard University Press.

——. 2002. *The Birth of Pleasure: A New Map of Love*. New York: Alfred A. Knopf.

The Psychobiology of Pleasure

An infant losing postural control and turning to self-comforting behaviors in response to the mother being Still-faced.

In Carol Gilligan's view, we follow developmental paths and live out culturally engrained stories that lead us to avoid relationships. By her account, we settle for sham relationships, all the while pretending that they are natural and real. We then dissociate, masking any sense of loss. Edward Tronick's "Still Face" research confronts us with the feelings behind the masks. As the figure above illustrates, in the presence of mothers who are Still-faced and out of relationship, infants show signs of distress and retreat into self-comforting behaviors. Older children and adults experience comparable distress when they are out of relationship with those around them.

Tronick offers the open systems theory as a framework for understanding why the loss of relationship is stressful, and why weathering relationship brings vitality and pleasure.

Meaning-Making, Open Systems, and Pleasure
EDWARD TRONICK

Pleasure, creativity, and development are related in ways that have to do with how individuals make meaning. The relationship is explained by principles that govern the operation of open biological systems,[1] of which we humans are but one example. These principles teach us that as open, complex systems, we connect with one another in order to maximize our organizational complexity, coherence, integration, and flexibility. We thrive in the messiness of human connection. Without it, we wither.

To say the least, a systems perspective is distant from the myths and metaphors of Carol Gilligan's *The Birth of Pleasure: A New Map of Love* (2002), but I hope to show that this distance is bridgeable. And ultimately I hope to show that Gilligan's Psyche acts in the most human of ways: as a seeker of both complexity and pleasure who understands that striving for and creating the new requires risking the old.

Linking systems theory and pleasure requires finding concepts that relate principles governing the operations of *any* kind of biological system to the operation of *humans* as complex open systems. For me such a concept is provided in Jerome Bruner's beguilingly simple assertion that humans are *meaning-makers* (1990), a concept easily linked to the idea of self-definition in dynamic systems theories of development (Stengers and Prigogine 1997). Humans, when thought of as meaning-making open systems, utilize energy to create complexly organized, coherent, integrated, and flexible states of consciousness. States of consciousness are psycho-biological states that contain the private meanings that individuals give to their places in the world. In the language of systems theory, states of consciousness are attractor states. These states are organized moment by moment by the individual and function to organize and anticipate the future based on the immediate present and updated past—that is, to organize the whole individual's movement into the world. An individual's states of consciousness generate intentions and actions, as when a complex set of reactions to the presence of a bear causes me to flee (Tronick 2007).

Meanings, the elements of states of consciousness, may be in, or more likely, out of, awareness. In fact, meaning may come into awareness only when it is violated. Few of us walk around with an awareness of our belief in the existence of things until we confront a magician who makes those things disappear. Indeed, though typically out of awareness, a state of consciousness always has a quality of impelling certitude that the world *is* the way it is perceived and understood. An eight-month-old in one moment is absolutely certain that a hidden object is gone and, in the next moment, when the object is brought into view, is absolutely certain that it exists. The two certitudes do not fit together, but, in separate moments, each is impelling.

Open systems theory teaches us why relationship, interaction, and connection are, as Gilligan suggests, necessary to human thriving. One of the first principles of open systems is that systems that successfully gain energy become more complex and integrated. By contrast, systems that fail to gain sufficient energy lose complexity and coherence, dissipate, and move toward chaos and death. Organisms, human or otherwise, are always engaged in a struggle against chaos, and thus in a struggle to gain energy.

But the term "energy" is too generic for humans. All systems struggle, not for just any form of energy, but for the particular forms of energy that they can utilize to increase their complexity. The food prey eat to provide energy for growth is not an appropriate energy form for predators that eat them, though once it is formed in the body of the prey, it can be utilized by predators for growth. The human struggle is for energy in many forms, but, most critically, it is for energy in the form of meaning. States of consciousness are generated by an embodied human mind as the world of things and people stimulates private meaning-making.

One of the most robust ways of expanding the complexity of an individual's state of consciousness is to create what I call a "dyadic state" of consciousness. Like psychologist Lev S. Vygotsky's zone of proximal development, these are social states (1978, 86).[2] They are the joint creations of two or more embodied minds bringing elements from each of their separate states into a shared dyadic state. As participants in this dyadic state, individuals appropriate new elements into their own state of consciousness, and as a consequence the complexity of each individual's state of consciousness grows.

Paradoxically, though systems principles suggest that organisms strive to maximize the coherence of their sense of the world, the dynamic social states that human beings seek to nourish their existence are always unpredictable and messy, and they may be contradictory and incoherent. This messiness is inherent to the process of meaning-making because there are many kinds of meanings to be integrated, limitations in the capacity of meaning-making systems, and many kinds of meaning-making processes (including affective, cognitive, memorial, linguistic, bodily, and psychodynamic processes). Nonetheless, the messiness of meanings is the ooze from which new meanings are created. Were states of consciousness fixed, nothing new could have been created, and complexity could not have been increased. An implication is that humans are more inclined to making meaning with each other, as opposed to things or events, because the meanings made between people are always messier. Dyadic states of consciousness are joint creations and, as such, bring together the messy, unpredictable, and inchoate features of each individual's state of consciousness. By contrast, individual states of consciousness are likely to be predictable and simple, such that while new meanings may be created, the process is one of diminishing returns. Thus, making meaning with others presents a greater possibility of the emergence of new meanings.

The effects of being restricted to solitary meaning-making are seen in the developmental deficits of the attention-starved infants in orphanages who were described by René A. Spitz as "failing to thrive" (Spitz and Cobliner 1965, 267–84). These infants were in an extremely pathological state in which there was a reduction of their attempts to act on and make sense of the world. Such a failure is a failure to fulfill the basic systems principle. It has often been noted that there is a resemblance of these deprived infants to infant monkeys raised on surrogates. It is easy to imagine how compromising food intake would lead to "malnourished" behavior, body, and brain. But in many cases we know that the nutrition and other "necessities" were adequate. The general consensus is that the absent "necessity" for these children was social stimulation. But stimulation is too dispassionate and too general a term. Stimulation could be anything of the physical or social world. So what were they really deprived of?

I believe these children were deprived of meaning-making. They were unable to form dyadic states of consciousness with others. The Spitzian infants were open human systems who, deprived of meaning-making, could neither increase the complexity of their states of consciousness nor maintain their existing complexity. They were failed open systems. When these infants are viewed as the little experiencing systems that they in fact were, we can see that they were incapable of making meaning as they had lost their capacity to engage with others or even with the world of things. Their self-organizing and dyadic capacities were so stunted that they could not make coherent sense of their place in the world. Perhaps more accurately, and even more insidiously, their impelling certitude was that they had no place in the world.

To further explore meaning-making, I have created an experiment to disrupt meaning-making in infants, children, and adults: the face-to-face Still-Face Paradigm. The Still Face precludes a dyadic state of consciousness.

As a result, individuals confronted with a Still Face suffer a lack of energy and complexity such that their state of consciousness dissipates (Adamson and Frick 2003; Tronick et al. 1978, 1–13). With young infants, we ask the mother to "freeze" while *en face* with her infant—to hold a Still Face and refrain from talking or gesturing. The (in)action of the Still-Faced mother precludes the formation of a dyadic state of consciousness because there is no exchange of meaningful affect and action with the infant—no creation of meaning. The infants are forced to make meaning with their own self-organizing abilities, and though they can do this for a while, their self-organizing abilities are limited and quickly fail. Initially, in response to the Still Face, infants act to reinstate their exchange of meaning by smiling at and gesturing to their mothers. But with the mother's continued lack of response, the infants disengage, look away, become sad, and engage in self-organized regulatory behaviors such as thumb-sucking in order to maintain their coherence and complexity and to avoid dissipation of the complexity of their state of consciousness.

The figure at the beginning of this chapter shows an infant during the Still Face who literally loses postural control, turns away, has a sad facial expression, and comforts himself with his hands in his mouth. What we see is a failed attempt to make meaning and a collapse of a whole set of systems including motor systems, attention systems, and self-regulatory maintenance systems. Though we cannot directly know the impelling certitudes of which an infant is capable in the face of the Still-Faced mother, it must be something similar to, "This is threatening," or perhaps "I no longer exist." As the Still Face continues, the infant's state of consciousness is likely to change to something like, "I must try to hold myself together." If these or similar interpretations seem doubtful, simply consider that the infant could apprehend the Still-Faced mother in other ways—as boring, playful, or novel—all of which we have found to result in reactions (e.g., lethargy, responsive play, or surprise) that are *not* seen during the Still Face. For the infant in the Still Face, there is meaning and certitude made by and expressed in his or her posture, actions, and affects, but the meaning is one that precludes gaining complexity.

More recent work with young children and adults makes it even clearer that what we are seeing with the Still Face is a failure to create meanings and form dyadic states of consciousness. In my laboratory we have developed a procedure for using the Still Face with children eight to fifty-four months of age (Weinberg 2002). In the first episode of this procedure, the child and the adult are seated on the floor and play with toys. This episode is followed by a Still-Face episode in which the mother "freezes" and does not respond to the infant. In the third episode, the mother resumes her normal play. The findings are as striking as our original Still-Face findings with infants. Young children respond to the maternal Still Face with heightened negative affect, expressions of confusion, and demands for change. Toddlers ask, "Why don't you talk to me?" or command, "Talk to me!" while simultaneously soliciting the mother's interactive behavior (e.g., pointing at her eyes, tapping or *almost* hitting the mother, making more and more urgent demands). In the end they may distance themselves from her and even appear to be in an internally focused engagement with their own thoughts about what to make of what is going on.

Importantly, and in keeping with their greater meaning-making capacities compared to infants, toddlers attribute states of mind to the mother (e.g., "Are you sleeping? Wake up!" or "Don't be afraid of the [toy] alligator!"). There is meaning in their words, in their affect, and in their actions that reflects their capacities for pretend play, cognition, language, mentalization, and complex affects—capacities not available to infants. Their impelling certitude is one of fearfulness and confusion at the break in connection. But the need for making sense of the world is so great that when play is resumed, some of the toddlers ask questions that attempt to make coherent sense of what happened with the mother (e.g., "Why didn't you talk to me?"), even though it brings back the painfulness of the experience.

Extending the Still-Face research to adults, one of my research assistants, Lisa Bohne, interviewed college students after they participated in an experimental role play. In this procedure, one student role-played as an unresponsive mother, and the other simulated being "in the mind of an infant." The "infant-persons" reported feeling anxious, vulnerable, angry, frustrated, sad, afraid, confused, and even "panicky." The Still-Faced "mother-persons" reported feeling guilty, distressed, anxious, depressed, ashamed, vulnerable, and confused. One reported, "It felt terrible to be so closed off from the infant. It made me feel depressed, and I'm sure the 'infant' did too after our interaction." Preventing an exchange of meanings and the formation of a dyadic state of consciousness disorganized each adult's own state of consciousness and generated a fearful, confused, and less coherent sense of the world. Importantly, these adults did not try to step away from their negative experience but, in more sophisticated ways than the toddlers, continued after the procedure to try to make coherent sense of what they had experienced. They talked with each other about their experience, and some of them apologized for what they had done.

The Still-Face experiments serve as a contrast to what happens during normal social engagement when meaning-making is successful. The contrast is needed because, like water of which the fish is unaware, meaning-making is for us an ongoing and continuous process of self- or co-creation. Self-organized meaning-making can be observed in the smile of the infant grabbing hold of an object that had been out of reach, in the exuberance of the newly walking toddler moving upright into the world, or in the announcement, "I did it!" by the five-year-old putting a last puzzle piece in place. There are also the "I did its" that continue throughout life when finally the sense of something is made. The *co*-creation of meaning is seen in the mutual smiling and cooing of mother and infant in face-to-face interactions. Their exchange is an example of a dyadic state of consciousness in which there is a mutual creation of new meanings. Other examples are the pretend play of the toddler with another person and the all-night conversations of adolescents. Social referencing (such as looking at other's reactions to an event to understand one's own reaction) by infants, children, and adults is a way of gaining meaning that leads to new and impelling certitude (Fonagy and Target 1998, 87–114).

What, then, is the link between open systems theory, meaning-making, and pleasure? After all, other species make meaning in the world and are also governed by first principles of systems theory. But what do humans exclusively do, or at least do more of compared to other species, that makes pleasure a consequence of their meaning-making as open systems? Humans, like other biological systems, strive to utilize energy to expand the complexity of their states of consciousness. However, I believe that humans always implicitly and sometimes explicitly have an *experience* of the extent to which their meaning-making fulfills systems principles. When humans are seen as *experiencing* meaning-making systems, the systems phenomenon of the dissipation or of the increase of complexity of their systems has powerful *experiential* consequences.

Dissipation, or losing of complexity, is a quality of systems. In humans it is a failure to make meaning that reduces the complexity of the individual's state of consciousness, and it has experiential consequences. When it occurs, the individual experiences shrinkage, anxiety, loss of self, and fear of annihilation. One's sense of self in the world begins to come apart. Spitz's infants were chronically deprived of the possibility of making meaning, and every level of their systems failed to grow and expand. Their experience was one of apathy, fearfulness, and sadness. This experiential state further amplifies their failure to make meaning. Infants, children, and adults, when confronted with a non-meaning-making partner in the Still Face, initially experience disappointment and confusion but eventually experience anger, sadness, and withdrawal. They also feel helpless and panicky in the face of the threat they experience to their ongoing self-organization. Although it is noteworthy that in the adult Still-Face study these experiential effects occurred in *role-playing* adults who knew that the situation was set up and unreal, nonetheless the effects were powerful because the experiment tapped into a basic primordial experience of failing to make a connection and experiencing a dissipation of self-organization. In these situations pleasure is not possible.

An increase in the complexity of a system also has experiential consequences for humans. When new meanings are self-created or co-created, the individual experiences an expansion of her own state of consciousness, a feeling of being bigger, and a connectedness to the action, idea, or person on which or with whom the new meaning was made. When creating new meanings, individuals—infants, children, adults—grow in every possible way and experience joy, interest, curiosity, and exuberance. Ultimately, I believe there is an embodied primordial experience of fulfilling a basic, life-governing principle: the success of making sense of one's place in the world and becoming more complexly organized. Often this feeling of wholeness, completeness, safety, and exuberance is out of awareness. Occasionally it is in awareness, and when it is, it is special indeed. But whether in or out of awareness, it is the experience of a deep, abiding pleasure.

Humans as meaning-makers have no option but to strive to increase the complexity of their states of consciousness. Were we to stop, we would dissipate and experience the terror of annihilation. Successfully creating new meanings increases our complexity and brings pleasure. However, it is not as simple as either success or failure, because striving to create something new requires taking apart something old. Taking apart the old organization to create something new reduces complexity in the short run, and the reduction is experienced as anxiety. This anxiety is increased because of the knowledge that there is no guarantee of ultimate success in the creation of new meaning. An apparent way to prevent the anxiety is to remain fixed and to not change, but, of course, such fixedness precludes the pleasure of expansion and the fulfillment of systems principles. Thus, the dilemma of striving to be a system that grows in complexity while risking dissolution is either to experience pleasure tinged with terror or to not strive to grow and ever experience pleasure. Healthy humans choose pleasure and terror.

Psyche has all the pleasure one could imagine, yet she chooses to look at Cupid because she *must* strive for the deep pleasure of expanding her knowledge of him and her relation to him, even at the risk of dissolution of the complexity she has already achieved. It is something she must do to be human. Her greatest pleasure comes when she dissolves the old and expands her state of consciousness. Thus, the myth captures the momentous and the everyday nature of meaning-making, the experience of pleasure, and, yes, even embedded systems principles. To create the new is to risk the old for the possibility of a greater pleasure, but not to create the new is surely to perish.

Notes

1   By "open systems" I mean entities that are perturbable or responsive to external entities.

2   The zone of proximal development is the space between a person's actual level of development and the level that person can achieve while working to solve problems with more capable guidance or collaboration.

References

ADAMSON, Lauren B., and Janet E. Frick. 2003. "Research with the Face-to-Face Still-Face Paradigm: A Review." *Infancy* 4: 451–73.

BRUNER, Jerome. 1990. *Acts of Meaning*. Cambridge, MA: Harvard University Press.

FONAGY, Peter, and Mary Target. 1998. "Mentalization and the Changing Aims of Psychoanalysis." *Psychological Dialogues* 8: 87–114.

GILLIGAN, Carol. 2002. *The Birth of Pleasure: A New Map of Love*. New York: Alfred A. Knopf.

SPITZ, René A., and W. Godfrey Cobliner. 1965. "Emotional Deficiency Diseases of the Infant." In René A. Spitz (ed.), *The First Year of Life: A Psychoanalytic Study of Normal and Deviant Development of Object Relations*. New York: International Universities Press, pp. 267–84.

STENGERS, Isabelle, and Ilya Prigogine. 1997. *The End of Certainty*. New York: Simon & Schuster.

TRONICK, Edward. 2007. *The Neurobehavioural and Social-Emotional Development of Infants and Children*. New York: W. W. Norton.

———, Heidelise Als, Lauren Adamson, Susan Wise, and Thomas Berry Brazelton. 1978. "The Infant's Response to Entrapment Between Contradictory Messages in Face-to-Face Interaction." *Journal of the American Academy of Child and Adolescent Psychiatry* 17: 1–13.

VYGOTSKY, Lev S. 1978. *Mind in Society: The Development of Higher Psychological Processes*. Cambridge, MA: President and Fellows of Harvard College.

WEINBERG, Katherine. 2002. "Preschoolers' Reaction to their Still-Faced Mother." Presentation at the International Conference on Infant Studies, Toronto, Canada, April.

Michael Tomasello's studies of the human gaze and of human pointing gestures provide some support for the notion that we are, as Carol Gilligan argues, "wired" for the pleasure of relationship. Our eyes are uniquely designed to facilitate nuanced intersubjective communication, and our uses of pointing reveal a unique consciousness of, and capacity for, intersubjectivity. Tomasello does not explore the subjects of pleasure and love. He sees our intersubjectivity as the thing that makes us capable of complex acts of collaboration, whether the collaborative aim is benevolent or hostile. But the collaborative and communicative capacities that he describes are exquisite. It is a short step to the conclusion that the exercise of these adaptive capacities brings pleasure, and not too great a leap to the hope that they facilitate love.

The Evolution of Cooperation
MICHAEL TOMASELLO

The Birth of Pleasure: *A New Map of Love* (2002) embodies a theory of human psychology grounded in the belief that the human species is specially and intensely relational. Carol Gilligan argues that we go against our nature when we accept uncritically the notion that separation is a central goal of human maturation. She asks us to question whether it is more in keeping with our nature to regard relational pleasure, rather than Oedipal anxiety, as the natural driver of psychosocial development. My research does not answer these developmental and psychoanalytic questions directly. It does, however, support the view that the human species has evolved and thrived because of special relational capacities. My colleagues and I have shown that the human species has a unique capacity for establishing the shared motivations and common mental ground that make complex acts of cooperation possible. This is revealed in studies of the seemingly mundane but deeply significant acts of following a gaze and pointing. These acts are cognitively and relationally significant because each requires an impressive feat of "mind reading." To follow a gaze is to track another's shifts in attention, and to communicate through pointing requires deciphering (or plotting) indirect signals that can only be made meaningful in a cooperative search for shared mental states.

THE COOPERATIVE EYE: TRACKING ATTENTION

Colonel William Prescott is said to have prepared his troops for a charge from the British Army at the Battle of Bunker Hill by telling them, "Don't one of you fire until you see the whites of their eyes." If the opposing army had not been British men but rather a horde of charging chimpanzees, the American troops would have been summarily overrun. Why? Because neither the chimpanzee nor any of the other two hundred and twenty species of non-human primates has whites of the eyes that can be easily seen. This means that we cannot track their gaze. If their eyes are looking in a direction other than the one in which their heads are pointing, we can easily be fooled about what they are looking at.

Human beings are very different. We can't fool anyone. The whites of our eyes are several times larger than those of other primates; this makes it much easier to see where the eyes, as opposed to the head, are pointed. Trying to explain this trait leads us into one of the deepest and most controversial topics in the modern study of human evolution: the evolution of cooperation.

The idea is simple. Knowing what another person is looking at provides valuable information about what she is thinking and feeling and what she might do next. Even young children know that when a person is looking at one toy and not another, she most likely prefers that toy and may reach for it. Professional poker players are often so worried about others reading their minds by reading their eyes that they wear sunglasses.

Evolutionarily, it is easy to see why it is to your advantage to be able to tell with maximum certainty where I am looking. You may use this information to detect food that you wouldn't otherwise have seen or to detect the dominant male that is approaching in a fight. But evolution cannot select the color of my eyes based on advantages to you. Evolutionary theory tells us that, in general, the only individuals who exist are those whose ancestors' actions were beneficial to *their own* survival and reproduction. If I have eyes whose direction is especially easy to follow, it must be of some advantage *to me*. If I am, in effect, advertising the direction of my eyes, I must be in a social environment full of others who are not often inclined to take advantage of this to my detriment by, say, beating me to food or escaping aggression before me. Indeed, I must be in a cooperative social environment in which others' following the direction of my eyes somehow benefits me.

Of course, it is possible that having large whites of the eyes serves some other purpose, like enabling me to advertise my good health to potential mates. But such an advantage would apply to other primates as well. Cooperation, on the other hand, singles out humans, as humans coordinate activities to do such things as construct buildings, create social institutions, and even, paradoxically, organize armies for war.

In a recent experiment, our research team has shown that even infants—at around their first birthdays, before language acquisition—tend to follow the direction of another person's eyes and not their heads. Thus, when an adult looked toward the ceiling with her eyes, head remaining straight, infants looked toward the ceiling in turn. However, when the adult closed her eyes and pointed her head toward the ceiling, infants did not very often follow.

Our nearest primate relatives, the African great apes (chimpanzees, bonobos, and gorillas) showed precisely the opposite pattern of gaze following. When the human pointed her eyes only toward the ceiling (head remaining straight ahead), they followed the gaze only rarely. But when she closed her eyes and pointed her head toward the ceiling, they followed much more often. It has been repeatedly demonstrated that all great apes, including humans, follow the direction of others' gazes. But in previous studies, the head and eyes were always pointed in the same direction. Only when we made the head and eyes point in different directions did we find a difference across species: humans are sensitive to the direction of the eyes specifically in a way that our nearest primate relatives are not.

Why might it have been advantageous for some early humans to advertise their eye direction in a way that enabled others to easily determine what they were looking at? One possible answer, what we have referred to as the "cooperative eye hypothesis," is that eyes that were especially visible made it easier to coordinate close-range collaborative activities in which discerning where the other was looking and perhaps what she was planning benefited both participants. When we were gathering berries to share, with one of us pulling down a branch and the other harvesting the fruit, it would have been useful, especially before language evolved, for us to coordinate our activities and communicate our plans by using our eyes and perhaps other visually based, prelinguistic gestures. The prelinguistic gesture of pointing would have been equally useful to early humans in a process such as gathering and harvesting fruit, and as we will see, it depends in its human form on a magnificent set of cooperative traits.

THE COOPERATIVE GESTURE: SHARING KNOWLEDGE AND INTENTION

Although there may be some variations of form (for example, in some cultures the norm is lip- or chin-pointing rather than finger-pointing), the basic interpersonal function of gesturing to direct someone's attention to something is very likely a human universal (Kita 2003). Pointing is functionally a special gesture in that directing someone's attention to something does not convey a specific meaning in the manner of most conventionalized, symbolic gestures. Rather, pointing can convey an almost infinite variety of meanings by saying, in effect, "If you look over there, you'll see what I mean." Suppose, for example, that we are walking down the street and I point to a bicycle. Am I pointing at the whole bicycle? Or the special kind of polyvinyl seat? Or the color? Or the metal material it is made of? The possibilities are limitless, and they demonstrate, perhaps surprisingly, that the pointing gesture can actually indicate radically different perspectives on one and the same perceptual situation. Pointing simply directs someone's attention to a location in the perceptual environment, but to correctly identify the intended referent requires that the communicator and the recipient *know together* that the indicated location is in some way relevant to some larger context they share. I will call this larger context "common ground"[1] or, sometimes, when I wish to emphasize the shared perceptual context, the "joint attentional frame."

To fashion a communicative pointing gesture or to recover its intended meaning is therefore an impressive feat of intersubjectivity. The communicating gesturer is asking the recipient to pay attention to something that they know together—to some common ground—in order to figure out what the communicator means. To expand my initial definition of the pointing gesture, it says, "If you look over there, you will see, as a result of knowledge that we share, what I mean." The recipient on the other side is required to recognize the request to attend to an object, to assume the common ground of something about this object that the recipient and the communicator know together, to cooperate by trying to figure out what the common ground is, and to cooperate further by trying to figure out what the communicator wants the recipient to do or learn or feel. To illustrate, suppose that you have been thinking about getting some special tires for your bicycle, but you did not discuss this with anyone, and the bicycle I am pointing to has tires of just this type. When I point to the bicycle, therefore, you will probably say to yourself something like, "He's pointing to a bicycle with just the kind of tires I need, but there is no way he can know this. So he must be pointing to something else." For you to interpret my point as indicating the tires, we must both know together that I have divined your need (Clark and Marshall 1981, 10–63).

The bicycle-tire illustration reveals another important feature of human pointing: it can go beyond indicating a referent to enable the recipient to feel or know or do something. In the illustration, the pointer may want to share the emotion of seeing the sought-after tires, or she may want the recipient to know that the owner of the bicycle can tell him where to find the tires, or she may be directing the recipient to go and ask the bicycle-owner where the tires can be bought. The definition of the pointing act should, then, be expanded further: "If you look over there, you will see, as a result of knowledge that we share, what I mean for you to feel or know or do."

The ability to "know together" creates an extraordinary intersubjective bond out of which we humans seem to have developed both an ability to cooperate and the trait of assuming—within limits, of course—that cooperation will be mutual. This assumption of mutual cooperation allows us to go beyond *knowing* together to *working* together, both in the communicative processes of referencing and deciphering the implications of common mental ground (Grice 1975, 41–48) and in carrying out the coordinated tasks that complex communication makes possible. Recent research with infants and other primates indicates that this capacity for cooperation is inherently and uniquely human. When, starting at the end of their first year, infants acquire the cognitive capacity to appreciate human intentions, to recognize the human phenomena of paying and sharing attention, and to have the motivation to cooperate or help, they begin to point communicatively (Tomasello et al. 2005, 675). The physical ability to make the finger-pointing gesture comes earlier, emerging reliably in infants as young as three months of age (Hannan and Fogel 1987, 187). However, as far as anyone can tell, infants at this age are not using this hand shape for any communicative function. Figuring out when infant pointing becomes communicative has been a tricky research challenge. It has been accomplished in experiments designed to isolate what I have now elaborated as the features of communicative pointing—the ingredients of an action that says, "If you look over there, you'll see [as a result of knowledge that we have in common] what I mean [for you to feel or know or do]."

"Look over There"—Referencing

The direction to *look over there* can be described more precisely as "intentional referencing"—as deliberately directing the recipient's attention to a particular object. Are infants able, after the age of twelve months, to give this kind of deliberate direction? It is clear that they understand how to respond to such a direction. For example, in the pre-established context of a hiding–finding game, an adult hid a toy in one of two buckets and then, subsequently, pointed to the toy's hiding place to help each child find it. Infants followed the direction in which the adult was pointing and also made the inference that she intended for them to attend to the bucket as location, as this was what was relevant to their joint activity in the hiding–finding game. Crucially for current purposes, in a control condition the adult held her hand in a pointing gesture toward the correct bucket (just as before) but while distractedly inspecting her wrist so that even though her actions resembled referential pointing, it was clear from her overall demeanor that she was engrossed in a completely different activity. In this case, infants did not find the hidden toy, presumably because they did not see the adult's behavior (including her protruding finger) as an intentional act of attention directing, or referring, within the context of some larger joint attentional frame or common ground. The same pattern of results was found for communicative versus distracted gazing at the correct bucket, showing that children did not ignore the adult's pointing gesture in the control condition above simply because she was not looking at the bucket (Behne et al. 2005, 492).

But are infants capable of their own acts of referencing? Or is it the case, as some have argued (Moore and Corkum 1994, 349), that infants who make pointing gestures do so only to call attention to themselves? We have designed studies to answer these questions. Pointing was elicited from infants by calling their attention to an event or object that was unseen by the adult with whom they were interacting—for instance, with objects such as puppets either suddenly appearing or engaging in interesting actions from afar. The adult's reaction was experimentally manipulated, and the infant's response to this reaction was observed. The main finding with respect to reference (more on this study with respect to   motivation below) was that when the adult responded to the infant's pointing gesture by simply and directly emoting to the infant but ignoring the referent, infants showed signs of dissatisfaction by repeating their gesture in an attempt at message repair, and they pointed less often over trials, again indicating dissatisfaction with the adult's response that ignored the intended referent (Liszkowski et al. 2004, 297). Even more directly, using the same basic methodology, we had the adult either correctly identify the infant's intended referent or otherwise misidentify it by alighting on a different object nearby (in both cases with positively expressed emotion and gaze alternation). When the adult correctly identified the intended referent, infants simply continued sharing attention and interest with her, but when the adult alighted on the incorrect referent, infants repeated their pointing gesture toward the intended referent in an attempt to redirect the adult's gaze (Tomasello et al. 2007, 705).

"Knowledge That We Have in Common"—Common Ground

The critical role of common ground or joint attention in infants' comprehension of communicative acts is illustrated in two sets of experiments. In the first set, we tested infants' reactions to the possibility of adding a new object to the mental world they shared with an adult. Twelve-month-old infants engaged with the adult in joint attentional interactions with each of two objects. The adult then left the room while the infant played with a third object with an assistant. When the adult returned and gestured ambiguously in the direction of all three objects, grouped together, and excitedly said to the infant, "Wow! Cool! Can you give that to me?" infants gave her the one that they had not shared with her previously during joint attention, thus illustrating their differentiation of objects previously shared and previously not shared with that adult (Tomasello and Haberl 2003, 906). Merely observing while the adult inspected the first two objects on her own was not sufficient for fourteen-month-old infants to know that she had experienced them; the sharing of attention to the objects was critical (Moll and Tomasello 2007, 309). These studies demonstrate that infants as young as twelve to fourteen months of age identify the referent of an ambiguous gesture in terms of some shared experiences they have previously had with the gesturing adult.

In a second set of studies, we focused more directly on how infants' responses to pointing are affected by the common ground they have with the pointer. In this study, eighteen-month-old infants and an adult cleaned up together by picking up toys and putting them in a basket. At one point the adult stopped and pointed to a target toy, which infants then picked up and placed in the basket. However, when the adult pointed to this same toy in the same way but in a different context, infants reacted differently: when the infants and adult were engaged in stacking rings on a post, the infants ignored the basket and brought the target toy back to stack on the post. The crucial point is that in both conditions the adult pointed to the same toy in the same way, but the infant extracted a different meaning in the two cases based on the two different joint attentional frames involved. And the "jointness" of the attentional frame is again a crucial component. Thus, in a control condition, the infant and adult cleaned up exactly as in the shared cleanup condition, but then a second adult who had not shared this context entered the room and pointed toward the target toy in the same way as the first adult in the first condition. In this case infants did not put the toy into the basket, presumably because the second adult had not shared the cleanup context with them. Rather, because they had no shared frame with this adult, they seemed most often to interpret the new adult's point as a simple invitation to notice and share attention to the toy. This was confirmed by having the two adults each play a different game with infants, in which case they interpreted each adult's pointing gestures as relevant to the particular game they had previously shared with that particular adult (Liebal et al. 2009, 264). This set of studies shows quite clearly that infants' interpretations of an adult's pointing gesture depend on their recently shared experience with that specific adult.

Although infants are able to use the concept of common ground, their grasp of the concept seems not to be as subtle as that of older children and adults. More precisely, they seem not to be able to manipulate the idea of knowing together, either in comprehending or in producing points. The manipulative phenomena that require us to posit deep understanding of the concept of common ground for older children and adults include, most conspicuously, hidden authorship and concealment—for instance, such acts as placing one's empty wine glass for the host to see (and fill), without revealing that this is what one has done. Adults engage in this kind of hidden authorship quite often in cases involving politeness or other forms of concealment, whereas one- and two-year-olds seemingly do not engage in this behavior at all.

However, it is possible that infants operate with a primordial understanding that contains the basic structure but not all of the adult details. There are several lines of evidence for this. First, from around their first birthday, infants clearly produce communicative acts "for" another person (or understand such acts as "for" them), as they make sure that they have the attention of the other, that they direct the act to them, that they make eye contact, and so forth (Csibra 2003, 447).[2] Second, when, in our hidden toy experiments, the adult in the control condition directed her extended index finger to one of the buckets as she distractedly examined her wrist, fourteen-month-old infants did not see this as a communicative act "for" them, and so they did not make the appropriate relevance inference (i.e., they did not see it as informing them of the location of the hidden toy, as in the experimental condition in which the adult pointed to the bucket "for" them). Third, we and other researchers have found that infants sometimes point even though the adult is already attending to the target referent, a behavior which could be interpreted not only as infants wanting the adult to attend to the object but also as an act of deliberate communication about the object (Moore and D'Entremont 2001). Finally, it has been found that children at thirty months of age correct adult misunderstandings, even when they (by accident) get the object they wanted, suggesting that they had both the goal of getting the object and the goal of communicating successfully with the adult (Markman and Shwe 1997, 630).

"I MEAN FOR YOU TO FEEL, KNOW, OR DO SOMETHING"—MOTIVE

The cleaning-up and stacking studies are relevant not only to infants' comprehension of the concept of common mental ground but also to their understanding that pointing has the motive of getting the recipient *to feel or know or do something*. The infants in these studies did not just recognize that they shared a game or a clean-up activity with the person pointing; they also understood that in the context of that activity the adult was pointing in order to get the infant to do something—to clean up in the cleaning-up context and to stack in the toy-stacking context. But do infants themselves point with the motive of getting the recipient to feel or know or do something?

We tested this by manipulating the adult's reaction to infants who pointed to puppets. The adult reacted to the infant's pointing gesture by:

(a) emoting positively toward the infant without looking at the puppet (Face condition),

(b) looking toward the puppet without looking at the infant (Event condition),

(c) doing nothing (Ignore condition), or

(d) alternating gaze between the infant and the puppet while emoting positively (Joint Attention condition).

Infants' reactions to these conditions were then noted in an attempt to establish the infants' motive for pointing. Results showed that when the adult simply expressed positive emotions to the infant while ignoring the indicated referent (Face condition), or when the adult simply looked to the indicated referent while ignoring the child (Event condition), infants were not satisfied. In comparison with the Joint Attention condition in which infants typically pointed for a long time, infants in these conditions (as well as in the Ignore condition) tended to repeat their pointing gesture more often within trials, apparently as persistent attempts to establish shared attention and interest. Moreover, infants in these conditions (as well as in the Ignore condition) pointed less often across trials than in the Joint Attention condition, apparently indicating growing dissatisfaction with the particular adult as a communicative partner since she did not respond by sharing the infants' attitude to the referent (Liszkowski et al. 2004, 297). Even more directly, using the same basic design, we had the adult correctly identify the infant's intended referent, but in different conditions the adult either expressed interest ("Cool!") or expressed disinterest ("Uh . . .") in the referent. When the adult expressed disinterest, infants did not prolong or repeat their pointing gesture within and across trials, presumably because they understood that the adult did not share their enthusiasm, as compared to trials when the adult expressed interest (ibid.). These results specifically isolate the infants' motive to get an adult to notice something and to share a feeling about it.

The puppet experiments involved expressive infant-pointing in which the motive was to share information and excitement about it. Infant-pointing has also been studied in contexts in which the motive for the gesture was an altruistic sharing of information. To have this motive, infants must have, first, an understanding that others can be knowledgeable or ignorant and, second, an altruistic motive to help others by supplying them with needed or desirable information. In order to test whether twelve-month-old infants point with such a motive, we placed them in various situations in which they observed an adult misplace an object or lose track of it in some way and then start searching. In these situations infants pointed to the needed object (more often than to distractor objects that were misplaced in the same way but were not needed by the adult), and in doing this they showed no signs of wanting the object for themselves (no whining, reaching, etc.) or of wanting to share emotions or attitudes about it (Liszkowski et al. 2006, 173). In a follow-up study, we presented infants once again with an adult searching, but in this case the two conditions differed only in whether the experimenter had seen the objects in their current location or not (one of them he had placed aside, whereas the other had fallen away unnoticed). In this case again, infants pointed more often to the object the adult had not seen in its current location (and they showed no signs of wanting the object or wanting to share emotions about it) (Liszkowski et al. 2009). These results suggest that infants sometimes point to achieve something other than sharing their excitement about a referent; they sometimes simply want to help the recipient by providing needed or desirable information.

We have seen that human infants point in order to get others to share their excitement about things. And we have seen that infants sometimes point altruistically to help a recipient in need of information. The most simple and perhaps most common form of infant-pointing has the motive of getting the recipient to do things for the infant, as when an infant points to a toy or a bottle that she wants. But it seems that infants sometimes point with the motive of getting the recipient to do something cooperatively. One indirect piece of evidence is that infants point to get recipients to feel things and to know things as early as they point to get recipients to do things for them (Carpenter et al. 1998). More directly—although the evidence is only for somewhat older children at thirty months of age—when young children request something from an adult, and the adult misunderstands them, but then, by luck, they get what they want anyway, they still attempt to correct the misunderstanding (Markman and Shwe 1997). This suggests that fairly early in their development, children understand that pointing works not by magically eliciting the desired response from the recipient but rather by a cooperative process in which the pointer informs the recipient of a desire, and the recipient comprehends this and agrees to meet the desire. We do not yet know, precisely when this understanding first occurs in infant development .

THE HUMAN DIFFERENCE

In their natural communication, humans' closest primate relatives do not point for one another (nor do members of any other animal species).[3] However, chimpanzees and other apes growing up in human captivity do learn to point toward food that is out of reach so that a human retrieves it for them (Leavens and Hopkins 1998, 95) and sometimes for other things they desire (such as locations to which they wish access). Approximately 60–70 percent of all captive chimpanzees spontaneously (with no training from humans) engage in this behavior when presented with the appropriate situation.

The pointing behavior of apes raised in captivity is used quite flexibly. For example, if several different types of food are available, chimpanzees will point to the most desirable one, and they will do so persistently until they get what they want (Leavens and Russell 2005, 291). Moreover, when some human-raised apes observe a human hiding food in an open area outside their cage, and another human comes by many hours later, they will point to the location where the food is hidden (Menzel 1996, 429). Finally, when apes observe that a human needs a tool to retrieve food for them, and then that tool is hidden when the human is away, they will point toward the location of the hidden tool when the human returns (Call and Tomasello 1994, 307). Even though this pointing is self-interested rather than cooperative, its indirectness is remarkable.

Yet, importantly, apes do not engage in pointing behavior, either for humans or for other apes, for the purely expressive purpose of sharing interest and attention or for the purely altruistic purpose of informing others of things they want or need to know. It is thus possible that ape-pointing for humans relies on somewhat different social-cognitive and social-motivational skills than human-pointing. One indication of this is that apes are not very skillful at comprehending informative pointing gestures.

If a human points and looks toward some food that an ape does not see, and by following the direction of the pointing gesture the ape comes to see the food, he will go get it. In this sense, one could say that the ape understands the human's gesture as an attention director. But a seemingly minor change in this procedure leads to drastically different ape behavior. In object-choice experiments like the hiding–finding games in which infants perform so well, apes generally perform quite poorly. They can be trained to do the task, and some apes—especially those with much human experience—seem to do a bit better than others. But very few apes understand the pointing gesture spontaneously in this context.[4]

Task failures may be explained in an almost infinite number of ways, but the results of a follow-up study considerably constrain the possibilities in this case. We conducted an alternative version of the object-choice task in which, instead of pointing, a human reached toward a bucket containing food but, due to the physical constraints in the situation, was unable to grasp it. Now the chimpanzees understood where the food was, whereas the exact same chimpanzees did not understand where it was in a standard version of the task (Hare and Tomasello 2004, 571). They were seemingly able to infer: she wants to get that bucket for herself; therefore, there must be something good in there. But they were not able to infer: she wants me to attend to that bucket for some reason relevant to our common ground. Thus, even though the superficial behavior of the human was highly similar in the two versions of this task—arm extended toward bucket—the apes' understanding of the human's behavior was very different, presumably because they understood her to be expressing a selfish intention rather than a cooperative, communicative intention.

What are we to make of the apes' behavior in these studies? One plausible interpretation is that they lack the ability to cooperate as humans do, either in their communications or in undertaking broader tasks. Human infants find the object-choice game trivially easy because they have created with the adult a shared goal of searching for the hidden object, which creates a joint attentional frame of things relevant to that shared goal, and also because child and adult mutually assume the adult is trying to be cooperative. In contrast, apes typically do not know what the human is attempting to communicate because, on our account, they have not created with the human a joint goal or joint attentional frame, and they do not share with the human the mutual assumption of partner cooperativeness. This means that the apes do not, indeed cannot, make the appropriate relevant inferences because they are unable to grasp the basic premise that the communicator is attempting cooperatively to inform them of something in their common ground that she thinks they will find relevant to their own concerns, even though they can make other inferences about what a human competitor is doing in a goal-directed act. And so apes simply do not understand why the human is pointing to the bucket, even if the communicative intention is overtly expressed. The gesture is an inexplicable, irrelevant act. The ape is searching for the food individually, and so when she follows the direction of the human pointing to the bucket, she says to herself, as it were, "A bucket. So what? Now where's the food?" The bucket is not relevant for her because she cannot comprehend that the human might be pointing altruistically to inform her of things he thinks she will find relevant.

Although we do not have as much solid data as we would like for some issues, there is a growing body of evidence that whereas apes do understand the basics of intentional action, they do not participate in shared intentionality.[5] Apes understand that there are intentional agents who make things happen. But apes are not motivated to share information and attitudes with others, nor do they comprehend when others attempt to communicate with these motives. Apes also do not share common conceptual ground or joint attentional frames with others, nor is their communication premised on mutual assumptions of cooperativeness among partners. Apes' communication, both with one another and with humans, is essentially individualistic. By contrast, human communication is cooperative in fundamental ways. In Gilligan's terms, it is relational. It is all about—and uniquely about—helping and sharing on common conceptual ground.

CONCLUSION

We humans have evolved to do many complicated things together. Our trackable gaze, to which infants attune even before language acquisition, and our capacities for cooperative communication, which infants share (again before language acquisition), surely facilitate relationship and collaboration. And it makes some evolutionary sense that engaging in such highly useful abilities would be pleasurable. If reproduction is pleasurable to a species, it is more likely that the species will multiply and survive; if cooperation is pleasurable to a species, it is more likely that the species will reap the benefits of cooperation. But cooperation, like reproduction, is double-edged. Just as reproduction can lead to perpetuation of a species, it can lead to overpopulation and a specie's demise. And the exquisitely functional human cooperative traits are as suited to fighting wars as to building houses, creating universities, or falling in love.

Notes

1   In this, I follow Herbert H. Clark (1996).

2   For infants' understanding of the communicative and pedagogical intentions of others, see Gergely Csibra (2003).

3   In the many tens of thousands of hours of observation of the four great species in their natural habitats, one anecdote of pointing has been reported for one bonobo individual (see Veà and Sabater-Pi 1998).

4   It is interesting that some domesticated animal species (especially domestic dogs) and human-trained animals (for example, human-

trained dolphins) are reasonably skillful in this object-choice task. For reviews, see Brian Hare and Michael Tomasello (2005) and Adam Miklosi and Krisztine Soproni (2006). The explanation for this at the moment is not clear, with one possibility being that they understand the pointing not as informative but rather as a command to go to a location.

5   For a review, see Tomasello et al. (2005).

References

BEHNE, Tanya, Malinda Carpenter, and Michael Tomasello. 2005. "One-Year-Olds Comprehend the Communicative Intentions Behind Gestures in a Hiding Game." *Developmental Science* 8: 492–9.

CALL, Josep, and Michael Tomasello. 1994. "Production and Comprehension of Referential Pointing by Orangutans." *Journal of Comparative Psychology* 108: 307–17.

CARPENTER, Malinda, Katherine Nagell, and Michael Tomasello. 1998. "Social Cognition, Joint Attention, and Communicative Competence from 9 to 15 Months of Age." *Monographs of the Society for Research in Child Development* 63(4) (SERIAL NO. 255): 1–143.

CLARK, Herbert H. 1996. *Using Language*. Cambridge: Cambridge University Press.

———, and Catherine R. Marshall. 1981. "Definite Reference and Mutual Knowledge." In Avarind K. Joshi, Bonnie L. Webber, and Ivan A. Sag (eds), *Elements of Discourse Understanding*. Cambridge: Cambridge University Press, pp. 10–63.

CSIBRA, Gergely. 2003. "Teleological and Referential Understanding of Action in Infancy." *Philosophical Transactions of the Royal Society* 358: 447–58.

GILLIGAN, Carol. 2002. *The Birth of Pleasure: A New Map of Love*. New York: Alfred A. Knopf.

GRICE, H. Paul. 1975. "Logic and Conversation." In Peter Cole and Jerry L. Morgan (eds), *Syntax and Semantics: Speech Arts*, VOL. 3. New York: Academic Press, pp. 41–58.

HANNAN, Thomas E., and Alan Fogel. 1987. "A Case Study Assessment of Pointing During the First Three Months of Life." *Perceptual and Motor Skills* 65: 187–94.

HARE, Brian, and Michael Tomasello. 2004. "Chimpanzees are More Skillful in Competitive than in Cooperative Cognitive Tasks." *Animal Behaviour* 68: 571–81.

————, and Michael Tomasello. 2005. "Human-like Social Skills in Dogs?" *Trends in Cognitive Sciences* 9: 439–44.

KITA, Sotaro (ed.), 2003. *Pointing: Where Language, Culture, and Cognition Meet.* Mahwah: Lawrence Erlbaum Associates.

LEAVENS, David, and William Hopkins. 1998. "Hand Use and Gestural Communication in Chimpanzees." *Journal of Comparative Psychology* 112: 95–9.

————, and Jamie L. Russell. 2005. "Intentionality as Measured in the Persistence and Elaboration of Communication by Chimpanzees." *Child Development* 76: 291–306.

LIEBAL, Kristin, Tanya Behne, Malinda Carpenter, and Michael Tomasello. 2009. "Infants Use Shared Experience to Interpret Pointing Gestures." *Developmental Science* 12: 264–71.

LISZKOWSKI, Ulf, Malinda Carpenter, Anne Henning, Tricia Striano, and Michael Tomasello. 2004. "12-Month-Olds Point to Share Attention and Interest." *Developmental Science* 7: 297–307.

————, Malinda Carpenter, Tricia Striano, and Michael Tomasello. 2006. "12- and 18-Month-Olds Point to Provide Information for Others." *Journal of Cognition and Development* 7: 173–87.

————, Malinda Carpenter, and Michael Tomasello. 2009. "Twelve-Month-Olds Communicate Helpfully and Appropriately for Knowledgeable and Ignorant Partners." *Cognition* 108: 732–9.

MARKMAN, Ellen, and Helen Shwe. 1997. "Young Children's Appreciation of the Mental Impact of Communicative Signals." *Developmental Psychology* 33: 630–6.

MENZEL, Charles. 1999. "Unprompted Recall and Reporting of Hidden Objects by a Chimpanzee (*Pan troglodytes*) after Extended Delays." *Journal of Comparative Psychology* 11: 426–34.

MIKLOSI, Adam, and Krisztina Soproni. 2006. "A Comparative Analysis of Animals' Understanding of the Human Pointing Gesture." *Animal Cognition* 9: 81–93.

MOLL, Henrike, and Michael Tomasello. 2007. "How 14- and 18-Month-Olds Know What Others Have Experienced." *Developmental Psychology* 43: 309–17.

MOORE, Chris, and Valerie Corkum. 1994. "Social Understanding at the End of the First Year of Life." *Developmental Review* 14: 349–72.

————, and Barbara D'Entremont. 2001. "Developmental Changes in Pointing as a Function of Parent's Attentional Focus." *Journal of Cognition and Development* 2: 109–29.

TOMASELLO, Michael. N.D. "Twelve-Month-Olds Provide Information to Help Others to Find Specific Objects." In preparation.

———, and Katharina Haberl. 2003. "Understanding Attention: 12- and 18-Month-Olds Know What's New for Other Persons." *Developmental Psychology* 39: 906–12.

———, Malinda Carpenter, Josep Call, Tanya Behne, and Henrike Moll. 2005. "Understanding and Sharing Intentions: The Origins of a Cultural Cognition." *Behavioral and Brain Sciences* 28: 675–91.

———, Ulf Liszkowski, and Malinda Carpenter. 2007. "A New Look at Infant Pointing." *Child Development* 78: 705–22.

VEÀ, Joachim J. and Sabater-Pi, Jordi. 1998. "Spontaneous Pointing Behaviour in the Wild Pygmy Chimpanzee (*Pan paniscus*)." *Folia Primatologica* 69(5): 289–90.

Carol Gilligan's work is rightly understood as feminist, but the feminist label can confuse as much as it clarifies. In a **Different** Voice (1982), *Gilligan's ground-breaking work in psychology, was rightly seen as a break from the too-common practice of theorizing human psychology on the basis of studies of the human male. But* In a **Different** Voice *was wrongly understood as supplementing male psychology with a distinct feminine psychology. Understanding that Gilligan is theorizing human psychology, Terri Apter reads* The Birth of Pleasure (2002) *not as a special statement about the mental life of women and girls but as something more momentous: a work of psychology that is deeply Freudian but that poses a profound challenge to central tenets of Freudian psychology.*

Gilligan's Challenge to Freud: Tribute and Deconstruction

TERRI APTER

"I have always been drawn more to psychoanalysis than to academic psychology," Carol Gilligan writes in "Recovering Psyche: Reflections on Life-History and History" (2004) and she goes on to explain that this affinity for psychoanalysis is at one with her affinity for literature. As an undergraduate she studied literature and experienced a"culture shock" in her graduate school days in psychology. She read Sigmund Freud as well as Anton Chekhov and Henrik Ibsen to alleviate her discomfort, for these writers allowed her "to retrieve a more nuanced and complex rendering of human experience" than she found in the articles that were set up as models for published research (ibid., 131–47).

The great writers have always been generations ahead of the psychologists in catching sight of central patterns of human development. They understand the essential links between history, society, and psychology, links psychologists all too often ignore as they proclaim universal or essential the developmental and behavioral patterns they discover. The challenge Gilligan presents to psychology is to bring the novelist's skills of observation and thick description to the realm of science. She demands that we keep all the dimensions of human personality in play, thereby avoiding the temptation to reduce the human psyche to any one of its many facets. Freud's vision, initially, respected this breadth. The case histories he wrote at the end of the nineteenth century read like short stories, and while Freud defensively notes that these case studies then may appear to "lack the serious stamp of science," he argues that the nature of the subject "is evidently responsible for this" (Freud and Breuer 1955, 160). He must follow the "intimate connection between the story of the patient's sufferings and the nature of his illness" (ibid., 161). For Gilligan, this is to Freud's credit. "Insights into the human condition carried by folk tales and writers across centuries," she writes, "begin to gain a footing in science, so that we see not only what happens or how it happens, but also why it happened over and over again" (2002, 219).

An awareness of a psychologist's need for artistic sensibility, for a clinician's eye and ear, and for an appreciation of the interplay between life history and history is central to understanding both the profound endorsements and the devastating challenges Gilligan presents to Freud in *The Birth of Pleasure*: *A New Map of Love*. For in addressing Gilligan's response to Freud, it is necessary to keep in sight both how she preserves and uses some of Freud's early methods and theories and how she criticizes and deconstructs later methods and theories. It is also necessary to see that she does not end her argument with criticism: in explaining where and how Freud went wrong, she replaces the Freudian template with a new paradigm of love and development.

Gilligan argues her case both for and against Freud by placing two case histories—that of Elisabeth von R., which was written in 1892, and that of Dora, about ten years later—as markers of the Freudian work she wants to take forward and the work she seeks to replace. She traces the significant shift from "the heady days of his early discoveries" to the establishment of psychoanalysis as a rigid theory. Identifying the theoretical pivot at which Freud broke faith with those initial discoveries that depended on sensitive listening, when his "picklock" technique was replaced by his own master code, she explains the social and psychological forces behind the shift in his theory from actual trauma to fantasy and toward the Oedipal complex. Then, in an elegant and creative repair-and-restoration job, she proposes a liberating alternative to the Oedipal myth in the myth of Cupid and Psyche, thereby finding a new paradigm of attachment and development. In consequence, Gilligan's account of repressed wishes and ideas, the interplay between society and psychology, the dynamics of conflict and resistance, and the construction of gender all challenge Freud's established theories.

THE EARLY CASE HISTORIES: LISTENING, LEARNING, AND RESPONDING

The case history of Elisabeth von R. is a fine example of what Gilligan calls "the heady days" (Freud and Breuer 1955, 135–82) of Freud's early discoveries, when Freud referred to his women patients as his teachers, and when "what they taught him gave him an insight not only into the workings of the psyche but also into the connection between the inner and outer worlds, the psyche and the culture in which it is living" (ibid., 138). Here Freud shows a respect for the clinical material—the observations of his research—that drives him to listen carefully to patients and to treat them as the authority on their condition. He explains: "The task on which I now embarked turned out . . . to be one of the hardest I had ever undertaken"; "the first question one asks oneself is whether the patient herself is aware of the origin and the precipitating cause of her illness" (ibid., 138–9).

The tools Freud uses as physician are tailor-made for the individual patient. Having located the source of knowledge in his patient, Freud's next task is to listen for what can be said but what, for some reason, the patient has difficulty voicing.

As he listens to Elisabeth, he "notes the points at which some train of thought remained obscure or some link in the causal chain seemed to be missing" (ibid., 139). What he hears when he listens are the telltale signs of dissociation—that is, knowing something but not being able to speak that knowledge—splitting off some knowledge from the knowledge that she can access. There are gaps in her memory. It is the combination of her knowledge, her failure to voice that knowledge, and her body's debilitating expression of her knowledge in the form of hysterical symptoms that persuades Freud that knowing is not enough. The patient with her "quick understanding and little resistance" nonetheless cannot access and integrate all her knowledge. Telling her story would alleviate her symptoms, since her ability to articulate her knowledge would relieve the body of its need to express her knowledge indirectly. But for her to access her knowledge so that she can articulate it, the dissociation—the split in her knowledge—has to be repaired.

Freud came to the crucial conclusion that a patient can only be persuaded to overcome a self-imposed or socially acquired silence in the context of a relationship in which it is safe to speak out. He therefore provided support and a responsiveness that instilled confidence: "The interest shown in her by the physician, the understanding of her which he allows her to feel and the hopes of recovery he holds out to her—all these will decide the patient to yield up her history" (Gilligan 2002, 219–20; Freud and Breuer 1955, 138). And while Freud enacts his role as physician by making "use of the technique of bringing out pictures and ideas by means of pressing on the patient's head," he notes that his technique would be "unworkable without the patient's full cooperation" (ibid., 153). In short, the physician has to engage with the patient and waylay her anxieties about possible punitive responses as she allows her thoughts to be spoken.

Having revised his old assumption that Elisabeth's secret was held within like some "foreign body" in favor of a belief that it was held in the form of knowledge, Freud decides to disbelieve the woman who says, "I don't know," or, "Nothing occurs to me." He suggests that she attend more carefully to her own thoughts and feelings so as to pick up what does occur to her. He addresses what might be her fears: that she might be wrong, that she might not be willing to confide in him, that she might not wish to face her own feelings, that her thoughts are insignificant. His authority as physician is to endorse her authority: you are the one who holds the key to your symptoms; your symptoms are physical expressions of your mind's knowledge; your knowledge must be spoken if we are to gain understanding; I will listen to what you say; it is safe to speak your mind.

In speaking her mind, the process of dissociation, the splitting of the mind so that parts of her experience become absent from her consciousness, is healed by association. Here lies the power of the talking or listening cure: what Freud discovered was the power of a confiding relationship (Gilligan 2002, 218).

LISTENING, RESONANCE, AND ASSOCIATION

This listening method—listening for what is said and what is silenced—has been adopted by Gilligan, and it is central to her research methods. Voice, she notes, is inherently relational. The sounds of one's voice change in resonance, depending on what we could call the "relational acoustics"—that is, whether one is heard or not heard, whether one is punished (by expressions of shock, outrage, or derision) or rewarded (with laughter, with understanding, with a response that opens out what's said rather than closing it off), and whether one fears one will be cast out for what one says (Gilligan 1986). What Freud provided, and what is always needed for direct speech, is resonance. "In the absence of resonance, or when the only resonance tells you you're crazy, you're wrong, you couldn't possibly know, this couldn't possibly happen, . . . the voice goes into silence" (Gilligan 2004, 145). Gilligan thus extends the significance of relationship beyond the therapeutic setting: to keep one's voice is, in a very broad sense, to live in relationships with others, to bring oneself into the world and influence one's human environment.

The consequence to a negative or punitive resonance—a resonance that "tells you you're crazy, you're wrong, you couldn't possibly know, this couldn't possibly happen"—is dissociation. Gilligan's work on "silencing" takes forward the nature of dissociation that Freud described in these early case histories. Freud was probably the first to use the phrase, often repeated in Gilligan's work with girls, "knowing and not knowing" (Freud and Breuer 1955, 165). Yet one must not lose sight of crucial differences: while Freud focuses on resistance of the conscious mind to thoughts and desires that are not consonant with one's sense of goodness, Gilligan focuses on resistance to the pressures to silence one's actual thoughts and desires. While Freud encourages free association to spot the repression of unacceptable thoughts (that is, thoughts which, if spoken, would be likely to be treated as unacceptable by others who uphold ideal or other abstract notions about what should be thought and felt), Gilligan focuses on the strategies by which we signal our knowledge even when we believe what we know cannot be expressed because we will be vilified, cast out, or ridiculed for speaking our mind. But while Freud focuses on the mechanisms of repression and Gilligan on resistance to the forces of repression, Gilligan converges with Freud in his attention to the body as a "speaker" for the knowledge that is not known—that is, for the knowledge that is split off from accessible thoughts.

In the absence of associated knowledge, there arises what Gilligan calls "the indirect discourse of symptoms." Freud described the symptoms of dissociation in terms of a mechanism of "conversion." The mind, as symbol builder, finds "speech" through the body, and psychic pain becomes physical pain. Although Gilligan turns to other psychologists and neuroscientists (particularly Antonio Damasio) to develop her argument that the mind and body are inextricably linked and that the conceptual separation of mind and body is based on an embedded cultural dissociation, she acknowledges that the foundation of her associative method for restoring dissociated knowledge is Freud's work on hysteria. For Gilligan as for Freud, the body is a would-be truth-teller, and the body belongs to a being who seeks relationships with others. "The implicit relational knowing of the human infant becomes the knowing that is carried by hysterical symptoms" (Gilligan 2002, 216). In this context, Gilligan's "challenge" to Freud is a creative use and extension of his methods, his discoveries, and his theories.

THE OTHER FACE OF FREUD: THE CASE HISTORY OF DORA

By the time Freud wrote "Fragment of an Analysis of a Case of Hysteria" in 1905, he no longer used a delicate picklock to access his patient's knowledge. He had become the master interpreter of the patient's words and symptoms, and he saw the patient's route to recovery through acceptance of his authoritative decoding (see Freud 1953b).

Dora, for whom Freud is able only to present a fragment of analysis, shares many of Elisabeth von R.'s courageous and appealing qualities. Elisabeth's father called his daughter "cheeky" and "cock-sure," warned her about her habit of "regardlessly telling people the truth," and feared that in consequence it would be difficult for her to get a husband (Freud ibid., 140). Dora is described by Freud as "in the first bloom of youth—a girl of intelligent and engaging looks." At sixteen years of age, when Freud first sees her, Dora is "a source of heavy trials for her parents." She suffers from low spirits and "an alteration in her character." While

Elisabeth has a mental constitution that "depart[s] from the ideal which people like to see realized in a girl," Dora looks to her brother, rather than to her house-proud mother, "as the model by which her ambitions had striven to follow" (ibid.).

Freud reports that Dora's symptoms are longstanding. As early as the age of eight, she had neurotic symptoms. At about twelve, she started suffering from migraines. She also had a constant cough and suffered from periods of loss of voice. In Freud's sessions with Elisabeth, he searched with the patient to recall a traumatic experience that was both covered over and expressed by physical symptoms. With Dora's coopera-tion, Freud brings to light two very disturbing and connected experiences, both involving compromising sexual advances by an older man, a trusted family friend.

The first approach from Herr K. (albeit the second to be revealed in the sessions with Freud) occurred when Dora was fourteen years old. Herr K. made a pretext for visiting Dora alone and "suddenly clasped the girl to him and pressed a kiss on her lips." At that moment Dora had "a violent feeling of disgust" and "tore herself free from the man." (ibid.). This incident—so confusing, and unpleasant, so out of keeping with the man's trusted position in the family and with the standards espoused by her parents' teachings and by social codes—was kept a secret until her ses-sions with Freud. Through the extensive case history, we come to learn, in addition, that Frau K. was having an affair with Dora's father, and that there may have been some (probably unspoken) agreement with her father that Herr K. be offered Dora in compensation. Hence, Dora's dis-gust could not protect her from further contact with Herr K. The two families continued to associate closely, bound, no doubt, by her father's love affair with Frau K. During one of the holidays taken by the two fam-ilies, Herr K. made another approach. Dora slapped him and challenged him and tried to reveal his betrayal, but he denied it and his denial was generally accepted.

Dora's symptoms—her migraines, her constant cough, her periods of loss of voice—might well be a conversion from the mental pain of being so inappropriately treated then driven to secrecy either through shame or through awareness that Herr K. would deny the truth. The body expressed her outraged knowledge that her father would lie about his own affairs and be willing to offer his daughter as a decoy. Her "loss of voice" would be the body's cry of declaration: "You will not allow me to speak the truth."

Though Freud shows exquisite sensitivity to the context in which Elisabeth's symptoms arose, he refuses to engage with the power of that context. Instead, he declares that Dora's behavior, at fourteen, is already hysterical because she felt disgust when Herr K. kissed her. "I should without question," he writes, "consider a person hysterical in whom an occasion for sexual excitement elicited feelings that were preponderantly or exclusively unpleasurable" (ibid.). He calls this a "reversal of affect" and is frustrated by the persistence of Dora's resistance to his overall explanations of her true ideas and wishes and his interpretation of her dreams. In fact, when Dora breaks off the analysis because she wishes to disengage from Freud's insistence that he holds the key explanation of her symptoms, Freud sees her action as revenge.

This is a far cry from the days when he looked upon his patient as the authority and found in her a teacher. While many writers have found Freud's analysis of Dora chilling, Gilligan's challenge is original in that she identifies how the change in his method—and the shift in his position as authority—join up with a shift in theory.

FREUD'S SHIFT IN THEORY AND BREAK WITH HIS PATIENTS

Gilligan's probing engagement with Freud turns to opposition when Freud realigns himself with patriarchy by formulating the Oedipus complex. The internalization of a father's voice becomes the foundation for morality and the bedrock of civilization. The obvious consequence of this realignment is Freud's conclusion that the stories women told him about incest and abuse as children must not, after all, be true but must be fantasies. Such events could not possibly be so common, he argued; the frequent reports he heard must have been reports of fantasies that screened the desire for sexual contact. To sustain his theory, Freud concluded that his patients' reports of their experiences had no truth-value. After all, he argued, in what he constructed as "the unconscious," there is no reality check, "so . . . one cannot distinguish between truth and fiction that has been cathected with affect" (quoted in Gilligan 2002, 227). In consequence, he disavowed what had become known as "the seduction theory," partly because he does not find it plausible that "in all cases the father, not excluding my own, had to be accused of being perverse." Incest remains central to his revised theory, but it is the child's wish for incest, rather than, in the seduction theory, a patriarch's licence. The physician who learns the truth from his patients is now lost.

When Freud abandons his neurotica—his theory linking neurosis with sexual trauma—and instead puts the Oedipus complex as the corner-stone of psychoanalysis, he ceases to listen to women talking about their experiences, which frequently included experiences of incest with their fathers. In the place of women's stories, he put the story of the young boy fantasizing about an incestuous relationship with his mother. In shifting the emphasis from reality to fantasy, a shift that follows what Gilligan identifies as "displacement," psychoanalysis lost its radical edge.

In shifting his focus from individual experience to the postulation of a universal fantasy, Freud took his clinical findings out of the context of history and culture. As a result, his theoretical grounding shifted from the reality of his patient's experience to a fantasy that is beyond any reality check and beyond social context. Freud's blinding himself to lived experience has a parallel in Oedipus's blinding himself in the myth. As Gilligan points out, in Freud's response to his father's death, he dreams of a sign that says, "you are requested to close the eyes." It is a blinding of knowledge: I will accept the laws of knowledge that you set down, Freud concedes as he places the Oedipal myth at the center of his theory; I will accept someone else as the authority over what I know. And so begins a process of dissociation that informs Freud's work and the accompanying construction of love and the unconscious. For now the unconscious is not primarily a container of knowledge that could anchor and confirm our responses; it is a container of dangerous impulses and fantasies, independent of life history and history. In consequence, Freud sees repression as necessary to avoid murder and incest and other kinds of mayhem whereas Gilligan, engaged by individual experience and historical context, sees repression as a mechanism that serves dissociation and impairs the psyche. She goes beyond Freud's view of what is necessary to society and registers the social benefits of psychological wholeness.

Oedipus, the hero of Freud's developmental template, is "the lone solver of riddles," and Gilligan suggests that this may be how Freud saw himself. He supplants the patient as the authority; it becomes his task to tell Dora what she really thinks and feels. When what is known and not known ceases to register the truth of our life histories, authority must be ceded to the expert who has mastered the "true" narrative. For Gilligan, this is the point at which psychoanalysis closes the door on Psyche in her representation as a seeing and speaking young woman; the woman patients who were Freud's teachers disappear from psychoanalysis. From this point, women's sexuality or desire is described as "veiled in an impenetrable obscurity," and women become a "dark continent" for psychology (quoted in Gilligan 2004, 133).

Also lost is the respect for individual differences and cultural contexts. Like the mythic Oedipus, Freud "universalizes his situation rather than looking at his [swollen] feet and asking where he has come from and where he is going" (Gilligan 2002, 226). Instead of taking one myth as a pattern among a wide register of common themes, Freud forges this as a universal template of development. From then on he neglects to ask the two primary questions that Gilligan insists any research must ask in order to hear what is said: "Who is speaking?" and "In what personal context and social historical context is the voice spoken?"

THE PSYCHOLOGY BEHIND THE BREAK IN FAITH

Why did Freud break faith with the voices of his patients?

Gilligan explains the quandary Freud faced: "In connecting women with their own knowledge, Freud [. . .] was breaking a cultural taboo, undoing a process of initiation by forging a method of inquiry that placed him in direct opposition to the fundamental rule of patriarchy: the claim on the part of the fathers to authority" (ibid., 219). She challenges but also understands: Freud was a man and a father, yet in his innovative work he aligns himself with women and uses their knowledge as he shapes his own. In so aligning himself, Gilligan reflects, "he finds himself in the position of women, isolated and embattled in his claim to knowledge" (ibid., 227).

The new, revised alignment with patriarchy is constructed by the very dissociation that Freud had learned to identify and to heal in his early case studies. But this was the price Freud agreed to pay to secure psychoanalysis as a respectable and mainstream enterprise. Freud, as researcher and clinician and theorist, would have to split off his knowledge about the impact of individual experience from his authoritative theories. He would uphold a theory in which splitting the love of the mother off from consciousness was a prerequisite of male maturity.

Love, in Freud's later theoretical frame, demands sacrifice and separation; maturity demands separation and splitting off the knowledge of connection. When what one should be in order to fulfill the ideals of maturity or manhood is so different from who we are, then we feel the need to fulfill a false ideal to be accepted and to find "love." When we seek love through a self constructed through dissociation, then the search for someone to love is also a search for a falsely constructed partner. Dissociation prevents direct speech and clear vision. What Gilligan argues powerfully for in *The Birth of Pleasure* is a new paradigm for true love—that is, a love that is sustained by clear sight rather than fantasy.

PARALLEL FINDINGS AND RETRIEVAL

From the beginning of her work as a psychologist, Gilligan honored Freud's early practice of ceding authority to the voices of women. "The key to discovery in the studies with girls," she explains, "lay in ceding to them the position of authority, approaching them as experts on their own experience, and they rose to the occasion" (Gilligan 2004, 139). In "Voices and Visions—An Overview" (1988), Gilligan, with her colleagues Lyn Brown and Annie Rogers, outlines methods that build on Freud. Gilligan describes her own methods in "reading" interview responses. She notes the telltale signs of dissociation in the increasingly repeated phrase, "I don't know," as she listens to adolescent girls; she also notes their resistance to pressures from society, from parents, from teachers to suppress their knowledge and to give way to the "knowledge" of the cultural authority (see Gilligan et al. 1988).[1] Her theory of adolescent development arises from what she hears; from what the girls she engages with say, omit, or cover; and also from the dynamics of interaction between girls and women in the more intensive theater and writing workshops that she organized with her colleagues. She identifies adolescent girls' resistance to the pressure that descends upon them as they move from childhood into adolescence, the pressure to embody cultural ideals of womanhood, of beauty, and of loveliness, both within and without. She refers back to Freud's *Studies on Hysteria* (1955) and is drawn by Freud's observations that the lost voice of hysteria is a voice that speaks from experience and by his demonstration that this lost voice can be retrieved.

In observing these patterns, Gilligan was fascinated by "the mechanism of splitting"—how children keep their voices from revealing their emotions; how they separate their minds from their bodies; and how they divorce themselves from relationships by silencing thoughts, wishes, and responses. But where does the honest voice go when it recedes into silence; what happens to the desire for relationships; how do we record our experience when we cannot afford to know what we know; and what happens to the sense of truth?

New Routes to Retrieving What Freud Found and Then Lost

In *The Birth of Pleasure*, Gilligan extends what she learned from girls as they move from childhood into adolescence and what she learned from Freud when he was a pupil of his women patients. She draws on her subsequent work with young boys, who at a very early age are initiated into tropes of maleness that involve dissociation of their knowledge of connection from their sense of who they should be. She also draws on her work with couples, in which the rites and rules of patriarchy often come between men and women and their ability to see one another, to speak openly to one another, and to assure one another of their connection.

This broad view allows her to identify dissociation as a common response to initiation into false ideals. In all of her work, she sees, as Freud saw when he hypothesized a creative unconscious, that what is repressed or silenced remains alive and effective.

The lost voices Freud was able to retrieve in his early patients are, in Gilligan's view, equivalent to Antonio Damasio's core self (see Gilligan 2004, 141). Core consciousness, or core self, reflects our ability to register our experience "from moment to moment, like a film running continually inside us, and also our awareness of watching the film that extends the sense of self into time and history, memory and identity" (Gilligan and Richards 2008, 195). This core self is distinguished from the autobiographical self, the self wedded to a story about itself, a self made up of prefabricated elements, elements informed by cultural and social building blocks.

Gilligan listens for the grounding in body and emotion that informs the core self, "the voice that speaks from experience and was not bound to a prefabricated story. It was the voice Freud retrieved in hysterical women who had become wedded to a false story. The stunning discovery of the *Studies on Hysteria* lay in the unsettling demonstration that a voice, seemingly lost, could be found" (Gilligan 2004, 140).

So, Gilligan is a follower of Freud as she works with girls, women, boys, men, and men and women as couples to identify the sound of the preinitiated voice, the voice that resists cultural scripts that shape self-deception and guide the stories we tell about ourselves. Her reading of the discourse of dissociation, like Freud's reading of the symptoms of hysteria, brings out the words that can heal.

But as Gilligan has reflected over her decades of listening to the preinitiated self and to resistance to prefabricated culture, she has come to challenge Freud's capitulation to culture in his break with the preinitiated voices of women and his construction of the Oedipal myth as the heart of development. Gilligan therefore challenges the psychoanalytic theory and the culture of love as sacrifice, and in her challenge she presents a revision, a myth to repair the splitting formulated by the Oedipal myth. She reads the myth of Psyche and Cupid as a resistance story and a map of transformation, a myth wherein the key players are a young woman, her lover, and his mother. Here the terms of development are shifted from splitting to association as essential to personal and societal health: human connectedness does not have to be sacrificed; love is fashioned not on displacement and idealization but on individual preference, honesty, and knowing.

The Birth of Pleasure presents a new paradigm whereby the relational self (a self that talks openly and directly to another and is seen for what he or she is) replaces separateness as the apogee of development. Gilligan links up her work with adolescent girls and young boys and married couples. She identifies splitting and consequent dissociation as conditions not of universal development but of development in a patriarchy, and she shows how patriarchy might be dismantled. Her brilliant exposé of the dissociation in patriarchal development and theory challenges not only Freud's shift in methods and theory but also the canonical assumptions about love and self that have been constructed by others (including her teachers Erik Erikson and Lawrence Kohlberg) and whose constructions feed into cultural notions of maturity and health, thereby perpetuating dissociation. Gilligan's "new map of love" provides routes to association and healing.

I end this discussion of Gilligan's challenge to Freud with a proposal for a revised reading of the Dora case, noting that Freud's ability to write a story too vivid to be contained by his dogma can be seen in this 1905 case history, too, as long as we view it through the frame Gilligan's work provides. While Freud depicts himself as badgering Dora to accept his interpretation of her responses to trauma and the meaning of her symptoms and dreams, he actually presents a case of a strong-minded young woman who makes a valiant effort to reclaim her voice.

Freud berates Dora for the trouble she gives him, for leaving him before the analysis is concluded, and for disputing his authority. But Elisabeth, too, ends her analysis with Freud before he judges her to be fully cured of her hysterical symptoms. Nor are they on good terms: Elisabeth is offended by his presumptuousness in trying to sort out her life. "Elisabeth," Freud writes, "would have nothing more to do with me." Yet, with Elisabeth he has "a kind of conviction that everything would come out right." He is intrigued to hear more of her and to see her, and when he does, he frames her as a dancer, whirling by him and having reclaimed her life (Freud and Breuer 1955, 160).

Freud's skill and honesty as a writer allow us to see a parallel in Dora. Several months after breaking off the therapeutic session, she returns. She says she is seeking his help again, but Freud notes that "one glance at her face, however, was enough to tell me that she was not in earnest over her request." What she wants to tell him is that she has confronted Herr K. and has forced him to acknowledge the truth of her reports of him. She also concludes her business by saying to the wife, "I know you have an affair with my father," and from Herr K. she draws an admission of the attempted seduction on their holiday that, previously, he had disputed.

Dora finds the courage to speak her mind, and her truth is acknowledged. In spite of Freud, perhaps, she has retrieved her buried voice and learned to trust her experience. The urge to speak what one knows and to overlay the autobiographical self with one's core self has a thrilling resilience. As Gilligan notes in her work with adolescent girls, when they were invited to speak their minds, "they rose to the challenge."

But the skill Dora and many others exhibit in voicing their knowledge may only be an interim recovery. Dora has been described as a lifelong neurotic, bitter and vengeful. The descriptions, if justified, indicate someone searching to retrieve what keeps slipping away. Indeed, the preinitiated voice described by Gilligan has a far more complex relationship to accessible knowledge than do the symptoms of the hysteric. Once seen and acknowledged, the hysteric's symptoms are unlikely to return in full, for the body need no longer be the speaker in disguise. Reclaiming one's own knowing in the sense of being able to name one's day-to-day experience, however, is a far more difficult task. Given the tenacity of ideals and abstractions such as national glory and patriarchal protection and manly pride that distort and cover individual knowledge, the resonance we need to speak from our core self is patchy, and we may come up against responses that remind us over and over again to hesitate before trusting the relational acoustics. The nightmare perpetrated by Freud in "Fragment of an Analysis of a Case of Hysteria" is of the apparent facilitator who says, "I want to know you and hear you; I am listening," but who then becomes the patriarch who says, "I know you, and you do not know yourself." In *The Birth of Pleasure*, Gilligan shows us remarkable resistance to a destructive paradigm, but she never underestimates its force.

Note

1   Listening for the discourse of dissociation, Carol Gilligan also listens for other things—different narratives of care and justice, for example, and she works on a coding system that refuses to cover the complexity of interview material (see Gilligan 1982).

References

GILLIGAN, Carol. 1982. *In a Different Voice: Psychological Theory and Women's Development*. Cambridge, MA: Harvard University Press.

————. 1986. "Exit-Voice Dilemmas in Adolescent Development." In Alejandro Foxley, Michael S. McPherson, and Guillermo O'Donnell (eds), *Development, Democracy, and the Art of Trespassing: Essays in Honor of*

Albert O. Hirschman. Notre Dame, IN: University of Notre Dame Press, pp. 283–300.

———. 2002. *The Birth of Pleasure*: *A New Map of Love*. New York: Alfred A. Knopf.

———. 2004. "Recovering Psyche: Reflections on Life-History and History." *The Annual of Psychoanalysis* 32: 131–47.

———, and David A. J. Richards. 2008. *The Deepening Darkness: Patriarchy, Resistance, and Democracy's Future*. Cambridge: Cambridge University Press.

———, Lyn Mikel Brown, and Annie Rogers. 1988. "Voices and Visions— An Overview." In Lyn Mikel Brown (ed.), *A Guide to Reading Narratives of Conflict and Choice for Self and Moral Voice*. Cambridge, MA: Harvard University Press, pp. 1–31.

FREUD, Sigmund. 1953a. *A Case of Hysteria, Three Essays on Sexuality, and Other Works*. London: Hogarth.

———. 1953b. "Fragment of an Analysis of a Case of Hysteria." In James Strachey (ed.). *The Standard Edition of the Complete Psychological Works of Sigmund Freud*, VOL. 7 (1901–05). London: Hogarth, pp. 7–122.

———, and Josef Breuer. 1955. *Studies on Hysteria*. London: Hogarth.

Methods for Recovering Pleasure

The lodestar of the work that culminated in Carol Gilligan's **In a Different Voice** *(1982) was a voice of resistance that she heard as she interviewed adolescent girls. In this voice, girls questioned cultural demands that they become muted and self-sacrificing as they become women. Gilligan has continued to pursue this voice of resistance by refining interview techniques to uncover it in the human sciences and techniques of close reading to uncover it in classical and postcolonial literature.*

The turn to classical literature for voices of resistance has been controversial. Peggy Cooper Davis, for example, worries about seeking liberation in "master" narratives, and Eva Canterella questions whether the ancient story of Psyche and Cupid can support a psychology of liberation.

Tova Hartman, following Gilligan, uses the story of **Iphigenia at Aulis** *to demonstrate close reading of the classics for the voice of girls' resistance.*

Of the many haunting impressions left by Iphigenia's eponymous tragedy, one that lingers with nagging poignancy and anxiety consists not of words but of a shift between words: not a startling phrase or vivid insight or fearless stripping of humanity down to its bones but a juxtaposition, unexplained and unresolved, between two speeches, two stances, two voices seemingly so at odds with one another that it is difficult to see how one character could possibly encompass them both.

Iphigenia speaks to her mother and father separately in response to the same fact of fate, decided in her absence and before the play even begins. To right a wrong she had no part in, for the reclamation of Greece's battered glory and her uncle Menelaus's limping pride, the Greek fleet must sail to Troy and reclaim wayward Helen from the suave, ardent charms of its prodigal son. The only problem is that there is no wind. The war goddess has engineered this infernal glitch, rendering the great fleet and its commander, Iphigenia's father Agamemnon, grounded and impotent to realize their revenge. She has, through a prophet, named her price, the sacrifice required for the ships to set sail—a maiden. And Agamemnon, in the "after-me" spirit of the consummate commander, has taken the burden upon himself and his daughter.

Learning of his decision, Iphigenia first responds by challenging her father and questioning the core patriarchal assumptions upon which his identity and Greece's identity have been built. She confronts him with a call for memory, for relationship, for love, and for a vision of the world in which these values take priority over such "natural," "objective" considerations as the glory and stability of the nation-state. When this plea fails, Iphigenia, in a farewell speech to her mother, appears to undergo a complete turnabout, espousing those patriarchal values and celebrating her role, in sacrifice, as their heroic guarantor. This reversal occurs within the space of a few pages, a few scant minutes of dramatic time.

What happened to Iphigenia? What brought on her sudden, and total, change of heart and mind? Do we meet, in this second monologue, a new improved daughter of Greece, a final (if belated) socialization success?

Or has she changed at all?

READING FOR RESISTANCE

The theme of adolescent girls being sacrificed and sacrificing their own emerging identities in order to save the lives of their fathers and maintain the social order their fathers feel they have been entrusted to uphold is one whose nuances Carol Gilligan's work has not only put on the map but also brought vividly into view. Confronted with a chasm between what they know about their relationships and "what is socially constructed as Relationship within a male-voiced culture," they are awakened to "the dangers in the prevailing conventions of relationship[,] . . . the encouragement of self-sacrifice or self-silencing[,] and the holding out of purity and perfection as conditions for relationship and the mark of good women" (Gilligan and Brown 1992, 29–30).

Gilligan's theorizing of dissociation and resistance has both fed and grown out of her voice-centered methodology and her insistence on listening for multiple voices in girls' accounts of their lives. She has guided us away from envisioning identity as something that can be tracked and staged and toward a more subtle, dynamic perspective that sees voice as one of the primary currencies through which identity is not only expressed but also formed. Voice does not exist outside the context of relationship and is thus inherently multiple, "chang[ing] in resonance depending on the relational acoustics" (Gilligan et al. 1990, 20).

In her own reading of Iphigenia (Gilligan 2002, 145–52), Gilligan sees this ancient adolescent's apparent surrender to patriarchy as an archetypal loss, and she wonders at "the similarity between the change in Iphigenia's voice as rendered by Euripides and the change we hear in the voices of contemporary girls" (ibid., 152). Iphigenia's initial stirring assertion of what she knows and her urging Agamemnon to cast aside cultural expectations and bravely reclaim what *he* knows comprises a "heroic attempt to resist the exigencies of patriarchal society." When this intimate act of self-exposure fails to move her father, she becomes racked by hopelessness, powerlessness, and shame. In response, she seems to flee from the knowledge that brought all of this on and, in the vacuum of not-knowing that dissociation leaves in its wake, to assimilate with chilling Stepford-like totality her culture's party line.

Gilligan's sensitivity to the quality and dimension of resistance implicit in Iphigenia's initial appeal highlights the kind of sophisticated listening her voice-based methodology enables. It also highlights the integral relationship between her methodology and her theory. In the following passage from "Remembering Larry," she describes her own process of tracing a subtle theme in girl's self-narrations, then framing that theme within theories of political and psychological resistance:

I came to a place where I heard girls narrating their initiation into not knowing. I then began to trace the psychology and the politics of resistance, observing girls' healthy resistance to losing relationship turn into a political resistance or struggle to stay in the human conversation, *to speak from their experience in the face of a construction of reality that made their desires sound selfish and bad and their knowing seem crazy or wrong.* Highlighting the political and moral dimensions of resistance made it easier to see the psychological processes of splitting and dissociation as responses to an initiation—the division of the world into good girls and bad girls (1997; emphasis added).

Gilligan's theory of political and psychological resistance opens up and demands a more complex and nuanced methodology of listening within which the interviewer must become sensitive to a multiplicity of voices in the narrator's accounts of their experience. The methodology she created for this purpose requires a "close reading" of interview transcripts for subtle, specific shifts in language and/or themes. It requires sensitivity to the multiple layers of meaning present within any life story. It "ask[s] about the relational story which is being told, and about the societal and cultural frameworks . . . to inquire into differences that are psychologically meaningful—one's body, one's experience of relationships and how one tells that story at a particular time, one's societal position, one's cultural groundings" (Gilligan and Brown 1992, 21).

One of the themes in girls' lives that is often silenced or muted in the stories they tell is that of resistance—the ways in which girls "refuse the established story of a white, middle-class heterosexual woman's life, a story all girls in this culture . . . struggle against, albeit in different ways" (ibid., 15). Taking Gilligan's methodology of listening for voice, together with her theoretical work on girls and their forms of resistance, we are led to read Iphigenia with an eye for the types of resistance she expresses and employs. In reading for Iphigenia's resistance, we will listen again to the voice she uses with her father and to what appears to be her total shift from poised petitioner to good-girl martyr, completely assimilated within the values of patriarchal Greece. We will hear the places of dissonance between her subjective knowledge of herself and her relationships and the "oughts" and "shoulds" of her culture. Gilligan's methodology enables us to revisit what seemed to be a voice of acquiescence in Iphigenia's final speech and conversation with her mother and to hear even there strains of resistance that crescendo as she approaches her death.

WHAT IPHIGENIA KNOWS

We ask first whether there is a voice of resistance embedded in the "good-girl" reassurances that Iphigenia gives her mother in her second speech. Iphigenia's mother has mustered the sympathy and commitment of Achilles, who promises to marshal all of his half-divine power to prevent Iphigenia from being harmed, even if it entails a fight to the death with the entire Greek army. During the conversation between Clytemnestra and Achilles, Iphigenia stands inside the tent, within earshot, and all three of them can hear the shouts of the not-distant mob crying unanimously for the young girl's blood and threatening to make short work of anyone who would dare stand in their way.

> CLYTEMNESTRA. Did they threaten you?
> ACHILLES. They said they would stone me.
> CLYTEMNESTRA. For defending my daughter?
> ACHILLES. For that, exactly.
> CLYTEMNESTRA. But who would dare lay a hand on you?
> ACHILLES. The whole Greek army, it seems.
> CLYTEMNESTRA. But the Myrmidons, your own forces—
> ACHILLES. They were the first to turn against me.
> (Euripides 1998, 296).

For the reader, it is uncanny and unnerving to see the speed with which Achilles, the hero of heroes, is cast into abject murderous disfavor by the people to whom he has devoted his life. From behind her tent flap, Iphigenia must hear both Achilles's dutiful, quixotic commitment to the mission he has and his stunned anxiety in the face of the mob's overwhelming response. Bound by natural law and subservient to the inscrutable demands of the gods, the assembled masses understand something that he cannot, at least not fully: What good is a hero when the entirety of their societal order is on the line? Though the reluctance that must have tainted Achilles's tone only becomes obvious to the reader in the (almost comically and transparently self-referential) relief with which he greets Iphigenia's decision not to enlist his services—

> I'm glad you don't rail
> at the gods any longer. That's a fight
> you cannot win. Instead, and rightly,
> you surrender to fate . . . I'd carry you off
> if I could, though I am glad not to fight the Argives,
> even for your sake. It's a terrible thing to die.
> (Ibid., 301).

Iphigenia surely would have heard it as he spoke. She would have heard the sudden skittishness invading the great warrior's pitch and begun to understand, as he had, just what they were up against—how deeply her sacrifice was required and what devastation and havoc would be wrought by her refusal to comply. This, I would argue, is one of Iphigenia's central epiphanies: while her first speech reflects the intuitive knowing born out of the relationship between daughter and father, what she overhears between her mother and Achilles forms the basis of a new sociopolitical knowing about her culture and its core ideology. She would have understood that the kind of resistance her mother has orchestrated, while not necessarily futile in the literal sense (Achilles claims, at least, to have the gods' blessings), ultimately accepts this ideology on its own terms. Clytemnestra, after all, does not reject the principle of sacrificing a maiden in order to jump-start the stalled military engine, only its application in this particular case.

> CLYTEMNESTRA (*to Agamemnon*). You should have made a counter
> offer when the seer came to you. "Acheans! Do you mean
> to sail against Troy? Then let's cast lots to see whose daughter
> dies." *That is justice*.

(Ibid., 289; emphasis added.)

Iphigenia sees that her mother's form of resistance (defense against one man by way of another, stronger man) and its ultimate goal (finding another girl to sacrifice in her place) do nothing to challenge the system whose rigid patriarchal foundations were exposing themselves to her in their rawest, most subterranean form.

> ACHILLES. "She must die!" they are crying.
> CLYTEMNESTRA. Doesn't anyone want to save her?

(Ibid., 295).

How, if at all, does this new knowledge get reflected in Iphegenia's subsequent interaction with her mother? Does she hold onto it? Can she know what she knows, or, to pose one of Gilligan's most powerful and influential questions, must she, for the sake of the relationship, for the sake of comforting her mother, stop knowing certain basic truths not only about her father but about her mother as well: that she is a participant in patriarchy? I suggest that Iphigenia continues to know, and this knowledge can be traced by reading for her resistance. Although she has no power ultimately to change her fate, she has certain powers to resist how her death is used by her family and culture and she uses these powers to speak the truth of a girl who knows intimately what the patriarchy is capable of doing.

Choosing Voice

In "Exit-Voice Dilemmas in Adolescent Development," (1988) Gilligan describes the tensions that girls face in negotiating identity coherence within a personal value system that prioritizes attachment over detachment, loyalty over separation, and care over justice, in defining one's emerging self by finding and expressing voice within relationships rather than by exiting them (141–58).

Gilligan claims that as a result of traditional psychology's "equation of progress with detachment and opposition" (ibid., 146), its theorists "typically have given priority to principles as the anchor of personal integrity" (ibid., 149). This prioritization of principles over relationship is not, however, unique to psychology. Rather, it is deeply ingrained in patriarchy. Thus Clytemnestra, who has assimilated patriarchal ideology, frames her argument to Agamemnon in terms of "justice," "law," and "right."

> Show me the law that rewards evil and condemns
> the virtuous to death. Do what is right.
> Let our child live.
>
> (Euripides 1998, 290).

Achilles, meanwhile, casts his lot with "reason."

> Reason is stronger than fear . . . He can't kill his child. You are
> his life's partner, mother of the girl . . ."
>
> (Ibid., 282).

When these principles fail to persuade Agamemnon, the only logical option is a further step in the direction of exit. In the case of Achilles, exit entails leaving his post as military leader to become an enemy to his own forces. In the case of Iphigenia, exit means something even more sinister: death at the hands of her own father and people.

The only choice left for Iphigenia is *how* to exit. Will she be meek? Will she bemoan her fate? What voice will she assume as she is driven to her tragic fate? Or will she remain quiet? Gilligan's opposition of the "neatness of exit" to the "messiness and heartbreak of voice" resonates with Iphigenia's plea to her father, her refusal to let Achilles fight for her, and her insistence upon making one last, "heartbreaking" speech (Gilligan 1988, 146). Playing out the exit option would have required nothing of Iphigenia other than keeping quiet; the deal between Clytemnestra and Achilles had already been sealed. But Iphigenia is unwilling to relinquish her vocal prerogative. Rather than stepping back into the silence of an exit that would do nothing to challenge the values that had brought this situation about, she takes a radical step into voice.

What makes Iphigenia such a remarkable protagonist is that she chooses loyalty knowing exactly what the outcome will be.

A PRISM OF VOICES

> Mother, I have something
> to say to you. Your anger with my father,
> what good will it do? . . .
> We should be glad for this stranger's courage.
> He would save me if he could. The men respect him,
> love him even. We must take care
> not to ruin his standing with the army.
> That would only weaken our cause
> (Euripides 1998, 299).

Taking Iphigenia's words in this speech at face value would lead one to conclude that she has undergone quite an about-face indeed. The audience is startled by the polyphony of a character that at first seemed simple and pathetic.

Potential sites of polyphony are not difficult to pinpoint. Concern for Achilles's standing in the army, for example, seems almost comical in light of the fate to which she has been consigned. Furthermore, the sudden declaration of loyalty in the first-person plural—"this would only weaken our cause"—is startling enough not only to make one wonder what cause, exactly, and whose, would be undermined by her remaining alive, but also to make one wonder if she is wondering it as well.

To say that Iphigenia speaks through a jagged prism of conflicting voices is not to deny that she is also sincerely attempting to comfort her mother or desperately attempting to convince herself. In a sense, after failing to resist patriarchy's values head-on, she now can be seen as reviewing the myths upon which she has been raised, trying them on for size. When she tells her mother, "If I have no fear it is because I have no hope," she betrays at the very least that she is not speaking out of pure ideological conviction. Devoid of hope, she gropes through her various adolescent identities—cultural good-girl, good-enough daughter, and "truth-teller"—for a resonant voice. Ultimately, her entire final speech and dialogue can be read coherently as expressing all of these voices.

Gilligan's claim about girls' multivocal tendencies can help to explain the discrepancy between the stance Iphegenia takes in addressing her father versus that which she takes in addressing her mother; it can also help us to make sense of the multiple, and seemingly opposing, strains in her words to her mother. As Gilligan puts it,

> The ability of girls to tell it from both sides and to see it both ways
> is not an illustration of relativism (the abandonment of an
> absolute truth) but rather a demonstration of girls' understanding
> of relationship raised to a cultural level and a provisional solution
> to a difficult problem of relationship: how to stay connected with
> themselves and with others, how to keep in touch with themselves
> and the world (1990, 529).

Euripides encompasses all of these voices within one character. It is
not the case that Iphigenia's first speech is "true" while the second is
"false." Both respond to different situations as Iphigenia understands
them. When Iphigenia determines that she has no hope of exit, her voice
becomes uncompromising, vigorous, and violent—a reflection of the violence that subsumes her. She goes from being Daddy's girl to being the
destroyer of Troy. As Aristotle pointed out, the transition is jarring, but we
need not follow Aristotle in considering this jarring effect a fault in the
drama. Rather, Iphigenia's apparent change is really the assumption of
voice in a situation where only a jarring, violent transition is possible.

Modern, Western developmental theory has insisted on stripping
voices down to a linear, staged progression wherein if multiple voices are
heard, one is privileged and the rest are discounted as false. It is Gilligan's
innovative intertwining of theory and method that allows us to *rediscover*
all of these lost, silenced voices in Iphigenia and in her countless real-
world, adolescent counterparts.

> You bore me for the sake of Greece . . . my death will bring you
> honor . . . I ask you not to cut your hair for me . . . I forbid you
> to cry . . .
>
> (Euripides 1998, 300).

Read from the perspective of a resistor voice, Iphigenia's speech to
her mother takes a sharp, truth-telling turn about halfway through. "You
bore me for the sake of Greece, not for yourself," she tells Clytemnestra,
and one has the sense that at this point, it is not for her own sake alone
that she is rehearsing the myths upon which she was raised. By reminding
Clytemnestra that her maternal commitment was never truly direct, that
it has always been mediated by her commitment to patriarchal myth,
Iphigenia raises the starkness of a radical choice for Clytemnestra: patriarchy or relation. Iphigenia appears to choose patriarchy, but she does so
in a manner so uncompromising and radical that her choice is disturbing.
Her choice to be the "destroyer of Troy" stands as an accusation of those
that are complicit in the social system that gives her only the options of
assuming the "manly" voice of war or of remaining silent.

In wielding this voice of accusation, Iphigenia deconstructs the simple good–bad/all-powerful–victim dichotomies between father and mother. On one level, her words of comfort express an understanding of her mother's powerlessness within the patriarchal scheme. However, when she tells her mother that her own imminent sacrifice is "all you could wish for me," she signals her awareness of Clytemnestra's complicity in Greece and its value system, exposing the facileness of her protestations (ibid., 301). "You helped to bring this about," she seems to says in effect, "and so you cannot suddenly act as if you don't know how it happened."

The good girl is speaking, but she is also choking on her good-girl speech; she is looking at her mother and seeing both a victim and an oppressor, and it is this double vision that she ultimately, simultaneously, describes.

Building on these themes of complicity and hypocrisy, Iphigenia then takes on a more explicit and more broadly cultural cast. When Clytemnestra starts to weep, Iphigenia asks her to stop in order not to weaken her resolve. It is perhaps the naive absurdity of Clytemnestra's response—"Whatever you ask. I'd never harm you"—that firms her daughter's final resolve to assume a voice, the voice of the "destroyer of Troy," that challenges her mother's view (ibid.). Iphigenia, in rejecting the traditional tokens of mourning and grief, startles her mother into considering her own position within the patriarchal order.

"Then I ask you not to cut your hair for me/or drape yourself in black" (ibid., 302). The request startles Clytemnestra, who has already begun to take on the familiar—and no doubt somewhat comforting in its familiarity—role of mourning mother. Iphigenia cuts off this option, as she literally cuts off her mother's bewildered objection:

CLYTEMNESTRA.	Why should you forbid this?
	When I have lost you—
IPHIGENIA.	Not lost. My death
	will bring you honor.
	(Ibid.)

Though on one level this assurance of honor can be read as another gesture of consolation, clearly there are darker, more complicated implications at play as well. After all, if Clytemnestra were in fact the kind of mother who resisted—who not only resisted her culture's military through ludicrous, last-minute heroics but also resisted its values—she would see no honor in this type of death. Iphigenia questions the meaning of a loss that is destined to be filled with honor. In what she knows will be her final utterance, Iphigenia voices punishing honesty, calling Clytemnestra out on where her loyalty really lies. "You will enjoy some of the honor that comes from my death," she seems to be saying, "even as you regret it. Because you accept the honor, you may not enjoy the comfort of mourning."

This indictment does not stop with her mother. As Clytemnestra stammers to process what she has just been asked ("You mean, I cannot mourn you?"), Iphigenia delivers convention another shattering blow:

IPHIGENIA.	Never! And I want no earth heaped over me.
CLYTEMNESTRA.	What, not bury you? What is there to do with the dead but bury them?
	(Ibid., 303.)

The request to remain uncovered in death would have been seen by her mother and her countrymen as an obscene flouting of cultural taboo. The very catharsis from which her mother could derive comfort and from which her father and society could achieve closure on this unseemly chapter of national history is what she denies them by disallowing the "natural" process of mourning. To paraphrase her statement of resistance, "my death will bring you honor . . . *therefore*, you may not cut your hair, cry, or cover me over; *instead* I will remain uncovered, defying ultimately the values of Greece."

Near the beginning of *Iphigenia at Aulis*, Agamemnon, explaining why he cannot save his daughter from her goddess-designated fate, makes a striking admission: "duty is hand-clapped over my mouth . . . only I am unnatural." Agamemnon does have some knowledge of what is natural and what is right; however, this knowledge for him is subsumed by duty, which silences everything and against which there is no resistance. Everything is covered over by duty.

Agamemnon effectively says, "I cannot know what I know and continue to be the commander of this army; duty does not allow it." Rather than offering comfort to her father, Iphigenia accentuates his dissociation by denying him the opportunity to mourn. After failing in her appeal to her father to allow love and memory to direct his decisions, and upon coming to terms with her mother's inability to save her, whether from weakness or partial complicity, Iphigenia assumes a voice that reflects with clarity the violence and dissociation of patriarchy, and her voice demands that they not turn away. When they have stripped her of her subjectivity and turned her into an object-for-the-sake-of, she responds by assuming the voice of the "destroyer of Troy," the ultimate subjective voice in her society. Since she was not honored as a daughter to her parents *or* to Greece, then she refuses to be mourned and eulogized as a daughter. If her father chooses his position as commander over his role as father, if memory and love cannot uncover the "hand-clapped" mouth of duty, then she will not willingly allow herself to be an object of passion after death. She will die, but at least she will not suffer her father's fate of being suffocated by values not her own.

In the context of a patriarchal society that leaves her few options, Iphigenia opts for a "messy" exit, one which leaves open the questions of voice and loyalty that a quiet exit, howsoever tragic it may be, would leave hidden. Is Iphigenia a dupe? A victim? An ironic resistor to a patriarchal order that she can only fight in death? Reading for resistance allows us to see that Euripides leaves these questions open, thus opening a space for questioning the patriarchal order that dooms Iphigenia to a tragic end.

References

GILLIGAN, Carol. 1988. "Exit-Voice Dilemmas in Adolescent Development." In Janie Ward, Jill McLean Taylor, and Betty Bardige (eds), *Mapping the Moral Domain: A Contribution of Women's Thinking to Psychological Theory and Education*. Cambridge, MA: Center for the Study of Gender, Education, and Human Development, Harvard University Graduate School of Education, pp. 142–158.

———. 1990. "Joining the Resistance." *Michigan Quarterly Review* 29(4): 501–36.

———. 1997. "Remembering Larry." Lecture presented at the Tenth Annual Kohlberg Memorial Lecture, Twenty-Third Annual Conference of the Association for Moral Education, Emory University, Atlanta, November. Available at: www.des.emory.edu/mfp/302/302gillkohl.pdf

———. 2002. *The Birth of Pleasure: A New Map of Love*. New York: Alfred A. Knopf.

———, Nona Lyons, and Trudy Hanmer (eds). 1990. *Making Connections: The Relational Worlds of Adolescent Girls at Emma Willard School*. Cambridge, MA: Harvard University Press.

———, and Lyn Mikel Brown. 1992. *Meeting at the Crossroads*. Cambridge, MA: Harvard University Press.

EURIPIDES. 1998. *Iphigeneia at Aulis*. Translated by Eliane Terranova. In *Euripedes 3: Alcestis, Daughters of Troy, The Phoenician Women, Iphigenia at Aulis, Rhesus*. Edited by David R. Slavitt and Palmer Bovie. Philadelphia: University of Pennsylvania Press., pp. 221–312.

Carol Gilligan's work relies on the results of highly systematized interviews. Her interview methodology is set out in a Listening Guide that is taught in an increasing number of academic disciplines at an increasing number of institutions. Niobe Way, an expert in the use of Gilligan's Listening Guide, uses examples from her studies of friendship among teenage boys to describe the Guide's function and form.

Reflections on the Listening Guide:
A New Method of Psychological Analysis
NIOBE WAY

In *The Birth of Pleasure*: *A New Map of Love* (2002), Carol Gilligan uses "I poems" to reveal the multilayered nature and complexity of the human psyche. In these poems, we hear the interior voices that compose the psychological worlds of girls, women, boys, and men. *I* poems are a component of the Listening Guide, an innovative set of tools that Gilligan and her students at Harvard University developed over two decades ago for analyzing psychological data. They developed these tools in response to a need for methods that analyze both implicit and explicit meaning and experience in the narratives of women and men. Until the development of the Listening Guide, analysis of psychological data was limited to methods like content coding that reduce the data to their explicit meanings. Yet Gilligan understood, as did Sigmund Freud and Jean Piaget, that to attend only to the explicit content of a narrative is to ignore the underlying, free-flowing logic of the psyche that informs and shapes that content. The Listening Guide is a method of psychological analysis that reveals "the nonlinear, nontransparent orchestration of feelings and thought" (Gilligan and Attanucci 1988, 233). In other words, it reveals that which is often left unspoken.

As a former doctoral student of Gilligan, I have been greatly influenced by Gilligan and her method of understanding psychological data and the human world and have been using the Listening Guide for the past two decades in my research on urban adolescents. This method has influenced not only how I analyze the data in my studies but also how I conduct my research and, more broadly, conceptualize human experience. In what follows, I will first describe the beliefs that inform the Listening Guide and how these beliefs have changed the way I understand the process of research and the analysis of psychological data. I will then describe the method more specifically and how I have applied it in my work.[1]

THE LOGIC OF THE LISTENING GUIDE

The Listening Guide is a voice-centered and relational approach to analyzing psychological data with girls, women, boys, and men. The voice, in Gilligan's work, is not merely a symbolic or illustrative device. It draws attention to the actual voice of the person speaking, with an understanding that speech is a physical act. The spoken word exposes both feelings and thoughts and implicates both the mind and the body. The Listening Guide also acknowledges the inherently relational nature of human experience, including the experience of doing psychological research. Here Gilligan adopts one of Freud's more radical insights that in the scene of analysis, the analyst does not possess the key to unlocking the patient's secrets or difficulties. Knowledge is only gained in the exchange taking place between analyst and patient. Research involves the encounter with—and the effort to make sense of—shared stories, actual bodies, and real voices. The patterns that are "found" by researchers are the result of relationships including those between the interviewers and interviewees. Interview narratives are never simply pure or unmediated representations of voices of the "other" but are jointly constructed.

In my own research, this relational assumption not only influences how I analyze the data but also how I conduct my interviews with young people. This focus on the relational nature of experience leads me to allow for, and indeed strive to permit, both stability and spontaneity in my interviews with adolescents. Although I always have a specific set of interview questions that I pose to each participant, there is a lot of room during the interviews for the adolescent and the interviewer to chart and follow new and unexpected paths. This semi-structured approach to interviewing explicitly acknowledges the interviewer's desire to understand a particular phenomenon or topic from the perspective of the interviewee and the interviewee's agency or power to introduce important new knowledge that the interviewer had not anticipated.

Attuning oneself to the power dynamics within the research is also central to this voice-centered, relational method. Shulamit Reinharz, a feminist sociologist, explains: "[B]y dealing in voices, we are affecting power relations. To listen to people is to empower them[,] . . . but before you can expect to hear anything worth hearing, you have to examine the power dynamics of the space and the social actors" (1988, 15–16). Although as an interviewer I have the power to choose the questions and to interpret the responses, the adolescents have the power of knowing their own experiences and deciding what to tell and not to tell me. We are engaged in a relationship in which each of us has power over what we say and how we say it. I do not carry as much power as has been assumed in psychological research because I am not claiming to know more than the interviewees about the meanings of their words. I do, however, have the power to decide what to include or focus on in my analysis and what to exclude.

Yet I carry this power with trepidation, realizing that I can misunderstand or misrepresent what adolescents are saying. This trepidation leads me to be especially careful to stick close to the interview texts. I quote from interview transcripts extensively so that the reader can hear the adolescents directly, rather than merely as paraphrases of their stories. I evaluate repeatedly my own interpretations and am wary of inference leaps that lead me away from the adolescents' actual stories and into the tunnel of my own, or my field's, expectations. Attuning ourselves, as Gilligan encourages us to do in the Listening Guide, to who is speaking, what is being stated, on whose terms, in whose language, and from what vantage point, increases the rigor of our research because it encourages us to see and hear the unexpected. Consequently, we are able to expand understanding of adolescents rather than simply confirm or maintain preexisting theories that may not accurately represent who our subjects are or what they believe.

Another assumption behind this voice-centered, relational approach is that the words of individuals cannot be separated from the cultural and societal context in which these words are embedded. To discuss how people speak about their world means to take into account and to understand that these experiences are intimately connected to their specific location in the world. And at the same time, a person can challenge, question, and resist—through, and with words—the culture in which these words have meaning. Holding such assumptions, I am consistently trying to understand what types of cultural and societal expectations, hopes, desires, and stereotypes are influencing the adolescents' stories as well as reflecting on my own questions, thoughts, interpretations, and comments during the interview. I am also paying attention to how adolescents might use existing words and expressions to resist specific cultural expectations and assumptions—those coordinates on the map of shared existence that have traditionally and unjustly allowed some stories to gain dominance over others. Here Gilligan and her students' methodological approach is congruent with the reflections of major feminist philosophers who have examined how women have to rely on the language of patriarchy in order not only to be heard but also to challenge its structures, all the while seeking new forms of expressions that are no longer marked by such hierarchical systems. Such insights during and following the interview process are then incorporated into the findings of my research.

THE WAY TO LISTEN

These basic assumptions regarding voice, relationships, power, culture, and context inform the method developed by Gilligan and her students

to analyze psychological data. The method consists of a series of sequential readings or "listenings," with each listening focused on a different
aspect of the narrative (Gilligan et al. 2003). The focus on listening rather
than the more traditional approach of "reading" texts draws attention to
the necessity of listening to what is actually being said in the interview.
The researcher becomes active in this process of constructing meaning by
listening carefully and engaging with the person being interviewed rather
than passively reading the text. The method requires the listener to attend
to a person's narrative at least four times, each time listening in a different way. Listening for a series of voices in the interviews stems from
Gilligan's belief that the psyche is "contrapuntal (not monotonic) so that
simultaneous voices are co-occurring" at all times (ibid., 159). The tensions that may exist among these simultaneous voices represent the
internal tensions of a psyche living in the world where the perceived needs
of the self may be in conflict with the perceived needs of others.

In the initial listening of the Listening Guide, the focus is on the plot
of the story that is being told and the interviewer's response to this story.
In addition, this step encourages the interviewer to reflect on how the
story or plot is shaped by the relational dynamics of the interview. This
first step is, in some ways, the most familiar to researchers of qualitative
data. Most qualitative methods of analysis focus on reading for the
explicit content or plot of the story. What makes this initial step unusual,
however, is the focus on the researcher—her responses to the interviewee
as well as to how the story is co-constructed. Focusing on the plot without
understanding how the interviewer shapes and responds to it reinforces
the misconstrued notion that plots or stories have no context and that the
researcher and interviewer are neutral and objective. However, active
engagement with the biases and responses of the researcher, interviewer,
and interviewee allows for new interpretations to be made.

In my research on friendships between adolescent boys, I am able to
hear how fifteen-year-old Raphael's stories of betrayal and hurt in his
male friendships are a reflection not only of his experience but also of the
context of his interview with me. He indicates directly to me that he
yearns for a close male friendship in which he can reveal his true thoughts
and feelings. (That indication is a part of his "plot.") With me, he appears
to have temporarily found such a space, and he thus enacts what he seems
to most desire in his relationships with other boys. He shows me that he
is able to be the way he wants to be in the context of safe space. Given my
interest in experiences of intimacy in friendships, I listen to his interviews
with my ears attuned to his desire for such friendships. His narratives and
my interpretations of his stories are a reflection of his desires, my desires,

and the space we have created together. My desire for him to want and to have close male friendships, as well as his explicit expression of desire for such friendships, become part of my interpretation of his friendships.

The second listening in the Listening Guide is focused on the voice of the *I*, or how a person speaks about her/himself. This step attends to the way the interviewees present themselves through the use of the first person pronoun by "picking up its distinctive cadences and rhythms" (ibid., 162). The researcher is asked to underline all the "*I* statements" in the interview text—which include the *I*, the verb next to it, and any word next to the verb that seems important—and create "*I* poems" that are constructed by linking together all of these *I* statements in the exact sequence in which they appeared in the text. For example, Victor, an African–American boy in one of my longitudinal studies of boys' friend-ships, tells me in response to my question, "Do you have a close or best friend this year?":

> I wouldn't say, I don't say I would. 'Cause I feel that a friend is going to be there for you and they'll support you and stuff like that. Whether they're good and bad times, you can share with them, you would share your feelings with them, your true feelings that's why I don't think I have any real close friends, I mean, things can travel around in a school and things would go around, and the story would change from person to person. Yeah, basi-cally, I hate it, I hate it, 'cause you know I wouldn't mind talking to somebody my age that I can relate to 'em on a different basis.

By listening to the *I* statements in Victor's story, I am able to discern his internal struggle and the ways in which he is able and not able to say what he feels and thinks about his own desires for male friendships.

I wouldn't say
I don't say
I would
I feel
I don't think
I have
I mean
I hate it
I hate it
I wouldn't
I can

In this *I* poem, I hear Victor struggling to express feelings of desire. This struggle is familiar to me as one who also lives in a culture where expressions of desire among boys or men are greatly discouraged. Yet, Victor is able to express such desires in this interview with me. This second listening reveals a conflict that Victor may be experiencing but is not articulating explicitly.

The third and fourth listenings in the Listening Guide are for the contrapuntal voices that are evident based on the first and second listening of the interview. Listening for the contrapuntal voices—taken "from the musical form counterpoint, which consists of the combination of two or more melodic lines"—offers a way of charting the multiple ways people understand and experience the world (ibid., 164). This process leads to a more direct response to one's research questions. The listener is asked to underline with a differently colored pen evidence of each contrapuntal voice. In her early work, Gilligan (1982) focused on the contrapuntal voices of care and justice. In my work, applying the first and second steps in the Listening Guide to boys' interviews about male friendships led me to focus on the contrapuntal voices of desire and resistance to that desire for male friendships. My listening for desire led me to underline statements both of explicit desire for close male friendships and of implicit desire, such as when boys described experiences of hurt by other boys and feelings of loneliness. I also underlined the boys' desire to express a desire for intimate male friendships. In underlining the resistance to their desire for male friendships, I focused on boys' expressions of "not caring" whether or not they had close male friendships, especially when these statements were followed or preceded by stories of hurt and betrayal by other boys. This is the same struggle between desire and resistance that was often revealed in the second readings' *I* poems, as boys struggled to articulate their desire and also struggled not to want to desire intimacy in their male friendships (Way and Chu 2004).

THE REWARDS OF LISTENING

The Listening Guide's multiple steps of listening to psychological data lead to new ways of understanding human experience. In my case, using the Listening Guide led to a reinterpretation of boys' friendships that challenged existing theories of boys' development. Most theories of human development have been based on what we can see and what we can quantify. Previously, when we listened to adolescent boys, we only listened to the explicit content as if their stories have only one meaning—as if they or we always say what they or we mean. When we begin to incorporate into our methods the belief that girls, women, boys, and men have psyches that inform what we mean, we begin to understand how it is that many of our existing theories of human development have missed a large part of what it is to be human.

Note

1 For a more detailed discussion of the Listening Guide, see Carol Gilligan et al. (2003).

References

GILLIGAN, Carol. 1982. *In a Different Voice*: *Psychological Theory and Women's Development*. Cambridge, MA: Harvard University Press.

————. 2002. *The Birth of Pleasure*: *A New Map of Love*. New York: Alfred A. Knopf.

————, and Timothy J. Attanucci. 1988. "Two Moral Orientations: Gender Differences and Similarities." *Merrill Palmer Quarterly* 43: 223–37.

————, Renee Spencer, Katherine M. Weinberg, and Bertsch Tatiana. 2003. "On the Listening Guide: A Voice-Centered Relational Model." In Paul M. Camic, Jean E. Rhodes, and Lucy Yardley (eds), *Qualitative Research in Psychology*: *Expanding Perspectives in Methodology and Design*. Washington, DC: American Psychological Association Press, pp. 157–72.

REINHARZ, Shulamit. 1988. "The Concept of Voice." Paper presented at the conference, "Human Diversity: Perspectives on People Context," University of Maryland, College Park, June.

WAY, Niobe, and Judy Y. Chu. 2004. *Adolescent Boys*: *Exploring Diverse Cultures of Boyhood*. New York: New York University Press.

Miriam Raider-Roth, who learned the Listening Guide as Carol Gilligan's student and now teaches it to researchers in the field of education, offers a second perspective on the structure and effects of a research process that is—necessarily and self-critically—both relational and subjective.

Listening to the Heartbeat of the Classroom: Bringing the Listening Guide to Teaching and Learning
MIRIAM RAIDER-ROTH

. . . an "I poem" [is] a sonogram on the psyche . . .
Carol Gilligan (2002, 40).

On a spring afternoon, in the quiet of her softly lit office in Larsen Hall, I sat with Carol Gilligan and confessed confusion.

"I don't think I can use the Listening Guide in my research," began my confession.

"Oh?" Gilligan looked at me, with wide eyes and a hint of a smile. Her surprise was understandable. My words were not consistent with our recent conversations. I had actually experienced an epiphany of sorts after using the Listening Guide to understand the relational dynamics of classroom life. All of a sudden, I could see and hear these dynamics in surround sound, as if someone had turned on a set of high-quality speakers in the room. It was an acute awareness that seemed to suddenly appear.

"The trouble with the Listening Guide is that it feels magical. One moment, I can't see anything, and the next moment, there's a powerful poem laden with meaning right in front of me. How can I use the method if I don't understand it?"

After a moment's pause, Gilligan responded, "Well, I think you know what you need to do."

I had a pretty good sense of what she was about to say: "You have to take this question seriously. You have to understand the magic. You may need to use the method to understand it, but don't let go of your question." Gilligan's directive reminded me of the rabbinic imperative from the "Passover Haggadah": *Tzeh ulmad*. Go and learn.

I took Gilligan's message seriously, and truth be told, it has taken me years to come to terms with the magic. This essay is an effort to explain my learning process, my journey in coming to understand the workings of the Listening Guide, and its capacity to tap into central relational dynamics in the world of teaching and learning. The dual act of both using and teaching this voice-centered relational methodology has provided me ample opportunity to experience and understand its power and has afforded me certainty of its rigor, robustness, and ability to voice thoughts and feelings that are central in understanding the relational dynamics of classroom life.

THE MAGIC OF ASSOCIATION

What is the nature and place of this awareness—this magical quality—in the world of research, and in teaching and learning? As an inherent quality of the Listening Guide methodology, what can this intangible dimension offer us that other methodologies cannot? I have worked and reworked this question since that spring afternoon in Gilligan's office. I will begin with my conclusion and then explain how I arrived there.

I believe that this magic reflects the beauty and mystery of the associative process that is central to the Listening Guide methodology. While association has found a respectable and central place in the world of psychotherapy, it is a much more suspect member of the research world. Association is subjective, personal, nonlinear, unpredictable, oftentimes surprising, and sometimes troubling. Association follows the connections, feelings, thoughts, questions, and images that occur as a person encounters another person, idea, place, song, scent, and so forth. This psychological process is at odds with the dominant paradigm of human science research, which is positivistic, rational, linear, generalizable, replicable, and large-scale. Indeed, the current paradigm endorses standardization, cultivation of a climate of depersonalization, and lack of connection. And yet, the very power of the associative process and the recognition of this form of thinking, knowing, and feeling for both the researcher and the participant is what I believe affords researchers unique access to the heartbeat of the classroom, to the pulse of relationship for teachers and students. In this way, the associative process awakens a relational stance and understanding.

It was in listening to a twelve-year-old boy named Jon that I first experienced the transformative power of the associative process in the Listening Guide, which kindled my ability to hear the relational dimension of the learning process. In the moments before I interviewed Jon, I sat in my car in the school parking lot while writing in my journal. I had two lines of questions I considered posing for him—his perspective on student self-assessment[1] and his thoughts about what it takes to trust what he knows.

My stated goals for this study had been to understand students' experiences of self-assessment, and, yet, I kept returning in my journal to questions of trust and knowledge. I decided to shelve the trust questions after thinking that my understanding of their place was not yet developed and that they would be too risky or derailing. I worried about confusing Jon (and myself). So I began by asking him whether opportunities in school to reflect on his learning were meaningful to him. He responded that they were only useful when he could compare self-reflections or self-evaluations over time.

At that moment I remembered a recent, informal conversation I had had with Jon when he told me that he was worried that he was not learning much in school that year. I did not fully understanding what had triggered this memory, but I decided to share it with Jon. He responded quickly and said, "I'm hoping that my teachers . . . will be able to show us what we've learned. But if they don't, I'm just going to have to trust myself and believe that I did learn."

His response stunned me, as he had built a bridge to the questions of trusting self and learning that I had decided to set aside. Somehow, following my memory or association had provided a trigger that led to this connection. This time, I set aside the self-assessment questions and followed Jon's thoughts and my curiosity.

We talked at length about times when he trusted what he knew and times when that trust was more fleeting. Just before he had to return to class, I asked him the question that I could not answer for myself— whether he saw a connection between trusting what he knew and student self-assessment. Once again, his response was illuminating: "Yeah, because if the kids trust what they know they can say, . . . 'Oh I know math. You know I can do long division. I can do decimals I can use decimals.' But if they don't know what they know, 'Ooh I'm not so sure about long division' . . . then they write things that really aren't true, but they just don't know it about themselves yet."

Essentially, Jon taught me that if children trust their knowledge, they can then locate what they know in their self-assessments and use this knowledge powerfully—such as by solving mathematical challenges. If, however, they do not trust what they know, they will assess themselves doubtfully and communicate to themselves and their teachers that they lack knowledge. Jon believes that they are communicating falsehoods about themselves because they don't have the trust to actually locate what they know.

In following my associations to Jon's prior comments and my curiosity about trust and knowledge, I was able to follow his thoughts, connections, associations, confusions, and emotions. Conceptually, I was able to understand that in the process of thinking about his own learning, Jon considered his relationship to the self, peers, and teachers. I learned that in order for Jon to trust what he knew, he needed to trust his teachers to guide his learning and to help him when his own trust in self faltered. Jon taught me that these relationships were bound with one another, and that trust in self was bound to trust in others.

Methodologically, I had learned that the researcher's associative process had to be taken seriously, documented carefully, and incorporated in the "trail of evidence" (Gilligan et al. 1995) that is required of the Listening Guide researcher. In interviewing Jon, I had seen that when I communicated my associations to him, he in turn made important connections between his ideas and my question. When a researcher's memories or associations trigger important pathways or bridges for the participant, they can indicate a level of connection and attunement between the researcher and the participant. Tracking these associations therefore allows us to follow the participant's pathways of thinking and feeling with which we connect.

The idea that the researcher's train of thought is "data" or "evidence" is a radical one in the current climate of educational research, which reveres objective, measurable, and replicable methodologies. Yet, the tradition of attending to the "listener" or reader's responses to another's narrative is well established in the world of psychotherapy, where counter-transference (the therapist's reactions and/or projection of their own rela-tional experiences and history) is viewed as key data in understanding the therapeutic relationship and thus the psychological processes of the patient or client (Rogers 1991).

Similarly, the reader's response to text is a crucial practice in literary criticism. In working to understand the dynamics of learning relation-ships, it is often the dynamics of the research relationship that shed light on the key issues being studied because the research relationship, as its core, is a learning one where the researcher is the learner. For example, in my own experience as a researcher, when interviewing a student who is struggling with painful knowledge that he has dissociated or disconnected from, I have found myself at times disconnecting or dissociating from the participant or the interview itself.

Recognizing these relational moves in myself has helped me under-stand and decipher my participants' thinking and feeling about their learning relationships. Association detects the peaks and valleys of the relationship, much like a heart monitor traces the rhythm of the heart. By following the researcher's associative process to an interview or narrative, we can draw one draft of a relational road map of the narrative. Similarly, when we follow the participant's associative logic, we render a different map. If we were to create (metaphoric) transparencies of these maps and place one on top of the other, we would render a multidimensional view of the narrative terrain. By inviting the researcher's associations, connections, memories, and confusions into the canon of acceptable data, we acknowledge the interplay of relationship in the research process and render a much more complex and rich view of the narrative.

When I listened to Jon, and as I followed my own associations and curiosity, I began to understand my own questions. I learned that a relational method could not only change what I could hear but could also change me as a researcher. It was not so much about discovering my findings. It was about entering a research relationship that was about genuine learning, where the researcher, like the learner in the classroom, comes away changed.

In listening to Jon, I realized that what I was labeling "student voice and assessment" was more accurately a detection of the relational dynamics in the classroom; understanding how the relationships between teachers and students shaped student learning and teachers' practice. Through subsequent interviews with other twelve-year-old children in Jon's school, I learned that they closely monitor the relational dynamics of their classrooms and adjust their spoken knowledge accordingly. Through their narratives, I heard children who concealed knowledge that did not seem welcome in their classroom and who held this knowledge steadfastly, albeit underground. For other students, the concealment had a higher cost, for they disconnected or lost hold of the knowledge when they felt it unsafe to say out loud. In short, I learned that in order for students to construct robust or trustworthy knowledge, they needed to learn in the context of trusting relationships. I developed a deep understanding of learning as an inherently relational process (Raider-Roth 2005a, b).

My experience with Jon and the research that followed taught me about the power of "discovery research." Gilligan speaks of the Listening Guide as discovery research—as sketching landscapes that had not yet been described in the literature (Gilligan et al. 2003). It is this discovery, this thrill of seeing something that had not been visible, that is the feeling-tone of the work. Early on, I had understood "discovery research" narrowly—that it was a process researchers engaged in by trying to unearth areas that had been overlooked or undetected, and that the goal was to describe the terrain of this new territory. While this is certainly an important goal of discovery research, it is also the self-discovery on the part of the researcher that makes the Listening Guide both so powerful and challenging to use. Like all creative processes, discovery requires an openness of mind, a tolerance for confusion, a comfort with discomfort, and an awareness that to enter a research process means to challenge one's questions, assumptions, and understandings.

Perhaps the most provocative issue that this discovery process raised for me was my legitimacy as an educational researcher in using a psychological and relational method. Somehow I felt myself to be a trespasser. What right did I have to listen so intently to the psychological logic of another person? While teaching and learning draw on fundamental psychological processes such as development, emotion, and cognition, attending to the dynamics of relationship seemed the purview of the clinician, not the researcher. And yet, the more I used the Listening Guide, the more I found it impossible *not* to listen in this way. That is, once I started listening for the logic of the psyche as expressed by the children I was interviewing, I could not screen out this voice without silencing what I was coming to hear and coming to know: the profound relational tones of classroom life and their centrality in the learning process. I realized that this kind of research was a deeply psychological enterprise, and that this kind of psychological and relational understanding was not trespass but a key building block in understanding teaching and learning. It was changing my identity as an educational researcher.

As I began teaching the Listening Guide, I observed doctoral students of education who were experiencing what I had experienced. In bringing their own questions to their inquiries, they often began to hear ideas and emotions they had not heard and to construct new understandings of their own practice. Even with these often thoughtful insights, they worried that a relational methodology was not theirs to use. Perhaps one reason for this is the remarkable historical absence of relational theory from mainstream literature on teaching and learning.[2] Students often ask me, sometimes in frustrated tones, how it was that they spent so many years in education without having been taught a relational perspective. I also encounter students such as Billy, a student in my course on Feminist Qualitative Methodology (focusing on the Listening Guide), who was moved to tears at the end of one class session. In reflecting on this class session, he wrote,

> I felt as if someone turned on a light and I could see myself in a research role. . . . Once I was opened up to feminist research and the Listening Guide, I immediately felt at home with research, and frankly my view of it. I can liken it to the experience of community or purpose one has when finding out she/he is not alone

(to discover those around you are also gay or lesbian or democrat or Latino, etc.). Simply, reading and discussing feminist research goals/methods gave me "proof" that how I had always felt about giving voice or projecting meaning was a legitimate and important mode/voice of research. My actual epiphany was quite emotional and I felt overcome with joy/validation. I suppose my feelings of validation were equivalent to what we hope our feminist research methods do—give voice and provide a venue. I now have my venue and a platform from which to better understand voice (my own and others').

As Billy so clearly articulates, as students integrate a relational perspective into their conceptions of teaching, learning, and research, they can locate their authority by finding the place and the need for a methodology that affords them access to fundamental but often unrecognized aspects of their own knowledge—and to their awareness of the relational dimensions of human life.

REFLECTION AND RELATIONAL THEORY AND PRACTICE

In my inquiry in bridging the worlds of teaching and learning, associative process, and relational theory and practice, I have returned time and again to John Dewey's theory of reflection. When considering why and how the Listening Guide can be such a useful research process for understanding teaching and learning, I have come to recognize that the Guide invites the key processes of Dewey's reflective cycle and, in so doing, marries thought and emotion, self and other, learning and action.

Dewey's theory of reflection teaches that in an effort to create new knowledge, the learner must be able to make connections to what she already knows, have experiences that allow her to construct new ideas, have a venue for articulating this emerging knowledge, and have an opportunity to act on this knowledge.[3] The logic of the four listenings in the Listening Guide methodology builds directly on this reflective cycle.

The first listening of the Guide asks the researcher to describe what she hears, the significant landmarks of the narrative at hand, the silences detected in the text, and the logic and contradictions she detects. The goal is to decipher and articulate the main "plot" lines of the narrative. The first listening also asks the researcher to pay close attention to her reactions, connections, associations, questions, surprises, and revulsions. Gilligan teaches that the "listener's response" helps the researcher locate her own story that is evoked by the conversation with the participant and helps the researcher keep her own story separate so that the analysis does not become a ventriloquy that uses the participant's words to tell the researcher's story (Gilligan et al. 2003). In the process of describing the "plot" of the narrative as well as locating the researcher's associative path, the researcher begins the process of connecting to her own prior knowledge and experiences with the learning at hand in the research relationship. In this way, the first listening functions as a key step in the reflective cycle, the place where the researcher describes what she sees and makes crucial connections to what she does and does not know, thereby allowing her to construct new ideas.

The second listening asks the researcher to listen to the voice of self that the participant brings to the narrative in relationship with the researcher. The researcher listens especially closely to the "I" voice of the participant by extracting, in sequential order, the "I phrases" (I + verb) from the narrative, such as "I want, I need, I see, I feel." In so doing, an "I poem" is formed. This process of listening closely to the "I" voice of the participant offers the researcher an opportunity to create and deepen a relationship with the participant and the text. Because of both the intensity of this listening, which I will discuss later in this essay, and the creative act of composing the Voice Poems, the methodology actually creates a whole-body, intensive experience that the researcher can engage in, hold, look back on, and build from. The idea of learning in experience is key to Dewey's concept of reflective thought and key to the process of building knowledge that is rooted in relationship with self and others (1963).

The third and fourth listenings, the contrapuntal listenings for the predominant voices in the narrative, provide an analytic and hypothesis-generating opportunity in the research process. In these listenings, the researcher listens for prevailing themes in the narrative that are in tension with one another. These tensions are often relational in nature and reflect the internal negotiations that the participant experiences when she speaks of relationship to self or others. When listening in this way, the researcher generates multiple hypotheses for what she suspects is occurring in the dialogue or tension between these voices. She may discover that two competing voices (such as the voice of knowing and not knowing) are acting out a drama in the narrative. In isolating these voices, she can listen for evidence of this hypothesis. In this act of creating and examining hypotheses, the researcher is engaged in the heart of the Deweyan cycle of reflective thought, where the learner generates multiple hypotheses for understanding the complexity of an educative experience and chooses a hypothesis to examine and explore further (Dewey 1933).

In the final synthesis stage of the method, when the researcher brings together her learning from the listenings, she has an opportunity to articulate her new knowledge and to take action as a result of this learning. Taking intelligent action is the final step in the reflective cycle (Rodgers 2002, 842–66). The action may lead to generating new theory, revising initial research questions, constructing the frame for follow-up interviews, building analytic structures to try out with other narratives in the study, or taking pedagogical moves to try out in teaching and learning environments.

While the reflective cycle, as described by Dewey and paraphrased in brief here, can appear linear in its construction, it is actually a true cycle in which the learner may go through the described steps many times, may enter midcycle, or skip a step only to return to it later (ibid.). The centrality of this process in the Listening Guide is to provide a researcher a frame—a map for the journey of the methodology. As described below, the associative process that is the bedrock of this methodology can lead researchers in a myriad of directions that potentially leave us inundated with possible routes to explore. Having the structure of the reflective cycle offers a grounding—an anchor for what can, at times, be a rocky voyage.

Assuming a Learner's Stance

By recognizing the inherent connections between the reflective cycle and the Listening Guide process, I am able to see the role of the researcher as that of a learner. It is this stance that I explicitly ask students to assume, because the traditional image of "researcher" often elicits a hierarchical stance of an imposing, all-knowing, authoritative figure who makes judgments of the other. In asking graduate students to become learners of those they study, I ask them to assume an altogether different stance. They approach their fellow teachers, students, and administrators with curiosity, ask genuine questions that stem from places of meaning-making, and try to understand that which they truly do not know. Students often experience this stance as a relief. When questioning their authority to inquire into the lives of others and the "validity" of their expertise to ask such questions, I teach them that it is their genuine curiosity, their authentic desire to learn from their participants, that grants them this privilege. It is a genuine "inquiry stance" that they are seeking (Cochran-Smith and Lytle 2001).

To assume this learning stance with others, researchers must apply this stance to themselves and listen carefully to their own questions, reactions, thoughts, and emotion. In "Teaching Shakespeare's Sister: Notes from the Underground of Female Adolescence," Gilligan describes a pivotal teaching moment when she asked her graduate students to "pose a real question, a question to which they really wanted to know the answer" (1990, 33). She writes about the effort that these students, especially the women, experience when trying to locate their own internal voices and clearing their minds of "good questions" or "important questions" (ibid., 8). It is this lesson about listening to the self and listening to what matters to the heart and mind of the self that I bring to my students. It is this lesson that makes the difference. When students start listening to themselves, they then begin to listen to others; they then begin to make connections between what they hear in themselves and what they hear in others. They see that recognizing what they know to be true about themselves and locating what they are genuinely curious about afford them the possibility of being able to listen to others' curiosity. Paying close attention to curiosity, a fundamental disposition in the process of reflection, sets the stage for paying attention to the pathways of association that will be generated as they listen closely to the experiences of others (Dewey 1933).

The drama of association begins when the students pose their questions to others and engage them in dialogue. As rooted in my learning with Gilligan, I ask students to listen carefully in their interviews to moments when their questions become the questions of their participants. When participants make the questions their own, they begin to shape the questions in such a way as to create a springboard for the stories they want to narrate. Together with my students, we consider the processes that change their questions. What can they learn by the shift in question? It is as if they have a vase of wet clay that they have rendered on a potter's wheel, and as if they then ask their participants to put their hands on the clay and continue the rendering process. It is this transformation that I ask them to watch. What happens to the form of the question? What happens to them as learners as they watch their questions change shape and meaning? Can they join this shared interpretive process? Do they resist it? Do they feel enriched or threatened? In this location of self, my students become aware of what they can see easily and where they may have blind spots. This alerts them to the places where they will have to be especially attentive so as to be as open as possible to their participants' stories. As they pay attention to the shifts in their questions, they are well poised to hear the stories their participants narrate.

In asking student researchers to assume the supplicant stance of learner, I am also asking them to assume a strength-seeking stance—the stance of looking for the goodness, the logic, the sense of the person they are studying. This approach is derived from the Listening Guide's philosophical stance (Gilligan et al. 2003). In my own work, it is also influenced by the work of Sara Lawrence-Lightfoot in her Portraiture methodology (Lawrence-Lightfoot and Davis 1997) and by the work of Patricia Carini on the Descriptive Process (Carini and Himley 2000). The common link among these three different methodologies, born in different disciplines (relational psychology, ethnography, and phenomenology), is the common search for the strength and resilience residing in human experience.

Perhaps the most overt lesson for me in this regard occurred during my first Listening Guide study. I was interviewing Maya, a brilliant twelve-year-old girl, about her experiences of learning; I was trying to understand the occasions when she trusted what she knew and occasions when that trust was harder to locate. During the entire first interview, she returned time and again to saying that she had "a lot of self-esteem" and therefore could not remember times when she did not trust what she knew. Halfway through this interview, I found myself tuning out and thinking that the interview had lost its footing. Connecting back to my own experience of being a twelve-year-old girl, I found it hard to believe that she was in a constant state of having "a lot of self-esteem." Ending the interview with a promise of another interview (as was the design of the research project), I slumped in frustration in a chair in the school office where I was conducting the interviews. The interview had felt aimless, and the thought of doing another hour like this one seemed like an obligation rather than a genuine inquiry.

Frightened by the emptiness I experienced in the interview, I picked up the office phone to call Gilligan. Much to my relief, her calming voice answered the ring immediately. I described the interview, the scene, my own failures as an interviewer. After listening, Gilligan asked in her gentle yet direct manner, "Did you ask her what having 'a lot of self-esteem' meant to her?" I was embarrassed and stunned. Not only had I *not* asked this question, I immediately understood what was lacking in this interview. My own reactions and associations to Maya's narratives were so strong that I had stopped listening. I could only incorporate her language into my own experience. I had not been able to step back to understand hers, to understand the meaning *she* was making in trying to construct her sense of self. I had stopped listening for the meaning or "goodness" in her words.

Herein was a lesson of the power of association, when it can derail an interview should it go unrecognized, and the centrality of the researcher's continual examination of the self. Only when I was able to locate my own twelve-year-old-girl experience and locate what self-esteem had meant to me then and what it meant to me as an adult woman was I able to listen and be fully present to Maya's experience of self-esteem.

In her second interview, I began by telling her that I had listened to the first interview and noticed this recurrent phrase. I told her that I wanted to understand what having a lot of self-esteem meant to her. In shifting my stance to one that listened for her meaning, her logic, and her strength rather than dismissing her with disbelief, I communicated that I was listening with connection rather than judgment. The result of this changed stance was remarkable. Maya and I entered into a conversation in which she described the great difficulty she experiences when talking about "not knowing" and the memories of trauma that get provoked. She described in vivid details her process of separating her knowledge onto two shelves: one "that's the horrible stuff" and the rest of her life that "becomes this other shelf." She described getting rid of the horrible stuff and said, "I don't think of it as part of my life anymore" (Raider-Roth 2005a, 78). Maya's striking portrait of the dissociative process helped me understand why her grasp on self-esteem was so central in her psychological logic and how it served as a fundamental buffer against her pain. Without assuming the understanding and strength-seeking stance that I did, I would not have been able to understand *her* meanings, *her* logic, or *her* navigation of her own relational terrain.

THE CENTRALITY OF AN INTERPRETIVE COMMUNITY

The move to call Gilligan on the phone—the need for another voice in my own research process—reflects the need for an interpretive community in the Listening Guide process. By assuming a learner's stance, I realized that what I learned from my research with children applied to myself as a researcher. That is, to build trustworthy knowledge in the research process, I needed to be learning in the context of trustworthy relationships. Early on, I believed that having an interpretive community was an ideal to aspire for but not a prerequisite of the Guide. The more I teach and use the methodology, however, the more I believe that it is a centerpiece of the process.

The centrality of this community stems from two significant demands in this methodology. First, in considering the data with other researchers from diverse walks of life, the researcher has the opportunity to see her blind spots and to recognize voices she may not be hearing because of her own personal or cultural lenses. Additionally, by inviting multiple interpretations of the text, the researcher can build a complex and nuanced understanding.

In my study of teachers' understandings of their relationships with boys, we experienced a turning-point meeting of our interpretive community, of graduate students and faculty (Raider-Roth et al. 2008). One member presented an analysis of a narrative in which a teacher, Anna, described her fraught relationship with Michael, an eight-year-old boy in her class. In describing her relationship with Michael, Anna repeated the phrase, "I have to let him go." She used this phrase in different contexts: letting him go from whole-class activities so that he could do his own thing, letting him go the following year to another teacher, letting him go to do his school work the way he wanted to do it rather than the way she wanted it done.

The person presenting this analysis suggested that the meaning of this phrase represented Anna's willingness to give Michael freedom, to follow his learning rather than her agenda, to loosen up her reins to see where he would take her. Another member of the group strenuously disagreed with this analysis and suggested that these words represented Anna's letting go of a relationship with Michael and her disconnecting from him. The research group debated these two interpretations at length and drew evidence from the narrative to support each interpretation. In a moment of clarity, the group realized that both interpretations helped us understand the complex dynamics of this teacher–student relationship. Anna's act of letting go held multiple truths that she was juggling in her relationship with Michael.

As I learned from Gilligan, the goal of the Listening Guide is to render the complexity of human thought and emotion, not to flatten or reduce to a monodimensional understanding. When we were able to hold both interpretations of Anna's thought, we were then able to appreciate the complexity of her relationship with Michael and the ways in which it was fraught, as well as the richness of her thoughts about Michael, her teaching, and issues of gender. In so doing, we were able to hear the depth of her narrative.

The interpretive community can assist the researcher in processing the intense emotional responses that can be triggered by the listening and associative processes. As a graduate student, I believed that my own strong reactions to my participants' interviews were the results of my own emotional disposition. While this may indeed be true, I have now watched many doctoral students use this method in their research, and many have similar experiences. They send emails, call, or appear at my office door with a slightly desperate tone or look, and they worry that they are too close to the narrative, that they feel stuck in the vortex of their participants' thoughts and emotions, that they fear this intense engagement will derail them from their work and will prevent them from seeing clearly.

I now understand this emotional spiral as a difficult and essential part of the Listening Guide process; it signifies engagement, relationship, connectedness, and resistance to the dissociative forces that would inhibit understanding. And yet, it is a dangerous moment in the research process because of the intensity of the engagement. It is a moment reflecting the profound relational nature of this research process. It is a psychological experience demonstrating the power of association. As the researcher becomes more attuned to the logic of another person's thinking and feeling, and as she listens closely to her own responses, connections, and memories, she may well confront ideas and emotions that had not yet been voiced by the participant or by herself. At this moment she must ask herself if she can or wants to hear these voices, if she can or wants to build this new knowledge.

Gilligan likens this moment to entering a dark room with the participant. You must ask yourself, "Do I have the courage and trust to explore this space with this person and to learn what I do not know?" It is at this moment that the interpretive community is essential to help the researcher understand the nature of the text that has grabbed hold of her, to help her articulate what she has heard and learned, to help her regain her footing and build an understanding from this fragile moment.

THE POWER OF ASSOCIATION

In my experience, the interpretive community is most needed when the researcher is engaged in the second listening, when the power of association in the Listening Guide is most intensely experienced. The nature of this associative power is complex and important to disentangle.

Listening to the logic of the "I voice," or the voice of the self that the participant shares in response to the researcher's questions, the researcher gains access to the participant's internal dialogue and psychological logic. Gilligan teaches that the second listening—the listening for the "I voice" in the narrative—is the distinguishing feature of this methodology, that it allows the researcher to magnify the participant's voice and to make it "magnificent." In this experience, the researcher can behold the logic and beauty of the self that the participant shares with her, at that moment in time, in response to the questions that are asked. It is the time, like the sonogram, when all of a sudden the magic can occur—when I can see and hear what was previously hidden or muted. Time and again, when I teach the second listening and we begin to extract the "I phrases" from the narrative into a carefully constructed list that ultimately reads as a poem, I can see the students' faces change from furrowed brows of confusion to wide-eyed gazes of comprehension, sometimes with tears, other times with a hand on the forehead while uttering something along the lines of, "Is this possible?" Oftentimes, there is a stretch of silence where we are taking in the new understanding. It is one of those extraordinary moments in teaching when learning and understanding are visible, readily apparent to all who share in the experience. And we begin the discussion of magic.

The second listening draws an outline of the logic of another person's thinking and feeling. As the "I poems" are constructed, this outline becomes visible, much like the outline of the head, arms, fingers, and toes suddenly appear in a sonogram of a developing fetus. The thoughts and feelings take shape and form, and they allow us to hold them and to react to them. We come into relationship with them. In entering the relationship, our own thoughts and feelings are stirred. The images of another's psyche (their thoughts, feelings, and inner experiences) evoke images of ourselves, our experiences, our other relationships. In recognizing the other, we look back at ourselves, and the associative process is in full bloom as we see where our minds go when we see the magnificence of another person. We follow the paths of our thoughts; we make connections and discoveries; we create new ideas. We return to the voice poems only to find new meanings that send us back to our own thoughts and associations. The second listening is a recursive process of association, recognition, and connection that leads to the generation of new knowledge.

It was in listening to Jon, the twelve-year-old we met at the beginning of this essay, that I first experienced this transformative nature of the second listening. In describing his learning in school, Jon told me of moments when he could and could not trust what he knew in school:

> To say, you know, I am learning something, you know, *because you might not be* [serious tone]. And usually you are when you have a teacher or something, but I mean sometimes it is a review for people. And sometimes you just gotta, you know, maybe it'll seem weird and you'll think you're really not learning anything, and you *know* you're not learning anything, just still gotta say I *am*. I am learning something and I'm gonna learn something and I'm gonna learn more and more and more.

Listening to this excerpt as it was spoken, I had a hard time understanding his meaning. He seemed to be contradicting himself, to be having a hard time deciding whether he was learning or not. The logic of his thinking emerged when listening closely to the way he was speaking of himself, using both the "I" and "you" pronouns to represent an internal dialogue:

I	You
I am learning	You might not be
	Usually you are
	You have
I mean	You just gotta
	You'll think
	You're really not learning
	You *know* you're not learning
I am	
I am learning	
I'm gonna learn	
I'm gonna learn	

By isolating these voices, I could hear an exquisite internal conversation between the "I voice" who was determined to learn and the "You voice" who was doubtful and skeptical. I was no longer confused, as I could hear and see his internal tension clearly. I was keenly aware of the magical quality of the Listening Guide that afforded me the transition from confusion to understanding, from hearing the narrative as an opaque text to a poetic conversation of the self. I now understand that the sudden awareness I developed resided in locating the logic and the meaning of these voices, which in turn offered me the opportunity to hear the melodies of Jon's thinking and feeling. Hearing the voices of the self that Jon shared with me in this interview helped me understand that this methodology tapped into a multidimensional, relational part of human experience that was at the core of teaching and learning.

THE RELATIONAL PRACTICE OF RESEARCH, TEACHING, AND LEARNING

The magic or awareness that the Listening Guide elicits stems from its ability to craft a place for both the researcher's and the participant's associations, connections, thoughts, and emotions. In this recursive process, the methodology can help make visible the foundational relational and psychological root system of human life. As educational researchers, our authority to uncover these lifelines of learning resides in our ability to listen carefully to the experiences of those who inhabit these learning spaces, to come into relationship with those who tell us their stories, and to follow the paths of our own thinking as we listen relationally. We are then able to construct understandings that illuminate ideas, emotions, and experiences that are at the core of teaching and learning.

In *Trusting What You Know: The High Stakes of Classroom Relationships* (2005a), I introduced the idea of the "relational learner" and drew empirically on my research with children as well as on the foundational work in relational psychology by Gilligan, Jean Baker Miller, Judith Jordan, and Irene Stiver. I suggested that for the relational learner in education, "the learning self is constructed and developed within the relationships of school" (ibid., 21). Drawing on the work of Miller and Stiver (1997), I argued that the developmental marker of growth is participation in mutually empathic, "growth-fostering" or learning-enhancing relationships. As I reflect on my learning from and teaching of the Listening Guide, I believe it is time to introduce the idea of the "relational teacher" and the "relational researcher," as both of these roles are central to the teaching and learning of this research methodology. Additionally, understanding the dispositions, practices, and stances of these relational roles will assist us in facilitating many more "comings home" or locations of self-experiences such as the one described by Billy earlier in this essay. Most importantly, with such theoretical models in place, we can help educate a new generation of teachers and researchers who are attuned to the logic of the psyche and who understand the essential pathways between this logic and human learning.

Notes

1   Self-assessment was defined in this study as classroom experiences in which students were asked to assess or evaluate their performance or their knowledge in school.

2   Recent scholarship has begun to apply relational theory to classroom life. For examples see Carollee Howes and Sharon Ritchie (2002), Lesley Koplow (2002), and Nel Noddings (2003).

3   For further reading on John Dewey's theory of reflection, see Dewey (1933), Harriet Cuffaro (1995), and Carol Rodgers (2002).

References

CARINI, Patricia F., and Margaret Himley. 2000. *From Another Angle: Children's Strengths and School Standards*. New York: Teachers College Press.

COCHRAN-SMITH, Marilyn, and Susan L. Lytle. 2001. "Beyond Certainty: Taking an Inquiry Stance on Practice." In Ann Lieberman and Lynne Miller (eds), *Teachers Caught in the Action: Professional Development that Matters*. New York: Teachers College Press, pp. 45–58.

CUFFARO, Harriet. 1995. *Experimenting with the World: John Dewey and the Early Childhood Classroom*. New York: Teachers College Press.

DEWEY, John. 1933. *How We Think: A Restatement of Relation of Reflective Thinking to the Education Process*. Boston: D. C. Heath.

————. 1963. *Experience and Education*. New York: Touchstone.

GILLIGAN, Carol. 1990. "Teaching Shakespeare's Sister: Notes from the Underground of Female Adolescence." In Carol Gilligan, Nona Lyons, and Trudy Hanmer (eds), *Making Connections: The Relational Worlds of Adolescent Girls at the Emma Willard School*. Cambridge, MA: Harvard University Press, pp. 31–51.

————. 2002. *The Birth of Pleasure: A New Map of Love*. New York: Alfred A. Knopf.

————, Jill McLean Taylor, and Amy Sullivan. 1995. *Between Voice and Silence: Women and Girls, Race and Relationship*. Cambridge, MA: Harvard University Press.

————, Renee Spencer, Katherine M. Weinberg, and Bertsch Tatiana. 2003. "On the Listening Guide: A Voice-Centered Relational Model." In Paul M. Camic, Jean E. Rhodes and Lucy Yardley (eds.), *Qualitative Research in Psychology: Expanding Perspectives in Methodology and Design*. Washington, DC: American Psychological Association Press, pp. 157–72.

HOWES, Carollee, and Sharon Ritchie. 2002. *A Matter of Trust: Connecting Teachers and Learners in the Early Childhood Classroom*. New York: Teachers College Press.

KOPLOW, Lesley. 2002. *Creating Schools that Heal: Real-Life Solutions*. New York: Teachers College Press.

LAWRENCE-LIGHTFOOT, Sara, and Jessica Hoffman Davis. 1997. *The Art and Science of Portraiture*. San Francisco: Jossey-Bass.

MILLER, Jean Baker, and Irene Stiver. 1997. *The Healing Connection: How Women Form Relationships in Therapy and in Life*. Boston: Beacon.

NODDINGS, Nel. 2003. *Caring: A Feminine Approach to Ethics and Moral Education*. Berkeley: University of California Press.

RAIDER-ROTH, Miriam. 2005a. *Trusting What You Know: The High Stakes of Classroom Relationships*. San Francisco: Jossey-Bass.

————. 2005b. "Trusting What You Know: Negotiating the Relational Context of Classroom Life." *Teachers College Record* 107(4): 587–628.

————, Marta K. Albert, Ingrid Bircann-Barkey, Eric Gidseg, and Terry Murray. 2008. "Teaching Boys: A Relational Puzzle." *Teachers College Record* 110 (2): 443–81.

RODGERS, Carol. 2002. "Defining Reflection: Another Look at John Dewey and Reflective Thinking." *Teachers College Record* 104(4): 842–66.

ROGERS, Annie G. 1991. "A Feminist Poetics of Psychotherapy." In Carol Gilligan, Annie G. Rogers, and Deborah L. Tolman (eds), *Women, Girls, & Psychotherapy: Reframing Resistance*. New York: Harrington Park Press, pp. 33–54.

In the course of a conversation with Carol Gilligan, legal scholar and cultural critic Zvi Triger questioned her decision to offer an account of the psychology of love that was based exclusively on the study of heterosexual love:

ZT: *I wanted to ask you about the theme of resistance with respect to gays and lesbians. Some readers have been disappointed that gays and lesbians were left out of* The Birth of Pleasure *(2002). I tend to disagree, because even before we "become" gay or lesbian or straight, we're all products of this culture and its tragic story of love. But I'm really interested in the way resistance plays out in gay and lesbian relationships, because there is a stream of thought that argues that gays and lesbians have the potential of eradicating patriarchy.*

CG: *My strategy was deliberate. I thought that gays and lesbians, by virtue of their sexuality, are necessarily in a position of resistance. Their sexuality is not going to fit into that main story even though they're absolutely washed in that story. I wanted to show that even if you went to where love is sanctioned, where there is no ostensible cultural impediment to love, to the so-called straight relationship, you have these psychic impediments. I'm very interested in your question. There were some gay couples in the therapy project that Terrence Real and I did, and I might have addressed their relationships explicitly. I remember someone saying to me: you should now write this book for gays. I don't think I'm the one to write a book about gay love, but I would find that a very interesting book.*

ZT: *And do you think that a queer* The Birth of Pleasure *will reveal that gay and lesbian couples are trapped in a hierarchical story as well?*

CG: *My book suggests that. And the reason is that gays were little boys, and lesbians were adolescent girls. I'm not saying that this comes out of sexuality. This is coming out of something between the psyche and the culture, from which gays are not exempt. The interesting question for me is how being gay and lesbian affects the possibility of resistance.*

Kendall Thomas presses the argument that The Birth of Pleasure *does, and should not, neglect the queer, and in doing so he opens a window on what a queer perspective might reveal. Thomas's critique resonates with Gilligan's earlier complaint that human psychology cannot be built on the study of exclusively male subjects. He argues that patriarchy is inextricably intertwined with—and is more richly understood in light of—homophobia. Then, taking up Gilligan's claim that love is the precondition for democracy, he draws on queer theory to argue that resistance is shallow unless it goes beyond the pursuit of freedom, preference, or pleasure to the pursuit of social harmony.*

The Methodological Costs of Exclusion
KENDALL THOMAS

This chapter describes my experience of reading *The Birth of Pleasure*: *A New Map of Love* while reflecting on the methodological commitments of what has come to be known as queer theory. I will focus specifically on three moments in *The Birth of Pleasure*, one from each of its three chapters, with an eye to exploring how queer method offers a useful, and to my mind indispensable, critical compass for negotiating the uncharted terrain through which Carol Gilligan's radical geography of love so boldly challenges us to journey. My claim in brief is that an explicit, sustained engagement with the methods of queer theory would have yielded a clearer and more complete cartography of the landscape where pleasure is buried than the map of love that Professor Gilligan draws.

The first moment in the text of the *The Birth of Pleasure* to which I call your attention comes in the opening chapter. Discussing her clinical collaboration with Terrence Real, Gilligan explains their studies of couples in crisis:

> We were interested more specifically in the tensions between love and patriarchy as they play out within and between women and men, generation after generation. And also in the challenges posed for couples by the changes brought about by women's liberation. Because I want to explore whether love in, and, of itself sets in motion a resistance to patriarchy, I have chosen to focus on heterosexual love, which is culturally sanctioned, rather than gay and lesbian relationships. Working for the most part with straight couples, Real and I came to an illumination that was unexpected (ibid., 15).

A queer reading would pose a number of distinct but related questions about this passage and its explanation of the choice to restrict its exploration of the tensions between women and men—to a heterosexual love that it sets up in opposition to the domain of gay and lesbian relationships. Since a queer reading of text attends not only to the substance of an argument but also to the language in which that argument is cast, we might begin by asking several questions: What are we to make of the discursive differentiation between heterosexual love on the one hand and gay and lesbian relationships on the other? Are gay and lesbian relation-ships to be understood as a form of intimacy which is not captured by the word "love"? More fundamentally, is it possible to imagine love in and of itself—that is, to imagine a pure love that has an existence outside the social identities that go under the names of sex, gender, and sexual orientation? Isn't such impossibility registered in the text by the apparent elision of love-as-such with heterosexual love? Why should the cultural sanction that attaches to heterosexual love operate as a restrictive limit on the investigation of tensions between love and patriarchy? What are the contradictions between, on the one hand, a theoretical constructivism that rightly insists that the tragic story of heterosexual love is just *a* story rather than *the* story and, on the other, a critical project in which the cultural sanction accorded in our society to heterosexual love congeals into the false necessity of natural law? Can we challenge the notion that the losses entailed by tragic heterosexual love are not fated or necessary without bringing homosexual intimacy and relationship into our field of vision? In what ways do the queer imagination and experience of love allow us to see and resist the sheer taken-for-granted-ness of what Michael Warner has called the "heteronormative?"

In its most radical formulation, queer theory contests the lockstep cultural alignment of sex, gender, and sexual orientation that underwrites the master narrative of patriarchy in the hope of destabilizing the cate-gorical hierarchy that patriarchy draws between heterosexuality and homosexuality as such. Indeed, for queer theory homosexuality is the constitutive outside on which the very idea of heterosexuality depends. In short, the force of the cultural sanction that attaches to normative hetero-sexuality would be altogether lost without the prohibition against non-normative heterosexualities. Heterosexual love then needs the story of a deviant and degraded heterosex.

Real quotes a Yiddish proverb in his book, *I Don't Want to Talk About It: Overcoming the Secret Legacy of Male Depression*: "The son wishes to remember what the father wishes to forget" (1997, 15). To put a queer spin on this proverb, we might ask, "Does the cultural sanction against homosexuality stem from an anxious, if unacknowledged, recognition that the homosexual wishes to remember, or the homosexual insists on remem-bering"—and I am using that word in all of its many potent senses—"what the heterosexual wishes to forget—namely, that homosexuality inhabits the very heart of heterosexuality, that it is the ether in which hetero-sexuality lives and moves and has its being?"

From this perspective, then, we might ask whether the focus in *The Birth of Pleasure* on heterosexual love doesn't unwittingly ratify and re-enact the symbolic violence against homosexuality that is the originary law of normative heterosexuality.

Attention to the questions that I've suggested would lead to opening the clinical scene to include, for example, not just homosexual couples but more complicated groupings of homosexuals which embody the networks and forms of affiliated kinship that are being forged outside the filiative form of the hierarchical, patriarchal family whose dynamic Gilligan so memorably charts. It might also lead to a deeper understanding of the place of friendship in love. That is to say, as Michel Foucault has told us, one can think about homosexual relationships as the practice of friendship as a lifestyle, which situates itself outside and against the bias of familial relation in ways that are, quite simply, revolutionary (1981).

The next moment to which I'd like to draw your attention is from the second chapter of the book. Gilligan speaks with a group of fathers about their young sons' ability to read emotional cues, especially of the fathers' anger:

> These fathers are trying not to intimidate their sons. They all know what they call, "the voice," "the Dad voice." "Do the voice," I say. Steve explains how you do it. "You lower your voice, speak loud," and Tom adds, "clearly and loud." "Forceful," Steve says. "Speak in your Dad voice," I say. Tom says, "No, I can't. I feel bad ordering them around."
> I recall the voices of the boys in their play—the partner, the good guy, the bad guy, the robber. They were practicing "the voice," ordering each other around, taking on the power that their fathers were questioning as they heard the detachment in the voice that spoke so clearly and loudly, as they thought about their own sadness and anger (Gilligan 2002, 65).

One of the central concerns of queer theory has been with the regulatory character of masculinity and the ways in which the male homosexual especially is situated in an abject relationship to that master narrative of normative heterosexual masculinity. My favorite example of this relay between masculinity and male homosexuality—between the construction of the image of male homosexuality and normative masculine heterosexuality—is a text from the psychoanalytic literature whose author has been described as the most famous mental patient ever. The text in question is *Memoirs of My Nervous Illness* (1903), written by Dr. Daniel Paul Schreber, a German lawyer, judge, and Senate President of the Dresden Court of Appeal.

As anyone who's read "Psychoanalytic Notes Upon an Autobiographical Account of a Case of Paranoia (*Dementia Paranoides*)" (1911) will recall, Sigmund Freud uses the Schreber memoirs to develop a theory of the catalytic role played by repressed homosexual fantasies in the mechanism of paranoia psychosis.

For Freud, the salient feature of the *Memoirs of My Nervous Illness* is a delusion of emasculation: Judge Schreber's belief that he was being transformed into a woman. As Freud tells us in the psychoanalytic notes, "Schreber's psychotic fantasy is triggered one morning between sleeping and waking by the thought that after all it really must be very nice to be a woman submitting to the act of copulation. This idea, "was one which Schreber would have rejected with the greatest indignation if he had been fully conscious," writes Freud (ibid., 13). Indeed, Schreber recounts in the memoirs that he initially construed his transformative un-manning as a conspiracy in which God himself had played the part of accomplice, if not of instigator. "This divinely ordained scheme," Schreber notes paradoxically, "was driven by purposes contrary to the order of things" (ibid., 19). Schreber's soul was to be murdered. And his transformed body was to be used like a strumpet.

Over time, however, the judge becomes aware that his emasculation is in fact part of a divine miracle and thus very much in consonance with the order of things. Schreber is forced to realize that the order of things imperatively demanded his emasculation, "Whether I personally liked it or no," (ibid., 20) because he had been chosen for something similar to the conception of Jesus Christ by the Immaculate Virgin.

The judge comes to interpret his un-manning as a sign that God has called him to redeem the world: "The further consequence of my emasculation could of course only be my impregnation by divine rays to the end that a new race of men might be created" (ibid., 20–21).

Schreber is eventually able to reconcile himself to the thought of being transformed into a woman, and he reports in lavish detail the hours he spends before the mirror "with the upper portion of my body partly bared and wearing sundry feminine adornments, such as ribbons, trumpery necklaces, and the like" (ibid., 21). Having transposed his dissonant sexual fantasy into a more harmonious spiritual key, Schreber finally accepts his calling. Schreber confesses that "a little sensual pleasure falls to my share when he inscribes upon my banner the cultivation of femaleness, and evokes that sensation of voluptuousness such as women experience, without which he cannot discharge his new maternal duty to keep God in a constant state of enjoyment" (ibid., 26).

It is thus that the unequal struggle between this one weak man and God himself is brought to a happy end. In Freud's formulation, what begins as a sexual delusion of persecution is converted in Schreber's mind into a religious delusion of grandeur. Now, there's clearly an opposition between the un-manning that Schreber initially resists but eventually embraces and the voice of the father which is, as Jacques Lacan tells us, "always already being—the voice of a judge, and the voice of the judge as a father" (1982, 44).

The passage just quoted from *The Birth of Pleasure* seems to me to register the anxiety of fathers—not simply about the vulnerability of their boy-children as men in the making but about the connection between that vulnerability and a certain image in the heterosexual masculine imagination of male homosexuality—an image that Leo Bersani describes in an extraordinary essay called "Is the Rectum a Grave?" (1987) Bersani argues that "the regnant representation of the gay male homosexual in the homophobic mind is that of a grown man, legs high in the air, unable to refuse the suicidal ecstasy of being a woman" (212). So, the voice spoken to these children—the voice practiced by these children—is part of the training script of homophobia by which masculinity—normative heterosexual masculinity in our cultures—constitutes itself.

Queer theory attends quite seriously to the mechanisms by which masculinity develops—what Real describes as a posture of contempt toward all that is associated with the feminine. And among the associations with the feminine in the homophobic male imaginary is this figure of a homosexual as a woman trapped in a man's body.

The relentless pressure that queer theory has put on the categories of masculinity and femininity—the destabilization, if you will, of that distinction and its costs in the regime of compulsory masculinity—could have been explored in *The Birth of Pleasure* through a more explicit and sustained engagement with this question of the queer.

Finally, the third moment is described in a very brief passage in the third chapter, where Gilligan writes,

> I am curious about the connection between love and democracy—the intimate joining of private and public life. Both love and democracy depend on voice, having a voice and also the resonance that makes it possible to speak and be heard. Without voice, there is no relationship. Without resonance, voice recedes into silence.

As the resonances of our common world are changing, as more voices come into the human conversation, we are re-writing our collective story, our history, coming to hear and to see ourselves and one another differently. Thus we step out of a frame. I write at a time when frameworks are shifting—the framework of love, the framework of marriage, what it means to be a human, a man, a woman, a person, a couple, a family, a member of the human community.

Collectively, we have moved to an edge of possibility. It has become possible to envision a democracy that is not patriarchal. It is more difficult to imagine a love that is passionate without becoming tragic. Leaving patriarchy for love or democracy sounds easy, even inviting. But it is psychically as well as politically risky. At least at first it seems to mean giving up power and control (2002, 230).

This passage about love and democracy seems to me to put squarely on the table the question, as Frederic Jameson has framed it (1983, 1–14), of pleasure as a political issue. And if we look at the history of struggles over pleasure as a political issue, particularly in the United States, we can say with some confidence that the foot soldiers in that battle have been gay men, lesbians, bisexuals, and transgendered people, those whose bodies—not simply their voices, but their bodies—have been marked as queer.

If the politicization of pleasure has anything to teach us, it seems to me to be this: the transformation for which it argues is not simply a transformation as so many thought during the 1980s and '90s that asks for recognition. It's not simply an identity politics, a me-too-ism. The challenge to consider pleasure as a political issue is the challenge not just to reconceive heterosexual love but to rethink and revision heterosexual love around the axis of homosexual love and, in doing so, to think in terms that Jameson writes of:

The proper political use of pleasure must always be allegorical . . .
[T]o fight for example on the terrain of the esthetics of the city, or for certain forms of sexual liberation, or for access to certain kinds of cultural activities, or for an esthetic transformation of social relations, or of politics of the body must always involve the dual-focus in which the local issue is meaningful and desirable in and of itself, but is also at one and the same time taken as the figure for utopia in general, and for the systemic revolutionary transformation of the society as a whole.

Without these simultaneous dimensions, the political demand becomes reduced to yet another local issue in the micro-politics of this or that limited group, or its particular hobby or specialization and a slogan that once satisfied leads no further politically (ibid., 13).

What I'm suggesting then is that in opening Gilligan's analysis to the method of queer theory, we're opening up to thinking not simply at the local level of love but to understanding love, in Jameson's words, as a general figure of utopia that is of an image for the transformation not just of erotic and intimate relations but of a more fundamental restructuring of the social formation as a whole.

References

BERSANI, Leo. 1987. "Is the Rectum a Grave?" *October* 43: 197–222.

FREUD, Sigmund. 1958. "Psychoanalytic Notes Upon an Autobiographical Account of a Case of Paranoia (*Dementia Paranoides*)." In James Strachey (ed.), *Standard Edition of the Complete Psychological Works of Sigmund Freud*, VOL. 12 (1911–13). London: Hogarth.

FOUCAULT, Michel. 1981. "Friendship as a Lifestyle: An Interview with Michel Foucault." *Gay Information* 7 (Spring): 4–6.

GILLIGAN, Carol. 2002. *The Birth of Pleasure: A New Map of Love*. New York: Alfred A. Knopf.

JAMESON, Frederic. 1983. "Pleasure: A Political Issue." In Frederic Jameson (ed.), *Formations of Pleasure: Formations Editorial Collective*. London: Routledge & Kegan Paul, pp. 1–14.

LACAN, Jacques. 1982. "Desire and the Interpretation of Desire in Hamlet." In Shoshana Felman (ed.), *Literature and Psychoanalysis: The Question of Reading Otherwise*. Baltimore: Johns Hopkins University Press, pp. 11–53.

REAL, Terrence. 1997. *I Don't Want to Talk About It: Overcoming the Secret Legacy of Male Depression*. New York: Scribner.

SCHREBER, Daniel Paul. 2000. *Memoirs of My Nervous Illness*. New York: New York Review of Books.

One of the principal data sources for The Birth of Pleasure (2002) *was Carol Gilligan's collaboration in couples therapy with Terrence Real. Real describes their collaborative process and how it worked against the hierarchal commands that locked their patients in tragic stories of love.*

Expressing one of the great psychological insights of the twentieth century, Carol Gilligan taught us that young girls are able to resist the patriarchal cycle and speak in clear voices about intimacy and fragility. But as girls are inducted into womanhood, they learn to join the conspiracy of silence and stop telling the truth about these things. What Gilligan is telling us in the twenty-first century is that both men and women can dismantle the code of gender division, learn to value the qualities we have called feminine, and break patriarchy's conspiracy of silence. In our clinical work together, Gilligan showed me the truth of this brave claim and transformed me profoundly, not only as a clinician but also as a person.

Gilligan and I have collaboratively worked with couples on and off for about five years. What I bring to the collaborations is a resonance with men's voices and with the experience of boys and men in the culture. And Gilligan made me see that I also bring a developed capacity to track the ways we inhabit the traumas of patriarchy—to see the injuries that are sustained by boys and girls in this culture and how those injuries continue to reside with us as adult men and women.

Gilligan brings to our collaborations a resonance with the voices of women and girls, but, more importantly, she brings a new and revolutionary capacity to track pleasure. Her stunning insight is simply that intimacy is pleasurable. By tracking pleasure in human interactions, we can use pleasure as a kind of marker gene: where there is pleasure, there is closeness and intimacy.

Gilligan follows neuroscientist Antonio Damasio in borrowing Seamus Heaney's phrase, "the music of what happens," to describe the pleasure of consciousness and intimacy. The study of infants reveals that closeness and intimacy are our natural state and our birthright (Damasio 1999). Little boys and girls both come into this world whole, connected, equally expressive, equally dependent, and equally good readers of other people's feelings. The state of authentic connection stays with boys and girls until we force them out of it—until the curtain of gender drops.

This curtain drops in complementary ways. For girls, Gilligan's research and other research tell us the curtain drops, roughly speaking, between the ages of ten and thirteen—in adolescence, when girls learn, in Gilligan's famous phrase, to "lose their voice" (Gilligan 2002, 178–9). They learn to stop telling the truth about relationships and about their place in relation to others.

The curtain of gender for boys, current research tells us, again roughly speaking, drops between the ages of three and five (ibid., 57–74). I tell parents that before our sons learn to read, they have already read the stoic code of masculinity, and they have already begun to follow its pro-scription that intimacy be avoided and denied. This doesn't mean that boys shut down in their capacities for intimacy and pleasure. It means that they have learned that it's not acceptable to express them.

So what happens at the juncture between intimate partners in this cul-ture? If intimacy and connection are pleasurable, why is there so much iso-lation, even within romantic relationships? When we commit to love, what is drawn out of us, like iron filings to a magnet, is every recorded wound of disconnection that's lodged in our body. What came to me in my work with Gilligan was what she has said so beautifully: moving into the simplicity of connection is frightening for both men and women because it requires that we face the possibility of a loss that is ahead of us rather than behind us. Moving into intimacy is frightening, but if we want to live fully, claim pleas-ure, and stay whole it is our job to move into that fear and stay there.

We don't properly equip either girls and women or boys and men with the tools to do that. That is, we don't equip ourselves to see and to overcome what I call "psychological patriarchy."

What do I mean by psychological patriarchy? I mean that patriarchy has and is maintained by a particular psychodynamic. This psychodynamic of patriarchy does not operate exclusively in interactions between men and women. Rather, it is a three- or four-phased cycle that is played out repeat-edly between two women, between a parent and a child, inside somebody's skull, between races, between cultures. It is perhaps best understood as three concentric rings that surround and progressively constrain us all.

The first ring of patriarchy is what I call "the great divide." We are in the grip of the great divide when we take the qualities of one whole human being, draw a line down the center, and say, "All of the qualities on one side are masculine, and all of those on the other side are feminine." Rationality is masculine; intellectual weakness is feminine. Stoicism is masculine; emotionality is feminine. Courage is masculine; care and concern are feminine. Voice is masculine; hearing is feminine. The list goes on. The great divide constrains us all, and it pushes us to behave according to gender or according to gendered assumptions about a role that we have assumed: men cannot be emotional; women cannot think; lawyers cannot listen; nurses are not heard.

The second ring in the patriarchal cycle is what I call "the ring of contempt": qualities designated masculine and feminine are not considered separate-but-equal in our culture. Masculine qualities are exalted. Feminine qualities are idealized in rhetoric and in limited spheres, but in most respects they are devalued. The essential relationship between the two sides of the patriarchal divide is contempt. What it means to become a man in this culture is to disown and devalue the feminine. And, as we'll see more clearly, when we reach the third ring of patriarchy, what it means to become a woman in this culture is to protect and value the masculine.

The third ring is what I call "the conspiracy of silence." And in some ways, it's the grimmest ring of all. The conspiracy of silence has a masculine side and a feminine side. On the masculine side, people operating within the rings of division and contempt split off their contemptuous "feminine" qualities and project them onto others, be they men, women, girls, or boys. This splitting off allows the person on the masculine side of the equation to deny feminine aspects of human character and the vulnerability and fragility that they imply. On the feminine side of the equation, whether the "feminine" side is taken by a woman, a girl, a man, or a boy, there is an instinct—a felt need—to protect the "masculine" counterpart's illusion of ruggedness.

Here is how the third ring operates. A man, for example, projects his disowned vulnerabilities onto a female partner and punishes her for it. Or, a man might project his disowned vulnerabilities onto a child. My father did this with me, and the psychological distortions caused by his denial of vulnerability were so acute that he became physically violent. When he was raging at me, my father was punishing the soft, vulnerable, tender parts of him that he had learned to hold in contempt.

One of the ugly realities of human nature under patriarchy is that at all cost, the unstable man—or whoever is in the masculine pose and living the lie of disowned fragility—must not be called to account. If you do call such a person into account, then you threaten to escalate things. While my father was hurting me, I was unable to express my own rage and pain. What I felt most was sorry for him; what I must have known at a deeper level was that if I challenged him, I would threaten his illusion of invulnerability and increase his rage. This is what I call "the unholy fusion of trauma." It entraps battered children; it entraps hostages; it entraps subordinated cultures; and it entraps battered women.

Similarly, I have found in my practice that as heterosexual couples begin to understand the dance of contempt, the disowning of fragility, and the lie of invulnerability, the confrontation of these realities may be seen as a healthy move for the woman, but it is usually seen only as a threatening move for the man. The couple fears confronting either the man's disowned fragility or his pose of ruggedness. If the disowned vulnerability is confronted, the fear is that the man will feel an unbearable shame and fall apart. And it will be her fault. If the disowning ego is confronted as grandiose and false, the man will either withdraw or attack.

One of the great paradoxes for men and women and boys and girls who are trying to stay whole in this culture is that connection itself is deemed part of the devalued feminine. Specifically, what we do with it is what I call "marginalization through idealization." We idealize love in principle, but we devalue it in fact. A culture that devalues love and connection is not built for intimacy. It is built for production, consumption, and war.

Gilligan goes right to the heart of patriarchy's marginalization of connection and love by taking on our culture's romantic mythology: the idea of romantic love as a tragic impossibility. As I remind couples in treatment, the one thing that the greatest lovers of Western civilization always do is die. There is a political message in that.

The romantic myth is very much like a Freudian neurotic symptom in that it both challenges the order and stands as a metaphor for the order. The romantic myth of doomed love challenges the order in its assertion of love, but it stands as a metaphor for the order in its lesson that love must end tragically. From the blood feud of the Capulets to the war of *The English Patient* (1992), lovers who are set against patriarchal values of war, honor, and "family values" are ultimately crushed by those values.

The extraordinary, revolutionary questions that Gilligan brought into her book *The Birth of Pleasure* and into my practice were several: What if love did not have to be doomed? What if love were not tragic? What if that was not the nature of things but *our story* about the nature of things? What if there was a story beneath this story? What Gilligan has emboldened me to see is that therapy must not be collusive with our patriarchal story; therapy must challenge that story and look for a new one. Gilligan has helped me see that as we move women into voice, into meaning, and as we pull men out of that horrible dance of contempt and into connection and wholeness, we are moving people out of patriarchy. In other words, moving individual men and women into intimacy is, by definition, moving them out of patriarchy. And that, by definition, is an insurrectionary act.

In writing about one of our shared cases, Gilligan reveals the clinical power of her revolutionary question. The case involved a man who was very distant from his wife. In treatment, this man recalled the tremendous pain of having been used by a mother who imagined him ill in order to act out a need to hide and sacrifice herself to parenting. The mother had taken him from doctor to doctor, and he had been subjected to a number of invasive procedures. Gilligan was sitting next to me, and she said, "Now tell me again about what things were like between you and your mother before this happened." And what things were like between this man and his mother before this happened was that he saw who she was. He said, "I saw the face beneath the face, and I was her pal." He used to stay home and bake cookies with her and be her pal. Underneath this bitterness, this victimization that he was now translating to all women—and specifically to his wife—there was an earlier relationship. And that's where Gilligan went because that's where the hope is.

Gilligan's question to our patient came from a solid conviction: it doesn't have to be this way. The gift for both of us was to be able to work with real couples who were struggling for their psychological lives and to take that supposition, "it doesn't have to be this way," and turn it into clinical action. And time and time again couples on the brink of disaster did just as we hoped they would: they returned to love and braved the difficulties of sustaining it.

References

DAMASIO, Antonio. 1999. *The Feeling of What Happens: Body and Emotion in the Making of Consciousness*. New York: Harcourt Brace & Company.

GILLIGAN, Carol. 2002. *The Birth of Pleasure: A New Map of Love*. New York: Alfred A. Knopf.

The Places to Look for Pleasure

Sigmund Freud shaped thinking about human psychology by embodying his central developmental theories in the old and resonant Oedipal myth. Freud used the realized prophecies of Oedipus's sexual union with his mother and murder of his father to stand for basic human desires. Oedipus's fate carried a warning that Freud took as a prescription for healthy psychological development: separate from the mother and internalize the law of the father.

Observing that the Oedipal myth tells the story of humankind as a story of mankind, and distrusting the injunction to separate from the mother and internalize the father's voice and authority, Carol Gilligan switches our attention to another ancient tale. She uses the story of Psyche and Cupid to celebrate the human connectedness that the maternal bond represents and to symbolize resistance to what she describes as a "Father Voice."

Does Gilligan—or did Freud—distort and misuse these ancient tales?

Eva Cantarella, a legal historian of the Roman period, questions Gilligan's reading of Psyche and Cupid as a story of liberation. She then asks whether Gilligan's theme of resistance to masculanized authority was foreign or familiar when Apuleius set down the first surviving written version of the Psyche and Cupid myth.

EVA CANTARELLA

I must confess that when I first heard Carol Gilligan's interpretation of the tale of Love and Psyche in a private conversation we had after one of her classes (when the book had not yet been published), I was very surprised. Until that moment, my reading of the tale had always been different. I first read it many years ago while I was writing my dissertation on Roman marriage, and I remember very well feeling disturbed by the story and by Psyche's behavior. To me, she was a woman abused not only by her patriarchal mother-in-law to be but also and especially by her lover, a man she continued to love despite his vile attitude and abject subordination to his mother. He was a mamma's boy: a man who never grows up, who goes home to his mamma when he is sick. This lover had abandoned her simply because she had disobeyed an order he had given without any explanation, reason, or justification. Blind obedience was what this man expected from Psyche. And in order not to lose him, to reconquer him, Psyche agreed to please his terrible mother and to undergo terrible ordeals. In particular, Psyche's behavior when Love abandoned her left me with an image that I found intolerable: Psyche hanging from one of his feet and trailing in the air in a situation that degraded her dignity.

Finally, in my eyes the end of the story (a happy ending, but a very costly one for poor Psyche) crowned a quintessentially patriarchal tale. Psyche married Love, and they bore Pleasure, but only with Zeus's consent, only thanks to the male divine character who, in return for his wedding gift to the couple (Psyche's immortality), asked Cupid to procure for him some nice girls, a typically patriarchal agreement between men.

Until Gilligan told me of her interpretation, I had never focused on Psyche's resistance. Only after our talk did I start to think that, perhaps, Psyche's story could be read in a different way. I knew that Gilligan had already dedicated an article, cowritten with Eve Stern, to Psyche's story (Gilligan and Stern 1988, 101–28), and I read it. Why is love so difficult to live, the authors ask. Their answer is: love is difficult because of our lack of knowledge.

According to Socratic principles, love requires self-knowledge. But within the framework of psychoanalytic theory (at least Freudian theory), self-knowledge is impossible for women. In "Three Essays on Sexuality" (1957), Sigmund Freud writes that only the masculine erotic is accessible through research. The erotic feminine life is veiled by an "impenetrable obscurity" (ibid., 151).[1] The only way to dispel our ignorance about the feminine erotic is to consider women as the subject, not the object, of a love story. Enter Psyche, the *protagonist* of the love story told by Apuleius in the second century AD.

A late myth recounts the well-known story of what happened when Psyche appeared on Earth, a young girl more beautiful than Venus, the goddess of love.[2] She was so beautiful that Venus, overcome by uncontrollable jealousy, ordered her son Cupid to make her fall in love with the most abominable of humans. Psyche, meanwhile, was terribly unhappy. Everyone venerated her as a goddess, as if she were a new Venus, but no one loved her or asked for her hand. Alarmed, her parents interrogated the Oracle, who said they must set her out on a distant rock to become prey to a monstrous serpent. She was taken there and was ready to die, but a gust of wind picked her up and carried her to a beautiful, empty palace. There, her every wish was granted by invisible hands and voices who served her as a queen. At night she was joined by a lover who made her promise never to look upon him. This invisible husband was none other than Cupid. He shut her up in the palace, unbeknownst to and against the orders of his mother. Psyche, during her long, solitary days, was homesick and wanted to see her sisters. She convinced Cupid to bring them to her. Seeing the palace in which Psyche lived, the sisters were overcome by envy. They convinced Psyche, now pregnant, that her mysterious husband was none other than the monster to whom she had been destined and that her child would also be a monster. The only way out, said the sisters, was to cut off the head of the husband.

Psyche was won over by these arguments and decided to break the promise she made to Cupid that she would never try to see him. Carrying a lamp for light and a knife to kill her husband while he slept, Psyche saw his face for the first time. She discovered that he was beautiful, so much so that her hands shook, and a drop of oil fell from the lamp and awakened Cupid. He reproved her for having violated his prohibition, and he flew away, abandoning her.

Psyche, desperate not to lose him, grabbed his feet and followed him in his flight until, exhausted, she fell to the ground. Every hope lost, Psyche tried to kill herself but was saved. Tormented by the curse and envy of Venus, to whom the wounded Cupid had fled, Psyche underwent terrible ordeals, the worst of which took her to the Underworld.

Cupid, meanwhile getting over his injury, was moved by Psyche's love and missed her. He persuaded Jove to grant her immortality. Psyche finally married Cupid and gave birth to a baby named Pleasure.

This, very briefly, is the story of Cupid and Psyche, regularly interpreted as an allegory of the transformation of a woman into a soul (the Greek meaning of the word Psyche, from Plato onward). But Gilligan says we should try to read it as the story of a mortal woman and a story of resistance.

Approaching Psyche as the subject of the story, Gilligan argues that the key to understanding it is her fight against reification (objectification). This began when she came to be venerated as a goddess (a situation she compares to death) and continued in the palace, where she lived a marriage in the dark, in silence, and in ignorance of her husband, of who he was, and of what he was like. Torn between the sweetness of her hidden love and a desire for human contact, Psyche despairs. The desire to know the truth about her relationship finally wins when she becomes pregnant. At this point, Psyche must protect herself and her child; she must know who the father is, so she disobeys Cupid's order. Rather than destroying her "love story" as Cupid had threatened, however, this disobedience transforms it into a "real story", not conditional upon blindness and silence as the previous relationship had been.

After reading and talking with Gilligan, I was ready to consider the story of Psyche and Cupid from a different perspective. I did this within the framework of my approach to the classics. Being a historian of Roman law, I started to think about the historical context in which Apuleius had written his novel: the Roman world, in the second century AD.

Of course, the roots of Cupid and Psyche's tale extend long into the past and very far from Rome. Its origin is controversial indeed. Does it come from Syria? Does it come from Iran, and is it a Greek elaboration of an Iranian myth? Furthermore, is it a cultivated myth (of Platonic origin, as has been suggested), or is it rather a popular saga, a folktale?

In the form known to us, the tale is elaborated by Apuleius, as proven by the many references to Roman institutions, an important example of which is the reference to the *metae Murtiae*,[3] the turning post at the southern end of the Circus Maximus (*Metamorphoses* 6.8.2). The great majority of Roman references, however, deal with Roman law. Born in Madaura in modern-day Algeria, Apuleius studied in Athens, Carthage, and Rome, where he was a practicing lawyer. His technical vocabulary demonstrates this: speaking of marriage, for example, he speaks of the Roman *confarreatae nuptiae*, a special ritual reserved to aristocrats and the highest priests (ibid., 5.26.7).

Other Roman laws quoted in the tale include a law on slaves and the so-called Julian law on adultery. When the fugitive Psyche asks for help, she is told that helping her would be against the law, which in fact prescribed major penalties for persons helping fugitive slaves. In the final part of the tale, Jove, a notorious womanizer, maintains that it was Cupid's fault that he had frequently violated the *lex Iulia de adulteriis*—a law enacted in 18 BC by Augustus in order to criminalize male adultery, which until that time was a feminine misbehavior punished within a household by the head of the family (ibid., 6.23.4).

Apuleius, then, tells an ancient Eastern story reset within the framework of his contemporary Roman world. But he modifies this ancient story, not only according to his personal poetic inspiration, and perhaps to his religious beliefs, but also taking into account his audience, its tastes, its expectations, and its mentality. He tells a story fit for a contemporary audience, which essentially shared Roman culture. The meaning of the myth in his novel might therefore be different than the meaning of the original tale.

Hence the question: could this audience (or part of it) have read the story as an indication, as a hint, of feminine resistance? Could Apuleius have had such a hypothesis in mind? Was feminine resistance conceivable in his world?

Under the influence of Gilligan's reading of the story of Cupid and Psyche, I considered whether there was evidence of feminine resistance in sources related to the world in which Apuleius lived and wrote. The answer is yes, there is evidence that feminine resistance was a historical reality in Apuleius's Rome and in the Romanized world of his time. Indeed, it had been a historical reality (although admittedly, not a universal one) since a couple of centuries before Apuleius wrote his novel.

Both the literary and the legal sources register stories of feminine resistance. I will start with the literary ones and with a story that goes back to the second century BC.

In 215 BC, a law, the *lex Oppia*, stated that women were not allowed to wear colored dresses or excessive golden jewelry. Twenty years later, in 195 BC, social tensions were less strong, and two magistrates proposed that this law be repealed. Perhaps women had suggested its repeal, but this is only speculation. What is not speculation is that the day this law was to be voted upon, the streets of Rome were filled with women protesting against the law and asking for its abrogation. The story is told by Livy in Book 34 of his *Histories*, and it is but one of many stories suggesting the existence of women determined to fight in defense of their rights (or privileges, as in this case).

The most important and direct literary proof of feminine resistance comes closer to Apuleius's time, in the life and writings of the poetess Sulpicia. Sulpicia was a noble and wealthy woman who lived in Rome in the age of Augustus.[4] She was educated and very opinionated, and she was in love with a certain Cerinthus. In that period, a woman who did not have a father was appointed a guardian who had to consent to her financial and personal decisions. She had to undergo this guardianship all her life, regardless of age. Sulpicia, who was under the guardianship of her uncle, Messalla, could not marry Cerinthus because Messalla would not give his consent. Needless to say, she was not allowed, either under the law or under contemporary social norms, to have sexual relations with him. Had Sulpicia not been a poetess, we wouldn't know how she reacted to this situation. But she was a poetess, and she wrote her love story in her poems, some of which survived and were included in Book 3 of the works of Tibullus (60–19 BC).

In these poems, Sulpicia does not stop at complaining of her uncle's desire (and legal authority) to control her behavior. She writes in clear words and with great pride that she has a sexual relationship with Cerinthus. Obviously, this was a social shame and a crime. But Sulpicia wants Rome to be aware of her relationship, and she writes:

> Love has come at last. The very idea
> that I'd hide it makes me more ashamed
> than openly confessing. Won over
> by my Muse supplication, Cithera's Goddess
> has brought him to me, placed him in my arms.
> What Venus promised, she has fulfilled.
> Let them tattle who have missed their chance.
> I'll not entrust the news to a sealed letter
> that none may read of it before my lover does.
> I loathe to wear a mask in deference
> to what the world may say. Let everyone hear
> That we have come together—each of us
> deserving the other
>
> (Tibullus 3.13).[5]

When her tutor wants her to spend her birthday in the countryside, she dares to oppose his orders and says explicitly that she wants to spend it with her lover—very unusual behavior for a Roman woman, indeed:

> My dreaded birthday is looming, and I have got to spend it
> there in the odious country without Cerinthus.
> What is more agreeable than the city? Is a country estate

a fit place for a girl or the fields
by the cold river Arno? Stop fussing about me,
Messalla, my kinsman, You are much too ready
to take me on an unnecessary journey.
Carried hence—I leave my soul and my senses behind
as I cannot exercise my own free will.

(Ibid., 3.14).

In a third poem, she addresses Cerinthus directly:

Light of my being, let me not be so passionately
desired by you as I guess I was some days since
if in the whole of my young years
I ever did anything quite so silly,
as I think it was
when I left you on your own the other night,
hoping to hide the fierceness of the passion
that all the time was burning within me.

(Ibid., 3.18).

Sulpicia's resistance had parallels in legal texts, to which I now turn. Papyri found in Roman Egypt, where interestingly, Psyche was a common feminine first name in Apuleius's time, document that women had begun to challenge the patriarchal power to choose their marriage partners.

In the second century AD, neither a daughter nor a son could marry without paternal consent. As the jurist Paulus writes, "Marriage does not exist unless everyone consents, that is those who come together and those under whose power they are."[6] Moreover, a father, having arranged a marriage, could also interrupt it, even against his daughter's will. This paternal right was abolished only in the second century AD, when the emperor Antoninus Pius (under whose reign Apuleius lived), prohibited fathers from interrupting their children's happy marriages (*bene concordantia matrimonia*) (Treggiari 1991, 460).

But the fathers did not give up their powers so easily. They went on insisting that their daughters leave their husbands' houses and come back to their paternal homes. Here, too, we find women resisting their fathers' orders, in this case going beyond poetic writing to the filing of petitions to local magistrates. In AD 186, for example, at Oxyrhynchus, a woman called Dionysia asked the local magistrate to prevent her father from interrupting her happy marriage by taking her away from her husband, as the father wanted to do. And she quotes precedents—other women whose similar petitions had been granted some thirty years ago.[7]

The highest moment of feminine resistance in ancient Rome was a well-documented and unprecedented act of civil disobedience. Worried about sexual morality, Augustus had passed a law, the *lex Iulia de adulteriis* previously cited, criminalizing adultery. According to this law, adulteresses were to be relegated to an island (usually, a small island in the bay). Since the law exempted prostitutes and pimps from punishment, Roman women decided to oppose it by registering themselves en masse as prostitutes. The story is told by Tacitus, Suetonius, and the jurist Papinianus and is recorded in Justinian's Institutes; it establishes Roman women as the protagonists of one of the first acts of civil disobedience in Western history.

Reading the classical sources, we find more than a mere suggestion of feminine resistance in the age of Apuleius—we find a historical reality. The extent of the resistance is unknown, but its reality cannot be questioned. I must confess that this historical evidence does not answer all of my questions about Gilligan's interpretation of the myth of Psyche and Cupid. Still, it does much to validate Gilligan's perception that a spirit of resistance was alive in Apuleius's time and discernable in Psyche's character and actions.

Notes

1 See Carol Gilligan (1995), where she relates the opacity of the feminine erotic in Freud's view to his "separation between the affectionate and the sensual in currents of the erotic life."

2 Apuleius's version of the myth, told here, uses Roman names for the Greek characters (Cupid, Venus, Jove); Gilligan's retelling prefers the Greek (Eros, Aphrodite, Zeus).

3 The reference has been taken as an indication that Apuleius wrote the *Metamorphoses* in Rome and for a Roman audience (see Apuleius 1983).

4 On Sulpicia's character and identity, see, among others, Jane McIntosh Snyder (1989) and Carol U. Merriam (1990).

5 Citations are to Tibullus, into whose corpus Sulpicia's works are incorporated (see Sulpicia 2000).

6 *Digest of Justinian* 23.2.2 (Paul, Ad Edictum 35), in Susan Treggiari (1991). See *Tituli Ulpiani* 5.2 ("A marriage is valid if . . . both parties consent, if they are independent, or their parents too, if they are in power"), in ibid. For a general discussion of consent to marriage in Roman law and practice, see *Tituli Ulpiani*.

7 The petition of Dionysia was among the papyri found at the excavation of the village of Oxyrhynchus in Egypt. Duke Databank of Documentary

Papyri, P.Oxy.: The Oxyrhynchus Papyri. Avaliable at: www.perseus.-tufts.edu/cgi-bin/ptext?doc=Perseus%3Atext%3A 1999.05.0181,237

References

APULEIUS. 1983. *The Story of Cupid and Psyche*. Edited by Louis C. Purser. New Rochelle, NY: Aristide D. Caratzas.

GILLIGAN, Carol 1995. "The Conquistador and the Dark Continent: Reflections on the Psychology of Love." *Dædelus* 113(3): 75–85.

———, and Eve Stern. 1988. "The Riddle of Femininity and the Psychology of Love." In Willard Gaylin and Ethel Person (eds), *Passionate Attachments: Thinking About Love*. New York: Free Press, pp. 101–28.

FREUD, Sigmund. 1957. "Three Essays on Sexuality." In James Strachey (ed.), *The Standard Edition of the Complete Psychological Works of Sigmund Freud*, VOL. 7 (1901–1905). London: Hogarth, p. 151.

MERRIAM, Carol U. 1990. "Some Notes on the Sulpicia Elegies." *Latomus* 49: 95–8.

OVID. 1986. *Metamorphoses*. Translated by A. D. Melville. Oxford: Oxford University Press.

SNYDER, Jane McIntosh. 1989. *The Woman and the Lyre: Women Writers in Classical Greece and Rome*. Carbondale, Ill.: Southern Illinois University Press.

SULPICIA. 2000. *The Poems of Sulpicia*. Translated by John Heath Stubbs. London: Hearing Eye.

TREGGIARI, Susan. 1991. *Roman Marriage: Iusti Coniuges from the Time of Cicero to the Time of Ulpian*. Oxford: Clarendon Press.

Kendall Thomas spoke as an outsider who felt invisible as he read The Birth of Pleasure *(2002). A queer man of color, he worried that Carol Gilligan's hetero-centric work cannot yield a full analysis of the human psyche. In arguments reminiscent of those Gilligan has made about studies of men that purported to be studies of humanity, Thomas urged that we cannot discover the human psyche in an exclusively heterosexual conversation.*

Like Thomas, Peggy Cooper Davis speaks of having felt invisible at times as she read The Birth of Pleasure. *As a feminist of color, she questions Gilligan's resort to "high-caste" Western literature for models of resistance to patriarchy. As a straight woman of color, she balks at Gilligan's invitation to celebrate postcolonial stories of rebellious love between higher-caste women and lower-caste men. Cooper Davis examines these reactions in search of insights about how race and caste figure in the perpetuation of patriarchy. And insights about why race and caste continue to be sources of division and simmering resentment between white feminists and feminists of color.*

Looking in Hard-to-See Places
PEGGY COOPER DAVIS

The Birth of Pleasure: *A New Map of Love*—indeed much of Carol Gilligan's work—grows out of her consideration of outsiders' voices and perspectives. It is most fundamentally a demonstration of what can be learned by considering the position of women in patriarchy, but it is also a demonstration of what can be learned by considering the position of the maverick, the political dissident, or the colonial subject. What follows is a reflection on how easily and how often the outsider becomes invisible, even to those who would honor her.

The Birth of Pleasure is centered on the story of Psyche and Cupid from Apuleius's *The Golden Ass* (1998a) and also importantly focuses on the work of William Shakespeare. In the first part of this reflection, I struggle with my instinct to redirect Gilligan's gaze from these valorized male writers, whom I associate with the patriarchal traditions of Greek myth and Elizabethan drama, to the harder-to-see lives and literature of women and other traditionally neglected outsiders.

The Birth of Pleasure also addresses writers who are more easily recognized as outsiders. Gilligan complements her analyses of classical literature with analyses of fiction that she describes as postcolonial, represented chiefly by Arundhati Roy's *The God of Small Things* (1997), Michael Ondaatje's *The English Patient* (1992), Jamaica Kincaid's *Annie John* (1985), and Toni Morrison's *The Bluest Eye* (1970). In the second part of this reflection, I consider Gilligan's interpretations of writers who conspicuously hold the insider/outsider position of being postcolonial subjects, straddling and blending colonial and indigenous cultures (or, in the cases of Morrison and Kinkaid, historically slaveholding and historically enslaved cultures).

Exploring Gilligan's treatment of classic texts, I find models of resistance that had heretofore been hard for me to see. Exploring Gilligan's treatment of postcolonial texts, I worry that she leaves invisible some of patriarchy's victims and some of those victims' strategies of resistance. I then try to draw a lesson about the value—and the difficulty—of being attuned to the full variety of outsider voices.

I begin with two confessions:

First, I have always been somewhat uncomfortable with "the canon." I enjoy ancient Greek literature and Shakespeare, but I would never go to these texts in search of liberation from color or caste or gender hierarchies. I think of them as what Audre Lorde called "the Masters' Tools" (1984).

My discomfort embarrasses me. I move in worlds in which the promise of canonical literature seems unlimited. Or limited only by ignorance or sloth. And Gilligan, whose work I greatly admire, insists that resistance to patriarchy should be inspired by voices of resistance in classical texts. But the discomfort remains.

Second, as I read *The Birth of Pleasure*, I was annoyed by what I saw as Gilligan's celebration of higher-caste women's love across color lines as a blueprint for liberation from patriarchy. As a woman of color, I struggle against being annoyed by stories of love between men of color and women of the "fairer" caste. But despite my struggles I find it hard to embrace these transgressive unions as models of resistance.

The resentment I feel in response to stories of love between "fair" women and dark men embarrasses me even more than my discomfort with classical literature. It feels like a betrayal of people I know and love who are in interracial life partnerships. It seems profoundly intolerant: What fault could possibly be found in love that upsets unjustifiable status hierarchies? My resentment feels petulant. It bespeaks a jealous insecurity rather than a healthy sense of self.

I have decided to swallow my embarrassment and force myself to take my discomfort and resentment seriously. I need finally to explain—or to get over—a pesky, subterranean, self-pitying sense that these feelings are justified. I need to find out what these feelings can teach me about caste, racism, and patriarchy. And about the often uneasy relationships between white feminists and feminists of color.

READING THE CLASSIC TEXTS: SEEING COMPLEXITY INSIDE

Like Eva Cantarella,[1] I was skeptical as I first tried, on Gilligan's invitation, to find liberation from patriarchy in the myth of Psyche and Cupid. I had several justifications for this skepticism. Gilligan suggested that Psyche hated her extraordinary beauty because she objected to being idealized. But Apuleius's text told me that Psyche was bothered by her beauty only because, although her more ordinarily beautiful sisters were married, "no king or prince or even commoner courted her to seek her hand" (Apuleius 1999, 77). Indeed, Psyche seemed to crave the beauty of a goddess. She defied Venus's command that she fetch a jar of beauty lotion unopened from the Underworld.[2] "How stupid I am," she said, "to be carrying this beauty-lotion fit for deities, and not to take a single drop of it for myself, for with this at any rate I can be pleasing to my beautiful lover" (ibid., 111).

Gilligan held Psyche up as a model of resistance, but I saw only two acts of defiance in the tale: filching the beauty cream and gazing at her husband's face. We have addressed the beauty cream. I had not seen Psyche's stolen gaze as resistance to a patriarchal code of detachment. I understood from the text that Psyche looked on Cupid's face because her jealous sisters had persuaded her that she should cut off his head.

After Psyche discovered that her lover was Cupid and he took wing, she clung, "a pitiable appendage" to his divine leg, until she could hold no more and fell to the earth (ibid., 93). This was a move that looked to me, as it did to Cantarella, like desperate and abject devotion rather than strength. Indeed, desperation seemed to be Psyche's persistent theme. At every trial, the girl seemed to become suicidal: when she first beheld Cupid, she tried to hide her offending dagger by "plunging it into her own breast" (ibid., 92); after Cupid's leg slipped out of her grip and she watched him fly out of sight, she "hurled herself headlong" into a river (ibid., 94). The trials that Venus put to Psyche set off more suicidal gestures. When Psyche was ordered to retrieve the wool of the golden fleece, she again decided to fling herself into a river (ibid., 106). When told to recover a vial of icy water from a lofty peak, she rushed up the peak and hoped that from its height she could "put an end to her intolerable existence" (ibid., 107). The order to retrieve a box of beauty cream from the Underworld led her to a high tower with, again, the thought of "flinging herself headlong" (ibid., 108).

And Cupid. He seemed an unfortunate partner for the bravely devoted Psyche. The old woman whom Apuleius assigned as narrator of the tale introduced Cupid as "that winged, most indiscreet youth whose own bad habits show his disregard for public morality. He goes rampaging through people's houses at night armed with his torch and arrows, undermining the marriages of all. He gets away scot-free with this disgraceful behavior, and nothing that he does is worthwhile" (ibid., 76). He had ensnared his father, Jupiter, in adulteries such that Jupiter's name, too, was "besmirched in common report by adultery and all kinds of licentious behavior" (Apuleius 1998a, 105). Jupiter married Cupid to Psyche to put an end to the boy's "lustful adventures on earth" (and, yes, for the "recompense" of a mortal "girl of outstanding beauty") (Apuleius 1999, 112).

But it was Apuleius's Venus who most troubled my efforts to see the myth of Psyche and Cupid as a guide to liberation from patriarchy.

Gilligan argued that an end to patriarchy required an end to the mandate that boys break from their mothers and denigrate the relationality that mothers symbolically represent. I had assumed that in this new, anti-patriarchal regime, healthy relationships among mothers, sons, and the wives and lovers of sons would have to be possible. Taking seriously Gilligan's critique of Freud, I assumed that the relationality of the nursery would somehow become a foundation for lusty partnerships rather than an endless source of lustful passion for forbidden partners.

However, Apuleius's Venus was "Oedipal" with a vengeance. When Psyche became known and revered as the New Venus, the Old Venus went into a growling fury (ibid., 76), entreated her son to destroy Psyche, and then kissed him "long and hungrily with parted lips" (ibid., 77). She summoned Care and Sorrow to whip and torture Psyche. She "flew at Psyche, ripped her clothes to shreds, tore her hair, boxed her ears, and beat her unmercifully" (Apuleius 1998a, 98). Reading all of this and following the tortuous trials that Venus set for Psyche, I could not help but fear that a little of Freud's civilizing detachment was needed.

I had similar reservations about Gilligan's claim that resistance to patriarchy was to be found in Shakespeare's later comedies. Gilligan marked *Twelfth Night* (see Shakespeare 1842) as a turning point in Shakespeare's work and argued that Viola, dressed as and modeling herself after her twin brother Sebastian, eroded the ground on which patriarchy sits by challenging its sharp gender distinctions and predetermined gender roles. Surely *Twelfth Night* offers us two of Shakespeare's most liberated women, with Olivia commanding a household and determined in her independence and Viola using the social license granted within her brother's identity to move more freely in the world—and to instruct both Olivia and the Duke in love. But, in the end, had Viola conveyed her message, or had she succumbed? In Act 2, Scene 2, Viola says these essentialist words to explain women's gullibility: "Alas, our frailty is the cause, not we! For, such as we are made of, such we be" (2.2.32–3).[3]

As Viola married the Duke—who announced himself prepared to kill Cesario in a patriarchal battle over Olivia, who said woman's love was only "appetite"; and who counseled marriage to a younger woman because man's affection could not hold, and women were like roses "whose fair flower, being display'd, doth fall that very hour" (2.4.38–9)—Gilligan saw the Duke united with his "saucy page" (Gilligan 2002, 214). But I sensed an imminent reprise of the final scene in *The Taming of the Shrew* (see Shakespeare 2010), in which the formerly saucy but now apparently tamed Katherina bids women, "vail your stomachs, for it is no boot, and place your hands below your husband's foot" (5.2.176–7).

What are we to make of Gilligan's uses of these texts and of others like them? Should we lecture her about the Masters' Tools? I was tempted. But on reconsideration I'm not so sure.

It occurs to me that focusing on the positive might be a key to understanding Gilligan's work. Gilligan often complains that her descriptions of adolescent girls struggling against pressures to hide their relationality are read as descriptions of shutting down rather than as descriptions of resisting. Of course, they are descriptions of both—descriptions of dissociation and loss of voice as well as descriptions of a marvelous capacity to resist the loss of voice. How the work is read is a matter of focus. Gilligan would have us focus on the resistance, for that is the difference between telling a tragic story and imagining a story of liberation. Or transformation. Or pleasure.

Perhaps focus is the key to our different readings of classic texts. Gilligan insists that relationship—or love—is a primary human capacity. She also insists that the human psyche resists isolation and hierarchy. If she is right on those two points, then rich works of literature—works in which characters are psychologically true—will reflect both a resistant tendency toward relationship and a conforming tendency toward isolation and stratification. These competing tendencies may play out more or less conspicuously depending on the status of the writer (and the status of the reader). Resistance may be, as Gilligan suggests, more apparent in the work of an insider/outsider like Apuleius or Shakespeare (and it may be more apparent to an inside/outside audience). But they should be present in any literature with well-drawn characters. The classic texts on which Gilligan draws, on repeated reading, reflect both resistance and layered isolation. It is instructive to look back on them with a willingness to focus on the positive and an appreciation that although their work is part of the patriarchal canon, Apuleius and Shakespeare each had the double consciousness of an insider/outsider straddling two cultures.

Apuleius straddled the world of Rome and the world of colonized North Africa. In his *Apologia* (1914) thought to have been given in defense against a charge of sorcery), he described himself as a "barbarian" and said:

> About my homeland, it is situated on the border of Numidia and Gaetulia. I am part Numidian and part Gaetulian. I don't see why I should be ashamed of this. . . .

> And I don't say this out of shame for my country. For even though we were once in a city belonging to the King Scyfax, when he was overthrown, we were given as a gift of the Roman people to the

King Massinissa, and now, with the recent arrival of resettled veteran soldiers, we have become a most magnificent colony. . . . Why did I offer this information? So that from now on, Semelianus, you may be less offended by me, and so that you may extend your good-will and forgiveness, if by some negligence, I did not select your Attic Zarat as my birthplace (Chapters 24, 25).[4]

It is remarkable how these words, mixing indigenous pride with a respectful deference to colonial power, foreshadow the double consciousness of the modern postcolonial subject. Apuleius was an erudite student of Greek, Latin, and Egyptian cultures, a brilliant orator in the tongue of his colonizers, and an initiate into the cult of the goddess Isis. He must, then, have lived and worked with contradiction and ambivalence. Looking back on Apuleius's tale with the possibility of contradiction and ambivalence in mind, it is easier for me to see resistance, strength, and a human leaning toward love set against a culture of domination.

I now see everywhere the message that clinging to life and love are natural—what nature and the gods support. Like all good heroes, Psyche has helpers and guides; all of them seem to be divinely motivated, and all of them steel her for life and love. There are the anthropomorphized helpers: the dagger that saves her from her first suicide gesture by "plunging out of her rash grasp" (Apuleius 1999, 92); the god-fearing stream that casts her ashore after the second (ibid., 94); the ants eager to assist "Cupid's wife" in the first of Venus's trials (ibid., 105); Jupiter's royal bird, who, "in veneration for Cupid's power," sees Psyche through the third trial (ibid., 108); and the tower (described in the Graves translation of *The Transformations of Lucius* as "divinely inspired"; see Apuleius 1998b, 139) that sees her through the last (Apuleius 1999, 109). There is Pan, the guide who tells Psyche, "[D]o not seek again to destroy yourself by throwing yourself headlong or by seeking any other means of death. Cease your sorrowing, lay aside your sadness, and instead direct prayers of adoration to Cupid, greatest of gods, and by your caressing attentions win the favor of that wanton and extravagant youth" (ibid., 95).

I notice that Psyche, a woman, is the protagonist who, despite fear and moments of hopelessness, succeeds at trials and achieves her goal. I notice that despite her forbidden peek inside the box of beauty, and alongside her wish to be married, Psyche did have feelings of resistance to being idealized as a New Venus. She protested that the admiration she received for her beauty was "such as is accorded to an exquisitely carved statue" (ibid., 77), and she ultimately accepted what she expected would be a monstrous marriage with these words: "Only now do I realize and see that my one undoing has been the title of Venus bestowed on me" (ibid.,

79). I see courage alongside naïveté in her effort to carry out the potentially murderous scheme devised by her sisters and to escape the fearful secrecy of being bound to a man she could not look on. Most importantly, I see that, despite Psyche's moments of suicidal despair, there is a thorough line of resolve in her story. This young girl, who saw that being designated the New Venus was her undoing, first runs from Venus's wrath, beseeching aid from Ceres, the nurturing goddess of agriculture (who had rescued her own daughter, Proserpina, from dangerous mischief hatched by Venus) and then from Juno, Jupiter's wife. But when both of these goddesses refuse to help, citing laws against harboring fugitives and ties of family and affection to Venus, Psyche gathers her courage and, not waiting for a guide or helper, makes this heartening speech to herself: "Why don't you show a manly spirit, and the strength to renounce idle hope? Why don't you surrender yourself voluntarily to your mistress and soften her savage onslaught by showing a humble demeanor, however late in the day? You never know, you may find the object of your long search in her house" (ibid., 102).

With this, Psyche's quest begins, and she is able to move through Venus's torture and trials to find Pleasure.

I revisit the image of Psyche clinging to Cupid's leg. The Graves translation does not call Psyche a "pitiable appendage"; it says that "she looked very queer carried up like that through the cloudy sky" (Apuleius 1998b, 118). It becomes possible to see holding on to love against all odds as an act of courage.

I also begin to see Cupid and his divine parents differently. When Cupid retreated to his mother, and mother and son turned their attention from the affairs of mortals, a white bird came to Venus to protest that because of their negligence, "[p]leasure and favor and elegance had departed from the world; all was unkempt, rustic, uncouth. There were no weddings, no cameraderie between friends, none of the love which children inspire; all was a scene of boundless squalor, of unsavory tedium in sordid alliances" (Apuleius 1999, 96–7).[5]

Venus was capable of being every bit as wanton as her son. (When Psyche completed her first trial, the Graves translation has it that Venus came to her from a feast "a little drunk, smelling of aphrodisiac ointments, and simply swathed in rose-wreaths" [Apuleius 1998b, 133].) Nonetheless, after hearing from the bird, Venus decides that she needs the assistance of her "enemy" Sobriety in dealing with Cupid. Sobriety must "empty his quiver, immobilize his arrows, unstring his bow, extinguish his torch, and restrain his person with sharper correction" (Apuleius 1999, 98).

Are we to imagine that Venus has put aside her jealousy and passion? We are not. Jealous temper bubbles in her very next words: "Only when she has sheared off his locks—how often I have brushed them shining like gold with my own hands!—and clipped those wings, which I have steeped in my own breast's liquid nectar, shall I regard the insult dealt to me as expiated" (ibid.).

Still, Venus seems prepared to stop tormenting Psyche and Cupid and tolerate a new equilibrium.

Are we to imagine that Apuleius's wanton Cupid will mellow? I doubt it. But it does seem that his anger about Psyche's disobedience softened, for the story of Psyche's trials is peppered with hints that his power protects her. Ceres and Juno try to dampen Venus's fury by taking Cupid's part because "they fear his arrows" (ibid., 99). The helper ants work to aid "this refined girl, who is Cupid's wife" (ibid., 105). The breeze that interrupts Psyche's suicidal gesture at the start of the second trial is described in the Graves translation as "divine" (Apuleius 1998b, 34). Jupiter's royal bird directs "his veneration for Cupid's power to aid his wife" (Apuleius 1999, 108). The tower that saves Psyche and guides her through the Underworld is "divinely inspired" (ibid., 109). And Psyche's final helper is Cupid himself, who rouses her from her Stygian sleep. Perhaps Cupid, like his mother, is in an uneasy alliance with Sobriety. And Loyalty.

The theme of an always ambivalent alliance with Sobriety is reprised when Jupiter softens to Cupid's entreaties and orchestrates a "happy ending" for Psyche and Cupid's story of love. Acting out of what he describes as his "usual moderation," Jupiter summons all the gods to announce his decision "that the hot-headed impulses of [Cupid's] early youth need to be reined in" (ibid., 112). "We must deprive him of all opportunities; his juvenile behavior must be shackled with the chains of marriage. He has chosen the girl, and robbed her of her virginity, so he must have and hold her. Let him take Psyche in his embrace and enjoy his dear one ever after" (ibid.,113).

Jupiter then made Psyche immortal, and she reclined with her suddenly lawful husband. Whereupon, a somewhat mollified but still vibrant Venus "took to the floor to the strains of sweet music, and danced prettily" (ibid.).

No hearer of this tale of Psyche and Cupid is likely to imagine that the tensions between Eros and Sobriety or between Old and New Venus have been resolved forever. But I have a new appreciation for the fact that the ending is happy rather than tragic. The white bird is vindicated as pleasure and favor and elegance return to the world along with weddings, cameraderie between friends, and the love that children inspire. And these gods will, I imagine, continue to dance between passion and sobriety and between envy and love, and they will revel with open eyes in what Gilligan describes as the changing weather of relationship.

Shakespeare's later comedies can be reconsidered in much the same way. Tina Packer argues that because of both his profession and his social class, Shakespeare was, like Apuleius, an outsider.[6] He was an artist at a time when artists were outcasts, and he is thought to have been the child of illiterate parents. Looking back on *Twelfth Night* with the possibility of contradiction and ambivalence in mind, it is easier, again, to see resistance and strength. In a lovely, recent production, Viola was portrayed as "this girl/boy who comes in through the side door of the theater instead of from backstage where everyone else comes from, and she's soaking wet in her pink dress, and her first line is 'What country, friend, is this?' And she changes everything."[7] Shakespeare's text supports the performance of this spirited Viola just as surely as it seems to confound it in Viola's essentialist confession of frailty.

Even in the present day, we have not learned to imagine ourselves out of hierarchy and patriarchy. It is reasonable, then, to expect that characters in literary works of the past will exhibit tendencies toward resistance and love, if they exhibit them at all, in a context of, and against the grain of, patriarchal culture. So it now seems to me—despite my longing for literature that would escape rather than simply resist the old paradigms, and despite my often deep discomfort with literature that lies solidly within those paradigms—that Gilligan is right to ask us to see, and celebrate, the vibrancy of contrasting voices in texts that have remained absorbing across centuries.

READING THE POSTCOLONIAL TEXTS: SEEING COMPLEXITY OUTSIDE

What I now appreciate as the outsiderness of Apuleius and Shakespeare is nicely matched by the authors Gilligan defines as postcolonial. Sitting between a dominant worldview and the worldview of the subordinated colonial subject, the writers of postcolonial fiction are, as Apuleius and Shakespeare must have been, aware that the dominant view is not universal. They are therefore uniquely open to alternative visions.

Although I was initially skeptical that Apuleius and Shakespeare, as classic authors, could show us the path away from patriarchy, I approached Gilligan's postcolonial authors with optimism. Indeed, the liberating power of two of them—Morrison and Kincaid—had struck me on first readings. But two things about Gilligan's uses of these texts irritated me: First, the strategy of accentuating resistance seemed to go a bit awry in Gilligan's analyses of Morrison and Kincaid. In her reading of Morrison, Gilligan seemed to accentuate resistance so insistently that she lost sight of the range and depth of the forces against which resistance was (sometimes hopelessly) pitted. And in Gilligan's reading of Kincaid, she seemed to overlook forces of resistance that I thought important and vibrant. Second, as I have confessed, I was irritated by what struck me as Gilligan's celebration of love between "fair" women and lower-caste men as a model of resistance. I refer specifically to the secondary story of love between an Indian noncombatant and a Canadian nurse in *The English Patient*'s sweeping account of war and dislocation and the love affair between a higher-caste Indian woman and a darker, "untouchable" man in *The God of Small Things* of an Indian family evolving within a culture of assimilation and Anglophilia. Both stories triggered deep-seated feelings about what people in communities of color often call the White Woman Problem.

Let us put the somewhat troubling second feeling aside for a bit while we consider how Gilligan's strategy of accentuating resistance plays out in her analyses of Morrison and Kincaid. (Perhaps when we return to the "White Woman Problem," we'll find that my two bouts of irritability had something of a common source.)

Seeing Struggle or Strife: *The Bluest Eye*

Gilligan cites Morrison's *The Bluest Eye* as a testament to what I will call the nursery—to the time and emotional place within which all but the unluckiest of us felt parental love and took pleasure in that feeling. She reminds us of Morrison's exquisite depiction of a coughing child's feeling inquiring and comforting hands—of the "somebody with hands who does not want me to die" (Morrison 1970, 7). This child, Claudia, and her sister Frieda are often our eyes in the world in which *The Bluest Eye* develops. Their feistiness reaffirms the message that they have known the playfulness and ease of residing in a parent's love—that there is in their mother's bustling, fussing, and singing and in their father's tense concern, "love thick as Alaga syrup" (ibid., 6).

But however eloquently *The Bluest Eye* describes the security of home and parental love, it is indelibly and more centrally about how home and parental nurture are corrupted by what Roy describes in *The God of Small Things* as "the laws that lay down who should be loved and how. And how much" (1997, 31). Family socialization is infected by lessons of caste. By lessons of social deference. And by lessons about who is ugly and who is not. Apart from Claudia's memory of hands that "repinned the flannel, readjusted the quilt, and rested a moment on [her] forehead" (Morrison 1970, 6), throughout the four seasons of *The Bluest Eye*, I recall only one other moment when either Frieda or Claudia feels their mother's touch. Frieda is hugged by her mother on the fateful day of Pecola's first menstruation, but this hug is an act of contrition. It is a second instinct, coming after the same hands have struck the child for "playing nasty" (ibid., 30). The accusation of "playing nasty" was leveled by Rosemary Villanucci, the first person we meet after the prologue. She is the white child sitting in a car eating bread and butter. The child who stirs herself to tell Claudia and Frieda that they can't come in. The child Claudia and Frieda would like to pummel if she would come out of the car. The mother's first instinct had been to credit Rosemary and to try to beat the nastiness out of Frieda.

Morrison depicts family lessons of caste most painfully in the stories of Cholly, Pauline, and Pecola Breedlove. The Breedloves lived in a dismal storefront "because they believed they were ugly" (ibid., 38). Pauline Breedlove "knew" from the day that her dark-skinned daughter Pecola was born that she was ugly. Pauline educated herself at the movies, forgetting "lust and simple caring" (ibid., 122), learning about romance and a dominant vision of physical beauty, and becoming a perfect servant. She found her worth in the approval of her masters and in doting on her pink and yellow little-girl charge. When Pecola disturbed the rabbit-slippered, pink and yellow child, Pauline knocked Pecola to the floor, slapped her, and evicted her with words "spit out like rotten pieces of apple" (ibid., 109). When the already defeated eleven-year-old Pecola aroused the tender loathing of her father Cholly, he raped her. Obsessed with a longing for blue eyes, Pecola steps out of reality. Becomes blue-eyed. But never blue-eyed enough.

As I considered this aspect of Gilligan's analysis, the issue of focus was revived. I had become persuaded that it was useful to focus on moments of resistance in the canons of patriarchal society. Still, it seemed wrong to cite a work so painfully explicit about the family's role in enforcing Roy's love laws only to focus on the relational pleasures of childhood and celebrate their recall. True, holding onto the relational pleasures of childhood is, under Gilligan's analysis, a key to psychic and relational wholeness. But avoiding a too-complete break from maternal values would not be enough to save *The Bluest Eye*'s children. They must learn to resist deprecation that flows with mothers' milk and somehow find what Morrison describes in this volume as the enabling power of self-love.

SEEING STRIFE OR STRUGGLE: *ANNIE JOHN*

When Gilligan speaks of *Annie John* (1983), Jamaica Kincaid's coming-of-age novel, it is to call attention to the painfulness of Annie's separation from her mother and the sense in which the mother supplanted a loving playfulness with distance and decorum. Again, Gilligan's reading seems right; Kincaid's text serves brilliantly to illustrate the trauma of being ousted from the nursery. Annie's mother does become less physical in her affection for the child, and she curbs Annie's instincts to dance, to roam the countryside, to play marbles, to engage with boys, and to climb trees. And it might fairly be said that, to borrow a portion of the near-perfect description of dissociation found in Claudia's concluding recollection of Pecola, Annie was forced to "switch habits to simulate maturity" (Morrison 1970, 163). But, here again, Gilligan has neglected aspects of the text that were strikingly important to my eye. Here, she seems not to accentuate resistance but to disregard her own admonition to keep a sharp eye for it.

There is a great deal of healthiness in Annie's growing. Her strong, sensual, beautiful mother, who quareled with her own father and left home, who swims off to distant rocks, and who has a secret that gives bite to Annie's return of the potent word "slut," didn't just impose decorum at a certain age (Kincaid 1983, 102). She gave Annie her first marbles, taught her to take her dreams seriously, and summoned the powerful traditional healer Ma Chess to bring her back to psychic health when she lost her way. Annie's parents gloried in the exuberant intelligence of this child who disliked obedient, eager-to-please students but was always chapters and conceptual leaps ahead in school. And they approved of her athleticism if not her dancing.

There is more. The support Annie got to resist adolescent socialization that went against her relational, high-spirited nature was matched—and no doubt reinforced—by the support that she and her peers got to resist colonial myth-making that disturbed a healthy, collective self-image among the descendants of slaves. Annie's parents—and perhaps her entire social milieu—seem to have supported the strong and positive sense of collective self that enabled Annie to resist the assimilation of norms that made no sense. As her mind races during a lesson about Christopher Columbus, Annie abandons the adolescent "I" for just a moment to tell us in the second-person plural that even though "sometimes, what with our teachers and our books, it was hard for us to tell on which side we really now belonged, the masters or the slaves," "we the descendents of slaves, knew quite well what had really happened" (ibid., 76). She goes on to assure us that right-thinking people would have behaved quite differently than the masters did: "[I]f our ancestors had gone from Africa to Europe and come upon the people living there," she explains, "they would have taken a proper interest in the Europeans on first seeing them, and said, 'How nice,' and then gone home to tell their friends about it" (ibid.).

Claudia, Frieda, Pecola, and Annie struggle to hold their voices as people of color just as they struggle to hold the pleasure of relationship with their mothers. The two struggles are entangled. If the mother has decided that she and her child are ugly, preferring what Morrison, writing after Kenneth and Mamie Phipps Clark's doll studies, defines as the world of Shirley Temple dolls, the child's voice dies at inception. Pauline remembers nursing the newborn Pecola: "A right smart baby she was. I used to like to watch her. You know they makes them greedy sounds. Eyes all soft and wet. A cross between a puppy and a dying man. But I knowed she was ugly. Head full of pretty hair, but Lord she was ugly" (Morrison 1970, 97–8). In the end, Pecola was reduced to madness: "She spent her days, her tendril, sap-green days, walking up and down, up and down. . . . Elbows bent, hands on shoulders, she flailed her arms like a bird in an eternal, grotesquely futile effort to fly" (Morrison 1970, 204). As years went by, "The birdlike gestures . . . [wore] away to a mere picking and plucking her way between the tire rims and the sunflowers, between Coke bottles and milkweed, among all the waste and beauty of the world— which is what she herself was" (ibid., 205).

Children do, as Gilligan suggests, crave holding on to the relationality of the nursery. But they have an equivalent craving for self-love. If children can hear self-love in their parents' voices and in their people's songs, they have a chance of holding on, of resisting the message when "the world itself" (ibid., 100) tells them that they and their kind are ugly. "If my mother was in a singing mood," says Claudia, "it wasn't so bad" (ibid., 25).

SEEING IN STRUGGLE: *THE GOD OF SMALL THINGS* AND *THE ENGLISH PATIENT*

Like Morrison's and Kincaid's novels, Roy's *The God of Small Things* and Ondaatje's *The English Patient* address the pains of caste hierarchy. Both involve stories of forbidden love. In *The God of Small Things*, we see life and love through the eyes of Ammu, an Indian woman who possessed both "the infinite tenderness of motherhood" and "the reckless rage of a suicide bomber" (Roy 1997, 44). Ammu was very much a colonial subject. She came from an ambitious family of Anglophiles, "[p]ointed in the wrong direction," as her brother put it, "trapped outside their own history and unable to retrace the steps because their footprints had been [figuratively] swept away" (ibid., 51), just as the footsteps of untouchables were required under the love laws to be self-erased as they left the presence of any person of a higher caste. Although Ammu has been schooled to elitism by her fiercely class-conscious family, she loves the darker-skinned and untouchable Velutha, who moved through life with "unwarranted assurance" and without conspicuous Anglophilia (ibid., 73).

Hana, the Canadian nurse of *The English Patient*, also finds love across lines of caste and color. Hana's Indian lover Kirpal is an ambivalent Anglophile, working comfortably with the British army, but only because he limits himself to the dangerous but noncombative role of finding and defusing mines. Although she has closed herself off from a world at war, Hana finds that she can open her heart to Kirpal, who, like Hana, goes to war zones to restore rather than to do battle.

Gilligan describes these forbidden love affairs as models of resistance. She speaks similarly about the monoracial but adulterous love affair that is the central mystery of *The English Patient*. Each of these affairs is in defiance of laws that lay down who you can love; and how; and how much. Each can be celebrated as a triumph of love over separation, solitude, and moral isolation. A triumph of love over detachment.

But in each case there is an Other against whom the lovers' triumph is an actual or symbolic betrayal. The central love story in *The English Patient*—the affair between the Patient and Katharine, his colleague's wife—makes this point dramatically. Katharine predicts that her husband will go mad if he discovers the affair. He does discover and goes mad, attempting to kill the three of them but leaving the Patient alive, later to be burned beyond recognition. Gilligan argues that the tragedy of the Patient's relationship with Katharine was not that it ended in death and disfigurement. The tragedy, she tells us, was that the Patient resisted Katharine's efforts to own and be owned—the tragedy lay in "the silences" by which the Patient in fact abandoned Katharine. When Katharine says that she will not continue to lie to her husband about the affair, the following conversation ensues:

> "What do you hate most?" . . . [the Patient] asks her.
> "A lie. And you?"
> "Ownership," he says. "When you leave me, forget me."

(Quoted in Gilligan 2002, 181.)

Gilligan argues that Ondaatje tells this love story backwards—in retrospect from the Patient's journal and from his morphine-clouded memory—to make it easier for readers to see that it did not have to end in death and tragedy. Easier to see that Katharine and the Patient might have avoided tragedy by declaring and holding onto their love. But, of course, to see the declaration of adulterous love as an avoidance of tragedy is to lose sight of the betrayed spouse. The husband's response to a declaration of Katharine's and the Patient's love might well have produced as much death and tragedy as did his response to the chance discovery of their love. But neither Ondaatje's nor Gilligan's account moves a reader to take the husband's perspective. I worry about Gilligan's capacity to erase the betrayed spouse in this way. As we will see, it is akin to the capacity to render the "Other" invisible in the stories of romance that cross lines of color and caste.

Erasure of the "Othered" partner is more subtle—and more invidious—than erasure of the betrayed spouse. It is symbolic rather than literal. It happens at the intersection of patriarchy and caste subordination.

Patriarchy and caste subordination both presume and resonate with so-called natural hierarchies. The most resonant of these presumptively "natural" hierarchies are those of gender and age. We justify patriarchy as a natural order. We justify caste subjugation by analogizing the position of the subjugated to that of women or children. Like women and children, subjugated adults are considered incapable of self-governance. They are emotional creatures rather than rational actors. They are childish or childlike, capable of violence or lust, but incapable of the controlled exercise of power. Their domination is therefore necessary and benevolent. They are naturally and mercifully kept in layered hierarchies: the higher caste stands above the lower caste. Within castes, men stand over women and adults stand over children.

In the Oedipal story, fear keeps these layers of patriarchal control in place. The mother becomes a moral hazard. Boys separate from their mothers and internalize a code of isolation. Girls suppress relationality in order to accept and defer to this code of isolation. The idealization of upper-caste women extends this Oedipal fear across castes. Like the mother, the higher-caste woman is desired and forbidden. Violating her is the ultimate transgression. And the ultimate trophy.

Gilligan reminds us that to be an ultimate trophy is to be an idea of beauty rather than a "lived-in" beauty; an idea of virtue rather than a human possibility. To regard oneself as an ideal is to dissociate from one's human self. But when the idealization of women functions in a caste hierarchy, it has a second effect that Gilligan does not mention. To regard a class of women as ideal is not only to deny their complexity and humanity; it is also to create, and to belittle, a class of Other women. When a couple breaks love laws that declare upper-caste women taboo, one can say that the couple has challenged the idealization of upper-caste women or accepted the denigration of lower-caste women. By the same token, one can say that it has challenged the denigration of lower-caste men or that it has potently dramatized the higher-caste man's need—and justified his power—to control. Since we are dealing with the logic of the psyche, we can imagine that these "contradictory" things happen simultaneously.

All love enacts resistance to the code of isolation, and in this sense all love is liberating. But so long as we accept patriarchy's idealizations and stratifications, all love will carry mixed messages. Love of "one's kind" will enact and maintain hierarchy's layers. Love for a superordinate Other will have the same effect. And love for a subordinate Other will imply one's own superiority and dramatize the lure of the forbidden. No matter how completely a couple has rejected caste hierarchy, the union retains all of its contradictory, symbolic effects.

We are right to join Gilligan in celebrating resistance, but it is also important to analyze fully the structures that make resistance necessary. An incomplete analysis will yield an incomplete response. To see patriarchy's full effect, we have to see it from every perspective. And we have to be mindful of how it is overlain with caste subordination. Patriarchy's objectifications and stratifications are hurtful at every level, and in the end they spare no one. They objectify and therefore demean all women. Within the logic of objectification, they further demean lower-caste women; not only are we objects, we are inferior objects. They deny lower-caste men's and all women's capacity for full maturity. And they suppress relationality universally, leaving us all—and often leaving men most tightly—locked in unnatural and crippling isolation. What would it take to pull out all the roots of patriarchy's evil? I think that it takes scrupulous effort against underestimating or ignoring any aspect of the pain and damage that patriarchy inflicts.

MOVING FORWARD: RESISTING HIERARCHY IN ALL ITS COMPLEXITY

I was right to push beyond my discomfort with classic texts. A less irritable reading does yield models of resistance.

Should I also push beyond my resentment on seeing love between upper-caste women and lower-caste men held up as a model of resistance? I should. Postcolonial theorizing about the psychic effects of symbols does not negate the courage of these unions. Nor does it speak necessarily to their health: cultural symbolism has an infinitely complicated role in any love relationship, and its role is as likely to be enriching as it is to be toxic or hurtful.

Still, my resentful feelings are deep and widely shared. And they are resonant with a layered patriarchy's supporting myths and practices. In our cultural imagination, women of color are rarely placed on pedestals by anyone of any color. Consider Shakespeare's acknowledgment of (and simultaneous rebellion against) Elizabethan standards of beauty:

In the old age black was not counted fair,
Or if it were it bore not beauty's name:
But now is black beauty's successive heir,
And beauty slandered with a bastard shame.

(Sonnet 127)

Or consider United States census data. The 2000 census reported that among black–white couples in the United States, 73 percent involved black men and white women, and the proportion was 80 percent for cohabiting couples. In 2005, census data indicated that nearly 70 percent of African–American women were living without a partner. It is not unreasonable to connect these data with the culture's image of the undeniably heroic Martin Luther King caught on FBI tapes in secret assignations with white women, during which he uttered the heartbreaking cry: "I'm not a nigger tonight!"[8] And it is not unreasonable to connect them with evidence from social psychology that African–American women are subconsciously associated with masculinity and generally perceived as being less attractive than Anglo-American women (Goff et al. 1908, 392–403).

Resentment is neither a constructive nor an appropriate response, but some discomfort with Gilligan's celebration of transgressive love is perhaps justifiable. It is here that my discomfort with Gilligan's selective attention to resistance and pain in Morrison's and Kincaid's postslavery novels converges with my discomfort with her celebration of transgressive love in Ondaatje's and Roy's novels of postcolonial India. Examining my discomfort teaches that it is hard for me to see the beauty and resistance beneath the surfaces of classic texts and hard for me to see the beauty and resistance in love that transgresses hierarchy's segregating laws. I have to work to shed self-referential blinders. Perhaps Gilligan and I have complementary difficulties.

Gilligan's analysis of postslavery novels focuses resistance to women's dissociation but shadows the pain imposed by caste hierarchy. While the resilience of Pecola Breedlove's feisty young neighbors is celebrated, Pecola's psychological destruction is all but ignored. Gilligan's analysis of postcolonial, cross-caste love stories has a similar effect: the higher-caste woman and the lower-caste man are focused and celebrated for their resistance, but the subordination of lower-caste women is nearly or entirely erased. Kirpal's Indian wife is seen only at the very end of *The English Patient*—a silent figure in the background as Kirpal looks away in reverie of his Canadian lover. The untouchable mothers and wives from the world in which Velutha somehow salvaged his "uncommon assurance" are never mentioned (Roy 1997, 73).

Morrison is right, I think, to tell us that self-love is a sure defense against subordination. But self-love does not come because it is called for. It does not come when parents and all the world tell a child that she is ugly. And it does not come easily to one whose passion is met with envy and suspicion. Self-love does not come easily to the invisible. It grows most naturally in a climate of empathy and respect. In communities in which the mutually reinforcing effects of all our unjustified hierarchies are acknowledged and undone. In communities able to achieve an advanced form of the relationality that patriarchy so effectively squelches.

Perhaps because of personal history, and perhaps because of a kind of genius, Barack Obama is a model of relationality and mindfulness. You can see this in his account of a simple incident. In the book *Dreams from My Father* (1995), Obama tells of feeling stunned when a black coworker came into their office wearing blue contact lenses. Obama was reminded of the moment during his childhood years in Indonesia when he began to understand racial hierarchy. Gazing wide-eyed at a magazine article describing a black person who had bleached his skin white, Obama, the child of an African father, had listened with a nine-year-old's wonder as his white American mother patiently and wisely answered his difficult questions. Years later, looking away from his suddenly blue-eyed coworker with embarrassment, Obama thought to himself, how can she learn to love blue eyes without hating herself? How can we keep the ranking—the degradation and idealization—out of our visions of Others? I don't know. But this journey has helped me appreciate the entrenched complexity of patriarchy's interlocking layers.

Notes

1 See Eva Cantarella, this volume, pp. 111–18.

2 Speaking of both, and after rescuing her from the nearly fatal consequences of the second, Cupid says, "Poor dear Psyche, . . . see how as before your curiosity might have been your undoing!" (Apuleius 1999, 112.)

3 References are to act, scene, and line. For the uncorrected text, "For, such as we are made, if such we be" is no better (Shakespeare 1842, 351).

4 Some have assumed that Apuleius was born to a Greek mother and a descendant of Plutarch, but so far as I know this assumption rests solely on the evidence that Lucius, the protagonist of the supposedly somewhat autobiographical *Metamorphoses*, describes his lineage in that way. Evidence of his North African heritage is usefully addressed in Helen E. Hagan's "Apuleius of Madauros" (2001).

5 Graves's translation of Apuleius's *The Golden Ass* is even more resonant with Carol Gilligan's interpretation. In it the bird "screamed," "the whole system of human love is in such complete disorder that it is now considered disgusting for anyone to show even natural affection" (Apuleius 1998b: 122–3).

6 See Tina Packer, this volume, pp. 141–6.

7 For this characterization of Viola, and for vastly enriching my readings of Shakespearian texts, I am indebted to Lizzy Cooper Davis.

8 This general subject is movingly addressed in Tracey Scott Wilson's beautifully balanced play *The Good Negro* (2010).

References

APULEIUS. 1914. *Apulli Apologia, Sive, Pro Se de Magia Liber*. Edited by Harold E. Butler and Arthur S. Owen. Oxford: Clarendon Press.

———. 1998a. *The Golden Ass*. Translated by Edward J. Kenney. New York: Penguin Books.

———. 1998b. *The Transformations of Lucius*. Translated by Robert Graves. New York: Farrar, Straus, and Giroux.

———. 1999. *The Golden Ass*. Translated by Patrick G. Walsh. New York: Oxford University Press.

GILLIGAN, Carol. 2002. *The Birth of Pleasure: A New Map of Love*. New York: Alfred A. Knopf.

———. 2008. "Commencement Address."Address at Mount Holyoke College, South Hadley, MA, May 25. Available at:www.mtholyoke.edu/news/story/5580663

GOFF, Philip Atiba, Margaret A. Thomas, and Matthew Christian Jackson. 1908. "Ain't I A Woman?: Towards an Intersectional Approach to Person Perception and Group-Based Harms." *Sex Roles* 59: 392–403.

HAGAN, Helene E. 2001. "Apuleius of Madauros." *The Amazigh Voice Magazine* 10(2) (Fall): 8–13. Available at: www.tamazgha.org/uploads/4/2/2/3/422318/amazigh_voice_vol10_n2.pdf

KINCAID, Jamaica. 1983. *Annie John*. New York: Farrar, Straus, and Giroux.

LORDE, Audre. 1984. "The Master's Tools Will Never Dismantle the Master's House." In *Sister Outsider*: *Essays and Speeches*. Berkeley, CA: The Crossing Press, pp. 110–13.

MORRISON, Toni. 1970. *The Bluest Eye*. New York: Holt, Rinehart & Winston.

———. 1992. *Playing in the Dark*: *Whiteness and the Literary Imagination*. Cambridge, MA: Harvard University Press.

OBAMA, Barack. 1995. *Dreams from My Father*: *A Story of Race and Inheritance*. New York: Times Books.

ONDAATJE, Michael. 1992. *The English Patient*. New York: Alfred A. Knopf.

ROY, Arundhati. 1997. *The God of Small Things*. New York: Random House.

SHAKESPEARE, William. 1842. "Twelfth Night." In J. Payne Collier (ed.), *The Works of William Shakespeare*: *The Text Formed From an Entirely New Collation of the Old Editions*. London: Whittaker & Co, pp. 315–420.

———. 2010. "The Taming of the Shrew." In Barbara Hodgdon (ed.), *Arden Shakespeare*. 3rd series. London: A & C Black Publishers.

WILSON, Tracey Scott. 2010. *The Good Negro*. New York: Dramatist Play Services.

Responding to Carol Gilligan's view that liberating insight can be found in times of political and social upheaval and in the voices of outsiders, Tina Packer examines Shakespeare as an outsider living in the turbulence of the Renaissance. Eva Cantarella found resistance among women at the emergence of the myth of Psyche and Cupid that supports Gilligan's claims for the myth's liberating power. Similarly, Packer finds in Shakespeare's life and times influences that support Gilligan's claims for the liberating power of the later comedies.

Shakespeare as Outsider
TINA PACKER

William Shakespeare is such a central figure in our western culture—and an influence in so many other cultures—that thinking of him as an outsider seems absurd. After all, everyone quotes Shakespeare. People of every political persuasion claim him as their own, and they can usually find some meaty and insightful words spoken by one of his characters to justify their own ideology. I do it myself all the time—mostly to prove Shakespeare is a good feminist. In fact, I created a performance–lecture trilogy called *Women of Will*: *Following the Feminine in Shakespeare's Plays*,[1] which is some nine hours of proving Shakespeare had a truly feminine perspective on life—even if many of his characters are chauvinist pigs par excellence. However, at this moment, I want to invite you to think about Shakespeare as Outsider—and within that definition of him, I want to claim that he knew that the most radical action a human being can take is to discover what really gives pleasure to the soul. This soul-deep pleasure has the power to heal our relationships and to give nuance, flexibility, and workability to societal structures—if not change them outright! To make this claim, I am going to have to try to define "soul" (always a tricky thing), and I will probably use something from Shakespeare to help me. And I want you to understand that I make the claim—and define "soul"— as an artist, not as an academic. I earn my living as a director, actor, teacher, and writer. I think of Shakespeare as someone who also had to earn a living, run a theatre, and nourish his own soul as best he could while worrying about bums on seats.

Shakespeare is usually taught in ways that reinforce a hierarchical organizational structure—there is someone in power who "knows" and is instructing and judging those who don't know. It is in some ways the same structure Shakespeare himself lived under from the ages of seven to seventeen. With one fundamental difference: as we shall see, Shakespeare was trained in the Art of Rhetoric. He was expected to stir up the desire to think, to persuade, and to influence others with his words. He developed his playwriting art through the use of rhetoric, and by doing so, he opened up some of the most transgressive questions of the day: What is the role of women in society? What is honor? What is God's law? Man's law? Which is more important, love or power? Where does the soul reside? What is language? Must we mean what we say? And so on. He created pleasure in questioning hierarchical order! Shakespeare was interested in awakening pleasure in new thinking, using both verse and prose to awaken insight in all his audience members—from every class and every gender, various religious persuasions, anyone who would pay the penny to get into the playhouse.

So the outsiders Shakespeare wrote about become archetypes of the fight against oppression then and now: Shylock, Othello, Caliban, and the women. As an artist, Shakespeare knew it was those human beings living outside the power structure who were best able to perceive that power structure. He knew that most individuals internalize the power structures they are born into and therefore think of them as natural, rather than inherited and constructed. It takes an artistic temperament to break through that patterning. The very essence of artistic talent is soul: the empathetic ability to awaken the senses so that they offer a perception that is different from the norm.

Shakespeare as Outsider

Shakespeare was writing on a cusp, at a time of change. It is one of the factors that make his text great: the paradigm is always shifting. He was writing during this raw time we now call the Renaissance, the rebirth. He did not call it that, nor did any of his contemporaries. All they knew was that it was possible to change structures and laws and to invent new ideas in a way that had not been possible for their forefathers. However, if you went too far, you'd get your head chopped off, so caution was advisable.

He was an artist living at a time when playwrights and actors (he was both) were not categorized as "artists." A playwright was a maker of plays as a wheelwright was a maker of wheels. An actor was legally categorized as a rogue and a vagabond who could be thrown into jail simply for being a rogue and a vagabond. Being a playwright and actor was dangerous. And Shakespeare knew it.

Shakespeare was part of an oral culture. His family did not read and write. In an oral culture, human beings speak and listen to each other with a deep intensity. This intense communication awakens relationships as it demands rapt attention in each present moment. The nuance, tone, duration, the onomatopoeic texture of the spoken word convey a wealth of information we can no longer conceive. There is soul contained in sound, as blues artists know. Our modern spoken words get flatter and duller with every passing year. The soul is passing out of language. In an oral/aural culture, you're not thinking particularly in perspective. Perspectives come in with literate culture. In an oral culture each human being's gut is out there, picking up every bit of information that it can. And theater is created in the oral. It is about living in these moments of now, now this minute, now. And now and now, and now some more.

But although Shakespeare's background, life, and art form belonged to an oral tradition with all the richness that implies, he himself was one of the new batch of boys. He was privileged to go to one of the new public schools set up by the good burghers of the town to educate their sons in the recently rediscovered Greek and Latin texts and to teach them to think clearly and deeply by practicing the art of rhetoric, the art of persuasion. Shakespeare's plays were written to affect people in the gut, in the immediate present, and to earn a penny at the door. His audiences had bodily reactions to what the actors said. Shakespeare's education, however, was for the most part cadenced, careful Latin. Like a colonial subject, he lived and worked in one culture and was taught in the language and terms of another. Shakespeare and his fellow students learned nothing about England in their education. They learned principally about the Romans, and while they did speak in English some of the time in the classroom, they spent many hours a day speaking and learning in Latin, with a bit of Greek and Hebrew thrown in. They were immersed in foreign texts. So language—how different people expressed different ideas in different languages—was one of the foundations of Shakespeare's education—six days a week, twelve hours a day. The method by which Shakespeare was taught affected him deeply. It was back and forth, back and forth between the teacher and the pupil: teacher recites, pupil recites; teacher speaks, pupil responds, translate this into English, translate it back into Latin, find another way to say it in English, another way in Latin. It was an actor–audience relationship of the most intense kind.

Then there was the memorization! The Art of Memory is one of the five parts of Rhetoric; Delivery (the actor's art) is another. Shakespeare had to memorize everything he learned. By the end of each day, the students had memorized everything that they had learned that day. And at the end of the week, they would repeat the whole week's texts, and then on Sunday, they went to church and heard the Bible and the sermon, and they memorized and repeated them. So is it any surprise that Shakespeare's brain contained all the texts he had learned in school— Ovid, Apuleius, Plutarch, Aristotle, Plato, Pythagoras, Cicero, Demosthenes, Virgil, and so on? And memory, of course, involves association and imagery. Learning this way creates many Proustian moments, associations that come up as you hear and rehear words. This associative process must have been at work as words from his everyday life mingled with words from the lives of Ovid, Plutarch, Apuleius, and the writers of the Old and New Testaments. The visceral pleasure of speaking and listening, the constructs of other languages, memory of the past, and the rhythm of repetition and sound are the foundations of Shakespeare's art.

By the 1590s, Shakespeare was living in London. It was a hundred years after the printing press was invented, and finally there were enough printing presses in the world that texts of every kind were flying out of the shops and into St. Paul's churchyard. St. Paul's churchyard was Barnes and Noble, Waterston's, and Borders all rolled into one. Shakespeare lived only a few streets away from St. Paul's, so he had access to almost every new text, and the texts went into Shakespeare's very skilled memorization tank, filtering into his plays. He became fascinated by man's "Godlike reason" and ability to observe the repeating patterns of human action and shifting power. He subtly weighed in on the furious public debate waged in St. Paul pamphlets on whether women have souls in their own right or souls that belong to their fathers or husbands: "Think you, in your soul, that Count Claudio hath wronged Hero?" asked the soldier Benedick (the big dick) of Beatrice (Dante's image of the feminine soul). "Ay, as sure as I have a thought or a soul," replies Beatrice without hesitation. "Enough, I am engaged!" Benedick believes the words of a woman, changes his loyalty away from his traditional, brother–soldier comradeship and takes on the feminine cause, thus turning around the story, previously heading toward full-scale tragedy, into a story of love restored, life engendered.

Let me try to pull some of these strands together. I think Shakespeare's visceral, relationship-oriented experience of language, the rhetorical form of the plays, his experience as a rogue and a vagabond, and his supreme sensibility, developed by being an artist, living in the rough and tumble of a commercial world, gave him the unique position he now holds in the world. He lived in the warmth and immediacy of an oral/aural culture, where words contained their emotional impact in their very sounds and created strength in direct communication. He lived in the reasoned cadences of the Latin language; he thought about events which had happened two thousand years earlier; he witnessed the bloodshed religious belief could bring; he knew monarchy was not the only way to organize a country. He was a rogue and a vagabond who wrote about many rogues and vagabonds (Autolycus and Thersites, for example), always testing the ground about how far they could speak out before they would get themselves killed.

Working under all of these influences, Shakespeare insisted above all that people use their godlike reason, their soul ("the better part of man"), the very essence of wo/man, the marrow of their bones (the place Elizabethans believed the soul resides), *to think individually*. He modeled individual thinking in every character he created. Each has a different worldview, each is a creator of reality, and all are played, no matter what their rank, by actors, rogues and vagabonds (who did everything they could in their own lives to acquire gentleman status and not to be subject to rogue and vagabond laws).

SHAKESPEARE'S WOMEN

The women in Shakespeare's plays offer the code to understanding Shakespeare the artist. Despite Elizabeth's status as the Queen (and she was clever enough to turn herself into an archetype: The Virgin Queen or Astraea, depending on whether you preferred a Christian symbol or a Greek one), women were outsiders. As a generalization (though it is a pretty good one), the women in Shakespeare's plays divide into two categories. With few exceptions, all the women strive to tell the truth as they see it, alter the course of the patriarchal story, and bring about love and reconciliation. If they stay in their frocks and are perceived as women, they are killed, they go mad, or they commit suicide. People are sorry afterwards, but the fundamental power structure does not change. But if the women disguise themselves as men, they are able to alter the story. Not only does no one die, but love, marriage, procreation, dancing, singing, and pleasure can take place. Whether it is Portia or Viola, Julia, Imogen or Rosalind, tragedy is averted. In the later plays, Shakespeare even has the daughters redeem the sins of the fathers, much as Antigone was able, to some extent, to lift the curse on her father Oedipus and the House of Cadmus.

Is it possible that the women's way of doing things in Shakespeare's comedies—telling the truth, keeping your sense of humor and your girl-friends, and being ready to be reconciled even with those who wished you dead, and then celebrating, dancing and singing—is it just possible that this is the way to the future sanity of the planet? On a conscious or unconscious level, do we, his audience, respond to his underlying message of sanity and health?

Is it possible that this great artist—possibly the greatest of all time—who wrote definitive texts that are never definitive texts, who is large enough to be embraced by people of all political persuasions, in many cultures, across genders, classes, religious beliefs, was creating a body of work, which when spoken out loud and remembered, awakens a state of consciousness in both speakers and hearers, releasing something in their psyches allowing them to understand and maybe even love each other? Is it possible that we would not just tolerate each other but that, in the present moment of now, on stage or in life, we might even find each other's difference fascinating and want to touch it and feel it, live it, and be changed by it?

The answer, of course, depends on our ability to achieve the best in both oral and literate culture. We must be able to talk and listen in the richest way. We must find power in spiritual and sexual communion (forever intertwined in Shakespeare's world). We must be curious about other mindsets and tolerant of uncertainty. And we must be open to persuasion, embracing the excitement of an invitation to think in new ways. It is only in taking these kinds of pleasure that the soul can sing and dance.

Note

1 Shakespeare & Co., *Women of Will: Following the Feminine in Shakespeare's Plays*. Performance, Lenox, MA, April 29–July 24, 2010.

Cupid's flight from Psyche represents, in Carol Gilligan's account, a culturally pervasive flight from relationship and pleasure. Wendy Steiner sees this flight from relationship played out in the history of modern art. Challenging those who complain of premodern artists' voluptuous objectification of women, Steiner decries modern art's sharp female forms as artistic dissociation. Searching for a way out of artistic dissociation, Steiner imagines encounters with beauty that are analogous to love. In passages that resonate with Edward Tronick's account of the open dynamic system in a state of vibrant growth, she describes both beauty and love as opportunities for encounters that yield the pleasures of complexity and growth.

Reimagining Beauty
WENDY STEINER

In *The Birth of Pleasure*: *A New Map of Love* (2002), Carol Gilligan writes, "The trauma that is inherent in patriarchy and that fuels its continuation is a break in relationship . . . This is the story we tell over and over again, the tragic story of love . . . To hear tragic love as a story immediately suggests the existence of other stories and also the possibility of new stories . . . It means to imagine an escape from tragedy" (19). When I came upon these words and Gilligan's interpretation of the Psyche and Cupid myth, I experienced one of those shiver-inducing intimations of a Zeitgeist. For I had published, just a year before, a book called *Venus in Exile*: *The Rejection of Beauty in 20th Century Art* (2001), which describes the twentieth-century arts as a programmatic breaking of relationship—from the communication between artist and audience arising in the experience of beauty.

Like Gilligan, I had used the Psyche and Cupid myth in my book as a countermodel of broken relationship. Early twenty-first-century artists, I argued, would liberate themselves from the sterile aesthetics of modernism by revalidating beauty, understood not as a thing or a property but as an interaction analogous to empathy and love. In the process, women, whose situation in society is inextricably linked to prevailing ideologies of beauty, would be reaffirmed at the center of value.

Let me try to fill in this sweeping hypothesis. The modernist avant-garde turned from the beauty previously symbolized by the female subject to a chilling sublimity, which they located in pure form on the one hand and in the self-mystifying fetish on the other. Here is Georges Braque's *Woman with a Mandolin*, painted the same year, 1910, as he stated, "I couldn't portray a woman in all her natural loveliness. I haven't the skill. No one has. I must, therefore, create a new sort of beauty, the beauty that appears to me in terms of volume, of line, of mass, of weight . . . I want to expose the Absolute, and not merely the factitious woman" (quoted in Steiner 2001, 44).

In D. H. Lawrence's hands, this Absolute becomes a terrifying picture of abstract, dehumanized will:

Marcel Duchamp, *Nude Descending a Staircase* (NO. 2) (1912)

Georges Braque, *Woman with a Mandolin* (1910)

Pablo Picasso, *Les Demoiselles d'Avignon* (1907)

What is interesting in the laugh of the woman is the same as the binding of the molecules of steel or their action in heat; it is the inhuman will, call it physiology, or . . . physiology of matter, that fascinates me. I do not so much care about what the woman *feels*—in the ordinary usage of the word. That presumes an ego to feel with. I only care about what the woman *is*—what she IS—inhumanly, physiologically, materially—what she *is* as a phenomenon (or as representing some greater, inhuman will), instead of what she feels according to the human conception (quoted in ibid., 38–9.)

Braque relocates beauty from female loveliness to volume, line, and mass. Lawrence shifts it from woman as a pleasure-filled, emotional being ("the laugh of a woman") to woman as fetishized power—a superhuman force that fascinates and overwhelms the mortal artist.

Both of these modernists were engaged in the dissociative process Gilligan has described in *The Birth of Pleasure*:

Our tendency when we lose something is to hold onto an image of that thing. . . . The pervasive images of women, idealized and degraded, reflect a pervasive loss of connection with women. Loving an image of woman rather than an actual person becomes a way of fending off the possibility of losing again, because an image can be held apart from relationship, and one woman can take another's place (2002, 151).

The modernists went one step further, reducing the image of woman to dehumanized form, indestructible because it is immaterial, pure, and ideal, or to a fetish, indestructible because it is merely borrowed—exotic, foreign, primitive, superhumanly powerful, sublime. After all, what cannot be possessed in the first place can never be lost.

We can see these two dissociative strategies in the most programmatic works of modernism. In Marcel Duchamp's *Nude Descending a Staircase* (1912), the female figure is remade as machine. René Magritte's *Attempting the Impossible* (1928) declares the act of painting a female subject impossible, and in his manifesto cover for the 1929 issue of *La Révolution Surréaliste*, "Je Ne Vois Pas La . . . Cachee Dans La Foret," he shows his fellow surrealists' eyes closed to the nude woman in their midst, with the word for her, "FEMME," omitted. Pablo Picasso replaces female beauty with both form and fetish in *Les Demoiselles d'Avignon*, the 1907 breakthrough to Cubism. In this work, prostitutes are recast as geometrical surfaces and African masks, and the viewer of these beauties is put in the position of being not a brothel client or a connoisseur of female loveliness, but an interpreter of a problem in space relations with a keen ethnographic awareness.

When artists explain the rationale for these dissociative procedures, they sound like Gilligan's patients. For example, the author Henry Adams, in 1900, wrote that he greatly preferred the eighteenth-century belief system in which he had been educated to the twentieth-century one lying before him. In that previous lost time, dominated by the symbol of the Virgin, woman "conceived herself and her family as the center and flower of an ordered universe which she knew to be unity because she had made it after the image of her own fecundity; and this creation of hers was surrounded by beauties and perfections which she knew to be real because she herself had imagined them" (Adams 1931, 459). But the Virgin has been replaced by the Dynamo, writes Adams, and when that happened,

> the stage-scenery of the senses collapsed; the human mind felt itself stripped naked, vibrating in a void of shapeless energies, with resistless mass, colliding, crushing, wasting, and destroying what these same energies had created and labored from eternity to perfect. Society became fantastic, a vision of pantomime with a mechanical motion . . . the dynamo became a symbol of infinity. . . . Before the end, one began to pray to it (ibid., 37).

Whereas Adams sees the female image of beauty as tragically lost, Leo Tolstoy sees it as something too ephemeral to value. "Is this [female] 'beauty' real beauty?" he asks. "Of what use is it? . . . [T]hin and grizzled hair, toothlessness, wrinkles, tainted breath; even long before the end all becomes ugly and repellent; visible paint, sweat, foulness, hideousness. Where, then, is the god of my idolatry? Where is beauty?" (Quoted in ibid., 36.) The modernists who followed Adams and Tolstoy declared the woman a failed symbol of artistic beauty, glorifying in her place abstraction, an "impersonal art" of form and fetish, assaults on the audience, shock, scandal, and absurdity. In its flight from feminine beauty, avant-garde art seems to cover a systematic and enthusiastic embrace of what Gilligan calls the tragic story of love.

What would it mean to return to beauty and love? To reimagine beauty in Gilligan's relational terms? The Cupid and Psyche story is instructive here; in it, the experience of Cupid's beauty incites Psyche's love and leads her to recreate herself in the immortal image of her beloved. Beauty and love are both interchanges between a Self and an Other. Psyche looks upon the sleeping Cupid and is awed by his beauty, but he flees from her unworthy gaze. She grabs his foot as he rises to heaven, but her mortal strength is insufficient to maintain the connection and she falls back into her lesser world. It is only after proving herself through heroic labors that she can ascend to heaven and unite with Cupid in producing the immortal child, Pleasure.

The borders between subject and object become blurred as Psyche, moved by Cupid's beauty, rises to become his equal. Something like this blurring happens in all aesthetic experience. In recognizing an Other as beautiful, the subject becomes displaced onto it, admiring it, giving herself over to it, becoming it in some temporary or virtual way. In love, this expansion of Self into Other feels like the ultimate gratification: finally we have what we need, what we always wanted; we have come home. And more, we have much that we did not even know we wanted. A lover is like a child or an explorer, discovering a world bigger than what she had previously imagined. The experience of artistic beauty involves a similar journey, accompanied by feelings of both self-confirmation and enlargement beyond the self.

Love and beauty create a sense of self-worth, presenting and affirming our value to ourselves through our response to an Other. Of course, in the experience of beauty, the artwork cannot return the rush of feeling projected onto it. But that doesn't mean the perceiver is like an unrequited lover, opening herself to someone who does not or cannot reciprocate. The structure of aesthetic experience is a projective opening for the audience, allowing us to inhabit the place of the missing Other, and in the process, to know and admire our value as the knower and admirer of an "immortal" Other.

Because the beautiful Other in art is a symbolic structure rather than a real person, we are free to observe ourselves moved by its beauty and therefore capable of being so moved. We say to ourselves,

> *That* is beautiful; *I* find that beautiful; for me, that is perfect (or ideal or wonderful). How amazing that that is what moves me, that I am capable of seeing its complexity (power, originality, charm)! I am like artist A or period P or society S, who were also attuned to that beauty. I find my sensibility aligned with theirs. But though I may find a psychic home in them, I am also unique. No other person feels the beauty of this artwork exactly as I do.

The experience of beauty is the recognition of value in an Other that we realize is also value in ourselves.

Perhaps if we were constantly feeling love we might not need the artistic laboratory of beauty to experience this revelation of self-worth. But no person can possibly provide every experience of value and self-knowledge we require. Aesthetic experience is crucial, I think, not because we are insatiable for love but because we are insatiable for growth and derive profound pleasure from it. The experience of artistic beauty is the experience of a pleasurable expansion of self-knowledge.

I am struck by how often we apply the word "beautiful" to people or things that expand our knowledge. When we love or admire or appreciate or learn, we feel as if the person or object that provoked this experience is beautiful. What they look like in purely visual terms is often irrelevant; however they look becomes beautiful to us. Maybe that is why people whose appearance conforms to an accepted ideal can sometimes seem so irritating; they appear to be making a claim on our appreciation before we have gone through the growth-inducing exchange at the heart of the experience of beauty. Some of us are only too happy to admire in this superficial way, perhaps needing the cue of a socially sanctioned ideal of beauty in order to respond at all. But the more we cultivate our sensibilities, the more we associate beauty with discovery and growth.

During the last couple of years, scholarly books and museum exhibitions devoted to beauty have proliferated, and more and more artists— often women—are using the female subject to rethink the place of beauty in art. They encounter a daunting array of opposition. Feminists argue that locating beauty in the female subject has led to the objectification of women, and that it is our duty to avoid "the temptation to be a beautiful object" (Steiner 2001, 126–7). For the continuing champions of the avant-garde, beauty and its feminine symbolism are throwbacks to an earlier, less rigorous aesthetic era when liking a painting was confused with liking its subject. The call to beauty is therefore nostalgic or prurient, a pandering to the unsophisticated beliefs of the public. And for those who think that art should be an engine for social amelioration, beauty is too complacent, too tied to gratification and bourgeois domesticity to incite change.

Despite the incompatibility of these various viewpoints, their cumulative effect is to make the female subject an aesthetic untouchable. Yet, for female artists and viewers—indeed, for everyone—art cannot go on with this model of alienation and shock and failed communication. The challenge for contemporary culture is to find a way through this bewildering rejection of the female image of beauty, so that Pleasure can be born again.

References

ADAMS, Henry. 1931. *The Education of Henry Adams.* New York: The Modern Library.

GILLIGAN, Carol. 2002. *The Birth of Pleasure*: *A New Map of Love*. New York: Alfred A. Knopf.

STEINER, Wendy. 2001. *Venus in Exile*: *The Rejection of Beauty in 20th Century Art*. New York: Free Press.

The Form of Pleasure

Anthony Amsterdam and Jerome Bruner see narrative as basic to how we humans construct and make sense of our lives. Working from this insight, Amsterdam sees the radical nature of Gilligan's use of ancient and postcolonial stories. By revealing the "storiness" of established narratives and by pointing to alternative stories, Gilligan unsettles received truths and invites the embrace of new ones.

Narrative as Possibility
ANTHONY G. AMSTERDAM

Carol Gilligan's methodology, like her subject matter, is complex. I will talk about only one aspect of it: the use of myths and literary works to explore how people come to terms with themselves and the world. This includes Gilligan's reading of the tale of Psyche and Cupid; of the myths of Oedipus and the patriarchal quartet that Gilligan speaks of as "Odysseus and Aeneas, Abraham, and Agamemnon"; and of five novels: *The Scarlet Letter* (1850), *Annie John* (1985), *The Bluest Eye* (1970), *The God of Small Things* (1997), and *The English Patient* (1992) (Gilligan 2002).

Even this one aspect of Gilligan's methodology resists reduction to a single procedure, for Gilligan is doing several things at once with these narratives. She is invoking or evoking them in the tradition of Freud as evidence of human psychological processes that she finds mirrored in them. Conversely, in the tradition of anthropologist Géza Róheim, she is explicating the stories themselves, interpreting their meaning by reference to basic movements of the human mind or spirit that they encode. The psychological processes that Gilligan sees reflected in the stories are, of course, quite different than those that Sigmund Freud or a Jungian such as Marie-Louise von Franz saw in the same or similar stories, and Gilligan's interpretations of the stories are quite different than those of anthropologist and psychoanalyst Róheim or those of a contemporary Freudian analyst of myths like Richard Caldwell. But the *purposes* for which Gilligan is examining the stories include those that led earlier insightful theorists of human behavior to attempt to understand it better by studying stories, as well as those that led earlier insightful literary critics to attempt to understand stories better through studying psychological theory.

These purposes are ambitious, each in its own right. But I mean to put them aside and to focus on another use that Gilligan makes of stories—a use that is more distinctive and radical. This is Gilligan's use of stories to transform *what is* into *something that could be* in order to enable a counter-transformation of *something else that could be* into *something that is*. Elementally, Gilligan dissolves the incommensurability between two planes of existence: our experience of life as it is, which we ordinarily take to be life as it must be, the inevitable human condition, and our vision of some better world that, lamentably, we were not born to inhabit. By translating both of them into the lingua franca of narrative, making stories out of both of them, she enables us to see that we are free to choose between them.

Gilligan is explicit about the transformation of *what is* into *what could be* when she deals with the myth of Oedipus, the story of tragic love that is the pillar of patriarchy: "To hear tragic love as a story immediately suggests the existence of other stories and also the possibility of new stories" (ibid., 19). Only tell the story with the consciousness that it *is* a story, in such a way that the artifices of its construction are made apparent, and "the tragedy becomes in the end surprising. Why, we ask, does this have to happen? Or, more radically, does this have to happen?" (Ibid., 169–70.)

Gilligan's use of the story of Psyche and Cupid serves the end of countertransformation—of accepting as possible and real a story of what could be, and there is a brief passage in *The Birth of Pleasure: A New Map of Love* (2002) that describes explicitly how this variant of her method operates: in discussing the novel *The English Patient*, Gilligan remarks that "[o]nly when we begin to tell a new story can we see rather than be enveloped in the old" (ibid, 185). So deeply is our experience of life embedded in narrative, and so deeply are the narratives of our culture woven into our conception of reality, that we must have some new stories *to step into* if we want to step outside the stories that we have always accepted as defining the human condition. We need new stories as a place to stand so that we can look at our life stories even momentarily from the outside, see that they *are* stories, and ask what kind of stories they are. Gilligan's reading of Psyche and Cupid as "an encoded map of resistance, showing how to get out of the Oedipus tragedy" does not serve simply to explore the possibilities of resistance (ibid., 22). It takes a first crucial step toward resistance by locating us in an alternative story—a reconnoitering post from which we can start to map the bunkers and blockhouses and barbed-wire fences that we need to find our way around if we want our resistance to have any hope of succeeding.

So Gilligan's technique of reading both patriarchal myths and tales of resistance goes beyond Freud's use of stories as the fossils of unconscious psychological process, and it goes beyond literary exegesis informed by psychological insight. It taps the force of narrative to do work for which narrative is humankind's specialized instrument: to explore possible worlds of *what if* (Amsterdam and Bruner 2000, 120–34, 231–9) and, by doing so, to give us the perspective needed to see that the world we have is not inevitable but contingent, the product of assumptions and choices that we and our culture are making and could make differently, albeit with difficulty.

Perhaps I am led to stress this facet of Gilligan's methodology because of the nature of my own work. As a lawyer, I spend most of my time these days representing death-sentenced men and women in an effort to get their convictions and death sentences set aside, and training other lawyers on the job. Those occupations make me peculiarly likely to appreciate that Gilligan's technique is adaptable to struggles beyond the struggle against patriarchy. To resist patriarchy is vital work—no less vital to men than to women, as *The Birth of Pleasure* makes clear. And it seems very likely, as I have heard Gilligan argue, that patriarchy is the root of other systems of privilege and domination and oppression that have been made second nature to most of humankind by the telling and retelling of old stories that, taken as realities, define how human beings need to treat one another (Lincoln 1999).[1] But however that may be, Gilligan's narrative-based methodology can serve us equally well in finding ways to get outside the many old, oppression-justifying stories which hold us in thrall.

When I teach at training conferences for lawyers who will represent condemned inmates in postconviction proceedings, the very first thing I say goes something like this:

> The key to successful postconviction litigation in death cases is *changing the picture*. By "changing the picture" I mean taking the image of your client's case as it was depicted in the appellate opinion affirming his or her conviction and sentence and turning it around, like turning a kaleidoscope, to break it down into pieces and to recombine those pieces into a new image, a new picture, a new story capable of catching the eye and the imagination and opening the minds of judges and clemency officials and even state attorneys who thought they already knew the whole story. Changing the picture is where every postconviction case inevitably starts: with a story that these people think has already been officially written and officially stamped true and officially stamped closed. Your job is to change that story, to reconstruct the world in which that story happened, to force people who believe they understand the story to *think about it in a new way* and to see enough new facts—facts that weren't exposed before or weren't put into focus before—so that the old facts make a new kind of sense and turn into a different story.
>
> There are two basic things to keep in mind here. *Thing One* is that the world is a mysterious and complex place where strange things happen and we understand very, very little of the why and the how of them. People make sense of the world, mostly, by taking

pieces of it and making a familiar story out them—almost always ignoring other pieces that don't fit the story. Once they have a first approximation sense of the most plausible story to explain any situation, then they dig in and find in the welter of facts and possibilities as much as they can to confirm that story while ignoring anything that disconfirms it. That is the ordinary process of police investigation and prosecutorial reconstruction of a crime. It is the ordinary process of every criminal trial. And the end result of a trial which produces a guilty verdict and a sentence of death is a story about the world that focuses on some things and disregards others, that organizes the facts in a particular scenario and declares that scenario the truth—and the whole truth—because judges and prosecutors and governors want to be comfortable in their own souls that when they put somebody to death they have got the story straight.

It is almost always possible to change that story because, as I've said, the story was constructed out of pieces of the world that were selected by police and prosecutors and courts for the purpose of making the story hang together, and it always omits other pieces of the world that might fit together differently to make a different story. But—and this is *Thing Two*—the story of your client's guilt and death-worthiness that is told in the direct appeal opinion and the trial record will not be easy to change. It will not be easy to change because of various legal doctrines limiting the grounds on which you can relitigate facts in postconviction proceedings. More basically, it will not be easy to change because it has been bought and sold and certified to be genuine—the official version of reality—by a lot of people (including not only the cops and the prosecutors and the courts and jurors but often witnesses and your client's own trial lawyers) who have a lot of ego and a lot of righteousness invested in believing that they got the story straight.

The only way to go about changing the story despite others' concerted belief in it is to develop *an alternative story that has enough initial interest to get people listening and enough ultimate plausibility to displace the official story of your client's guilt and death-worthiness.* This means coming up both with new facts—or at least with a radically new slant on previously known facts—and with a new story line that ends with the sparing of your client's life and makes better narrative sense as a story of wrongs righted and justice done than the story told at trial and on direct appeal that nails your client as the perpetrator of an ugly crime and a slime bag who deserves to die.

Now, this is easy enough to say, but in my experience it is very difficult for even the most creative lawyers to believe and work with *in the abstract*. The only way to get the idea across and get to work using it is to pore over the factual details of individual cases and actually start to develop alternative stories that can give you a perspective grounded *outside* the officially sanctioned story of the defendant's crime and character. Then, from those reconnoitering posts, it becomes possible to see the fault lines in the official story. As our reconnoitering posts, we often use detective stories and other fictional works from high and low culture, much as Gilligan uses myths and literary works.

In *Minding the Law*, a book that Jerome Bruner and I published some years ago, we took a rather similar approach to a number of decisions of the United States Supreme Court by looking for what stories were being told. For example, we examined the opinion in *Freeman v. Pitts*, the principal decision of the Supreme Court terminating the desegregation efforts launched by *Brown v. Board of Education* less than forty years earlier (2000, 143–64). We read the *Pitts* opinion as telling a story commonplace in myth and literature—the story of the Conquering Hero Turned Tyrant—with *Brown v. Board of Education* cast in the tyrant's role. We detailed how the *Pitts* opinion dressed *Brown* in this role by using the storytelling conventions that Aeschylus and Seneca and Alfieri used to portray the demise of Agamemnon, that Sophocles used to portray the demise of Creon of Thebes, that Shakespeare used in *Julius Caesar*, and *Othello* and *Macbeth* and *Coriolanus*, and that Racine used to tell of Nero's downfall in *Brittanicus*. In this stock plot, certain compositional devices lead the audience to perceive that a once-noble hero has finally overreached the powers he deservedly won and has become a dangerous dictator who must be cut down in the name of liberty, which is exactly what the Supreme Court in *Pitts* does to its venerated *Brown v. Board of Education* ruling.

As another example, we examined an opinion of Supreme Court Justice Antonin Scalia in *Michael H. v. Gerald D.*, a family-law case concerning the parental rights of an out-of-wedlock, biological father (ibid., 77–109), and we detailed how it reenacts the traditional patriarchal story of villainous adultery, a story that is a domestic version of the cosmic combat myth (ibid., 83). Unsurprisingly, at the end of Justice Scalia's tale, the adulterer is cut down and cast out, just as Mordred is by King Arthur, as Claudius is by Hamlet, as Huwawa is by Gilgamesh, and, ultimately, as Satan will be by God.

In both of these Supreme Court opinions and in others, it is made to seem that the justices have no real choice but to reach a result dictated by the application of relatively uncontroversial rules of law to the facts of the case before them. But reading the opinions as works of storytelling exposes how and how much the facts of each case were constructed—and the applicable rules were selected—as a function of the stories that their authors chose to tell, instead of telling others that they might have chosen.

The point of parsing judicial opinions in this way is closely akin to Gilligan's point in her use of myths and literary texts. It is to observe that the orderings of our institutions and relationships and lives, which we are accustomed to accept as imposed upon us by the iron rules of law or logic or necessity or scarcity or history or the human condition, are, after all, stories that we tell ourselves about ourselves and could tell differently. It is to awaken our imagination to the possibility of telling other stories. It is to acknowledge the extreme difficulty of departing from the stock plots and scripts through which we largely understand the world. And while we recognize that difficulty, it is nevertheless to insist that we are responsible for making choices whenever we opt unthinkingly to live our lives within the confines of time-worn tales without considering what we might become by taking on the arduous and painful work of recomposing them.

Note

1 On the reification of a culture's stories, see Bruce Lincoln (1999, 149): "The misrepresentation of culture as nature is an ideological move characteristic of myth, as is the projection of the narrator's ideals, desires, and favored ranking of categories, into a fictive prehistory that purportedly establishes how things are and must be."

References

AMSTERDAM, Anthony G., and Jerome Bruner. 2000. *Minding the Law*. Cambridge, MA: Harvard University Press.

GILLIGAN, Carol. 2002. *The Birth of Pleasure: A New Map of Love*. New York: Alfred A. Knopf.

LINCOLN, Bruce. 1999. *Theorizing Myth: Narrative, Ideology, and Scholarship*. Chicago: University of Chicago Press.

Kendall Thomas challenged Carol Gilligan's methods as too particular. The burden of his essay was to open a window on what The Birth of Pleasure (2002) *might have revealed had it looked beyond heterosexual love and utilized the insights of queer theory.*

Kenji Yoshino sees Gilligan's work as universal. The burden of his essay is to demonstrate the power of her methods when applied to the study of homosexual love. He appropriates two of these methods—shifting subject positions and altering cognitive style—to explore the relationship between patriarchy and the queer subject.

Shifting subject position is akin to the "race-switching" strategy that critical race theorists have long used to expose the effects race has on social interactions. A judge in a race discrimination case is asked to recuse herself because she is potentially biased in favor of the plaintiffs. How, we ask, would the request read if we imagined the judge white and therefore potentially biased in favor of the defendants? Yoshino demonstrates the importance of subject position shifts in Gilligan's work. He then shifts the study of patriarchy and the dissociation by which it is sustained to a queer subject position. Adopting a second and equally characteristic Gilligan method, Yoshino works in—and defends—an associative rather than a linear, cognitive style.

The Arguments and Argots of Pleasure
KENJI YOSHINO

Carol Gilligan's *The Birth of Pleasure*: *A New Map of Love* uses the Cupid and Psyche myth as the portal to many places. Cupid falls in love with Psyche but will only make love to her in the dark. Psyche's jealous sisters populate that darkness with horrible imaginings, saying her lover is a monster. Terrified, Psyche violates Cupid's injunction not to look at him and finds he is a beautiful god. Yet the light she casts is itself embodied and drips oil on his skin. The wounded Cupid reproaches her and flees. Psyche sets out to find him. After many travails she finds her way back to him and gives birth to a daughter named Pleasure (Apuleius 1989).

Gilligan reads this myth as one about overcoming dissociation. In each of us, she argues, is a voice that could also be called a knowledge, a self, an instinct that feels natural or authentic. We are prevented from speaking in this voice by a culture that constantly overrides it. Dissociation is the tectonic slide between what we know and what we are told we know. That slippage occurs in the myth when Cupid tells Psyche that love and light cannot coexist. Psyche knows this cannot be the case. In lifting the lamp, she seeks to exit dissociation.

This reading is revisionist. Traditional interpretations cast Psyche's need for ocular proof as a failing, specifically a gendered failing akin to the curiosity displayed by Eve or Pandora (Norris 1999, 112–34). By succumbing to their curiosity, these women destroy an idyllic state. Unlike Eve or Pandora, however, Psyche ultimately forges a finer world than the one she dissolved. This distinctive feature of the Psyche story makes it an apt archetype for Gilligan. Psyche vindicates her violation of the patriarchal law by having that violation lead to the birth of Pleasure.

The Psyche myth frames Gilligan's multiple depictions of the triumph over dissociation. Dissociation is so pervasive that it often appears not to have an outside. To imagine the world beyond it is like imagining the outside of an egg from within. Gilligan employs the Psyche myth as a bird would use a beak, beating and beating at a complete surface. The myth enables two related ways of surmounting dissociation: a shift in subject position and a shift in cognitive style.

The shift in subject position is a familiar one for Gilligan. Having famously reimagined moral development by focusing on the subject position of young girls, she now reimagines love in a similar way. She hears in the voices of adolescent girls an authenticity that disappears as they age, a self-knowledge that sinks into self-estrangement. Her reimagination makes her use of the Psyche myth particularly apposite, as Apuleius portrays Psyche not as a woman but as a girl, a virgin in all senses of that word. When we read the myth, it is easy to dismiss Psyche's voice, which is petulant, querulous, naive. But to do so *tout court* would be a mistake, for her voice has the virtues of its vices, a plain-throated knowledge that stands "before the law," temporally and spatially (Kafka 1948; Butler 1990; Schultz 1992). By taking the subject positions of archetypal and actual girls seriously, Gilligan pinpoints the moment before dissociation.

A shift in style attends this shift in subject position. *The Birth of Pleasure* does not pursue the traditional paths of scholarly exposition. It moves metonymically across psychological case studies, memoirs (Proust's *Remembrance of Things Past*, Anne Frank's *Diaries*), fiction (Michael Ondaatje's *The English Patient*, Arundhati Roy's *The God of Small Things*), and autobiographical material about the author's own childhood. The book's nonlinear style prosecutes its substantive claim that we cannot reason our way out of dissociation.

While seemingly particular, both the subject position and style of this book gesture toward the universal. Like Psyche's story, Gilligan's is gendered. Yet, while Gilligan aligns dissociation with patriarchy, she underscores that men as well as women are trapped therein. Similarly, we can see in the idiosyncrasy of Gilligan's texts a universal plea to reflect on our own beloved and peculiar texts. The book is Romantic in its belief that an individual, sedulously described, is the best and perhaps the only path to apprehending our common humanity (Izenberg 1992, 15).

We can see the breadth of this Romantic ambition by taking Gilligan's paradigm beyond its explicit subjects. In the balance of this essay, I show that Gilligan's antipatriarchal subject could just as easily be a sexual minority living under the strictures of "don't ask, don't tell." I also show that her antipatriarchal language could just as easily be a literary language asserted against the language of law.

1

One need not look far for gay dissociation. To hold same-sex desire in this culture is almost by definition to "hear with particular clarity the tension between a first-person voice, an 'I' who speaks from human emotional experience, and a voice that overrides what we know and feel and experience, that tells us what we should see and feel and know" (Gilligan 2002, 9). The inaugural voice is again the child's voice, speaking most literally about pleasure, about desire. The overriding voice is the voice of the culture that refuses to acknowledge childhood sexuality, particularly same-sex sexuality (Ruskola 1996, 269–329). To take but one covey of examples, Shakespeare's plays are full of adolescent relationships of passionate   erotic intensity, out of which one or both parties must be carefully schooled: Helena and Hermia in *A Midsummer Night's Dream*, Polixenes and Leontes in *A Winter's Tale*, Antonio and Sebastian in *Twelfth Night*, Celia and Rosalind in *As You Like It*, Antonio and Bassanio in *The Merchant of Venice*.[1] These plays could be read as ur-texts of Lacanian theory, in which absorption in similitude is cast as a form of infantile narcissism that must be overcome (Lacan 1977).

Dissociation pursues gay individuals into adulthood. As Eve Kosofsky Sedgwick puts it, the closet has an attendant epistemology:

> *Don't ask*; *You shouldn't know*. It didn't happen; it doesn't make any difference; it didn't mean anything; it doesn't have interpretive consequences. Stop asking just here; stop asking just now; we know in advance the kind of difference that could be made by the invocation of *this* difference; it makes no difference; it doesn't mean (1990, 53).

Incanting the cant of dissociation, this passage describes the suppression of erotic knowledge, which often stands as a synecdoche for all knowledge. Like Psyche, the homosexual subject is told to make love in the dark.

Published in 1990, Sedgwick's fugue on dissociation anticipates the military's 1993 "don't ask, don't tell" policy. Prior to the enactment of "don't ask, don't tell," the military was governed by a 1981 executive order stating that homosexuality was "incompatible with military service" (U.S. Department of Defense 1993). When elected, President Clinton vowed to lift this ban. The ensuing backlash resulted in a compromise, known in popular parlance as "don't ask, don't tell" (Gordon 1993; Shenon 1997). The conventional understanding of the policy is that gays can serve in the military so long as they remain in the closet.

"Don't ask, don't tell" is a codification of dissociation in both an overt and a covert sense. The codification of overt dissociation is inherent in the policy's requirement that gays (and straights) in the military disown their knowledge. Everyone knows there are, and have always been, gays in the military. Yet no one can say so. The visual register of the Psyche myth shifts into an aural one: the darkness of "don't see, don't be seen," transmutes into the silence of "don't ask, don't tell."

Like Psyche, we are encouraged to populate that imposed ignorance with monsters. In 1993 congressional hearings about the policy, military experts testified that the presence of even one open homosexual would destroy the cohesion of an entire unit, with dire consequences for national security (*Boston Globe* 1993; Taylor 1993; *Seattle Times* 1993). The evidence we have flatly belies this claim—open homosexuals have served without incident in the militaries of other countries and quasi-military organizations in our own (Larrabee 1993; Perkins 2004; Files 2005; Lyall 2005). When we lift the lamp on the homosexual service-member, he looks less like a monster than a sleeping lover. What is most intellectually (as opposed to morally) offensive about the military policy is that the scheme itself, by summarily excluding openly gay service members, prevents anyone from testing the predicates of its apocalyptic vision.

The statute also requires a covert form of dissociation. In its treatment of the three moving parts of gay identity—status, speech, and conduct—the policy is more complicated than its popular uptake suggests. Unlike the 1981 executive order, the statute does not penalize homosexual status per se; the old language deeming homosexuality to be "incompatible" with military service is absent from the statute's operative language. The policy also does not make self-identifying speech, standing alone, a ground for separation. Such speech only raises a presumption that the individual has engaged in homosexual conduct. If that presumption remains unrebutted, the service-member will be discharged but for the conduct and not the speech. Self-identifying speech here is taken up for its confessional value, as if I said, "I am a bank robber," and then left unrebutted the presumption I had robbed a bank. In these ways, the policy is at pains to tie its sanctions to overt homosexual conduct.[2]

This division of gay personhood into status, speech, and conduct has been touted as progress for gays because it means at least some aspects of gay identity (status and speech) are protected. Yet that division should also be viewed as a covert form of dissociation with which many gays are all too familiar. Gay life is full of such self-estrangement: the eye does not see what the hand does; the mouth does not speak what the soul is. In this sense as well, the policy did not spring from the head of Congress but grew organically out of an underlying culture.

The overt and covert forms of dissociation are usefully distinguished because conventional gay rights litigation resists the former but not the latter. Just as Gilligan takes up the antipatriarchal subject position of girls, lawsuits challenging the military policy have adopted the perspective of gays. By arguing that gays have equal protection, speech, and due process rights to serve openly in the military, these suits frontally attack the social contract of "don't ask, don't tell."[3]

Yet even as it challenges the overt form of dissociation, such litigation often colludes in the covert form. By taking up status claims under the equal protection guarantee, speech claims under the First Amendment, and conduct claims under the substantive due process guarantee, such litigation reenacts the dismemberment of the gay body. In the *Steffan* case, which preceded "don't ask, don't tell" but anticipated its logic, pro-gay litigators argued that Joseph Steffan could not be separated from the Naval Academy because the Academy had no proof he had engaged in homosexual conduct. Steffan's victory in appellate court (which was later reversed) bought Steffan the right to be gay but not the right to engage in same-sex sexual conduct.[4] That victory had all the opulent self-estrangement of a cubist painting.

Conversely, those who challenge covert dissociation find themselves forced to assent to its overt forms. Liberal judge Stephen Reinhardt has rejected the status–conduct distinction: "To pretend that homosexuality or heterosexuality is unrelated to sexual conduct borders on the absurd."[5] In his view, however, this rejection of covert dissociation required him to sustain the military policy. Under this view, we must choose to perfect the suit or the self.

We should not discontinue such litigation. On September 9, 2010, a district court struck down the "don't ask, don't tell" policy.[6] (The case is now pending appeal.) If gay rights advocates can win on every claim, we can reconstitute the gay self much as Isis reconstructed Osiris after fishing his body parts out of the Nile. We should also hold open the possibility that litigation might not need to dismember the gay self in this way. Yet the pervasiveness of this form of dissociation in law stands as a caution that conventional solutions often accede to the troublesome predicates of the problems they seek to solve. Sometimes resistance offered in a dissociative language only announces our capture by that language.

2

We begin to see why Gilligan makes her case against patriarchy in unconventional terms. Law is perhaps the quintessential patriarchal language, often favoring (*pace* Holmes) logic over experience. As captured in Charles Lamb's famous musing, "Lawyers, I suppose, were children once" (2003, 7). Lawyers are a paradigmatic case of the dissociated adult. Yet, law here stands in for a much broader discourse of rational argumentation, a discourse that may be so allied with dissociation it cannot be deployed against it. The virtue of more metonymic enterprises such as literature or psychology is that they provide a way of overcoming covert dissociation.

Such metonymy has a peculiar power to offend. Reviewing *The Birth of Pleasure* in the *New York Times*, Emily Nussbaum writes,

> Gilligan makes little distinction between actual individuals, fictional characters, and mythical metaphors, or for that matter, between one culture or time period and another . . . Her elaborate reading of the Cupid and Psyche myth lacks critical context: when Psyche receives advice from a water reed, Gilligan argues, this is the feminine principle teaching her to gain patriarchal power (golden fleece) by using a roundabout method (pluck wool from the brambles once the sun goes down). But just such inverted riddle-solving is a classic mythological trope for men as well: Jason, for one, fights Medusa by using his shield as a mirror (2002, 14).

What makes these scabrous sentences so striking is that they are preceded by Nussbaum's pledge of support for at least some of Gilligan's feminist projects. The sympathy Nussbaum expresses for Gilligan's substantive positions sets into relief her antipathy to Gilligan's style.

Nussbaum's paragraph is an odd vehicle for a charge about a lack of rigor. First, Nussbaum errs when she states that Jason kills Medusa. It is of course Perseus who does so. Second, Nussbaum's position that the Medusa story is *not* about the "feminine principle teaching [a protagonist] to gain patriarchal power" is hard to defend. It is Athena (or in Roman mythology Minerva) who gives her shield to Perseus (Apollodorus 1921). One could make the argument that Athena, the virgin goddess of war and wisdom, often embodies patriarchal principles in Greco–Roman mythology. But if Nussbaum wishes to cast Athena as a patriarchal figure, she would have to show an awareness that Athena plays a role in this myth. In the end, the only plausible way Nussbaum can distinguish the Medusa myth is by pointing out that it is a male rather than a female protagonist who follows the feminine principle. While true, this no criticism of Gilligan. As Nussbaum acknowledges earlier in the review, one of Gilligan's core theses is that men as well as women can learn by leaving patriarchy.

On a single page, Nussbuam makes the kinds of mistakes I have not been able to find in multiple readings of Gilligan's book. This suggests that a lack of rigor may not be the primary source of Nussbaum's disquiet. While I can do no more than speculate here, it strikes me that the discomfort may arise from Gilligan's decision to give her argument its full extension, resisting dissociation not just in substance but in form. Nussbaum is like the lawyer who is entirely pro-gay but who never wants to argue outside the law most conventionally construed. There are merits to this position; to have scholars arguing against patriarchy in traditional terms stops the mouths of those who would say feminists can only win the game by changing the rules.

Yet something is also lost: the language in which a position can be most ambitiously taken. There is no reason to think powerful social forces like patriarchy or homophobia affect only the arguments we make, leaving the argots in which we make them unaffected. To the contrary, I suspect we can only separate "argument" and "argot" here for heuristic purposes. For this reason, if Gilligan had argued in conventional terms, she would have risked undercutting her thesis in its elaboration.

Moreover, once Gilligan has done her work, it becomes easier to see that the "law," literally or figuratively construed, could accommodate her insights. Law seems to refuse metonymic language because of its violence (Cover 1986, 1601–29). It would be hard for us to contest this inverse relationship between force and fancy, for when we exert coercion on human beings around us, we have an ethical obligation to place certain strictures on our imaginations. But the law, in fact, sometimes self-consciously deprives itself of violence to permit more aggressive acts of imagination. Dissents, dicta, hortatory laws, legislative resolutions, international law, and legal scholarship are but a few of the locations where legal actors relinquish force to permit the play of fancy. Law, then, is not monolithic but self-consciously contains spaces in which it can depart from its most conventional registers. So it is that many of the most imaginative or literary opinions in *U.S. Reports* are dissents. And so it is that Gilligan's book can be read as a dissent against patriarchy, in its argot as well as in its arguments.

This insight does not preclude us from criticizing Gilligan. But it does encourage us to remain open to the possibility that some arguments can be made only in languages different from the ones we are used to speaking and hearing. One reason it is hard to write a book like Gilligan's is that it is so easy to ridicule from the complacent vantage secured by guild norms. But in struggling against that difficulty, Gilligan's project is no different from the project of authenticity itself.

Notes

1 For criticism on William Shakespeare's same-sex erotic relationships, see W. Thomas MacCary (1985), Joseph Pequigney (1992), Lawrence Danson (1994), and Steve Patterson (1999).

2 National Defense Authorization Act for Fiscal Year 1994, U.S. Code, VOL. 10, SECTION 654 (1994).

3 *Able v. United States*, 155 F.3d 628 (2nd Cir. 1998); *Philips v. Perry*, 106 F.3d 1420 (9th Cir. 1997); *Richenberg v. Perry*, 97 F.3d 256 (8th Cir. 1996); *Thomasson v. Perry*, 80 F.3d 915 (4th Cir. 1996).

4 *Steffan v. Aspin*, 8 F.3d 57, 63, 70 (D.C. Cir. 1994), reversed by *Steffan v. Perry*, 41 F.3d 677 (D.C. Cir. 1994).

5 *Watkins v. United States Army*, 847 F.2d 1329, 1361 n.19 (9th Cir. 1988) (Reinhardt, J., dissenting).

6 *Log Cabin Republicans v. United States*, Case No. CV 04-08425 (C.D. Cal. Sept. 9, 2010). Available at: http://online.logcabin.org/dadt-9-9-2010-decision.pdf

References

APOLLODORUS. 1921. *The Library*, VOL. 2, BOOK 4, CHAPTER 2. Translated by Sir James George Frazer. Cambridge, MA: Harvard University Press.

APULEIUS. 1989. *Metamorphoses (The Golden Ass)*, VOL. 1, BOOK 5. Edited and translated by J. Arthur Hanson. Cambridge, MA: Harvard University Press.

BOSTON GLOBE. 1993. "Stormin' Norman Takes his Stand; Presence of Gays Destroys Unit Cohesion, Schwarzkopf Tells Senate." 16 May, p. 67.

BUTLER, Judith. 1990. *Gender Trouble: Feminism and the Subversion of Identity*. New York: Routledge.

COVER, Robert. 1986. "Violence and the Word." *Yale Law Journal* 95(8): 1601–29.

DANSON, Lawrence. 1994. " 'The Catastrophe is a Nuptial:' The Space of Masculine Desire in *Othello, Cymbeline*, and *The Winter's Tale*." *Shakespeare Survey* 46: 69–79.

FILES, John. 2005. "Rules on Gays Exact a Cost in Recruiting, a Study Finds." *New York Times*. 24 February, p. A21.

GILLIGAN, Carol. 2002. *The Birth of Pleasure: A New Map of Love*. New York: Alfred A. Knopf.

GORDON, Michael R. 1993. "Pentagon Spells Out Rules for Ousting Homosexuals; Rights Groups Vow a Fight." *New York Times*. 23 December, p. A1.

IZENBERG, Gerald. 1992. *Impossible Individuality: Romanticism, Revolution and the Origins of Modern Selfhood*. Princeton, NJ: Princeton University Press.

KAFKA, Franz. 1948. "Before the Law." In *The Metamorphosis, In the Penal Colony, and Other Stories*. New York: Schocken, pp. 148–50.

LAMB, Charles. 2003. "The Old Benchers of the Inner Temple." In *Selected Writings*. Edited by J. E. Morpurgo. New York: Routledge, pp. 4–14.

LACAN, Jacques. 1977. "The Mirror Stage as Formative of the Function of the I as Revealed in Psychoanalytic Experience." In *Écrits: A Selection*. Translated by Alan Sheridan. New York: Routledge, pp. 1–7.

LARRABEE, John. 1993. "Wanted by Boston Police: Gay, Lesbian Recruits." *USA Today*. 30 August, p. A3.

LYALL, Sarah. 2005. "British Navy Seeks More Gays and Lesbians." *International Herald Tribune*. 23 February, p. 2.

MACCARY, W. Thomas. 1985. *Friends and Lovers: The Phenomenology of Desire in Shakespearean Comedy*. New York: Columbia University Press.

NORRIS, Pamela. 1999. "Curious Women: Eve, Pandora, and Psyche." In *Eve: A Biography*. New York: New York University Press, pp. 112–34.

NUSSBAUM, Emily. 2002. "Ms. Lonelyhearts: Carol Gilligan Offers a Unified Feminist Theory of Why Love Falls Apart." *New York Times*. 30 June, p. 14.

PATTERSON, Steve. 1999. "The Bankruptcy of Homoerotic Amity in Shakespeare's Merchant of Venice." *Shakespeare Quarterly* 50(1): 9–32.

PEQUIGNEY, Joseph. 1992. "The Two Antonios and Same-Sex Love in *Twelfth Night* and *The Merchant of Venice*." *English Literary Renaissance* 22(2): 201–21.

PERKINS, Laura. 2004. "Gay and Lesbian Police Recruitment Yields 300 Candidates." *San Francisco Chronicle*. 9 April, p. F10.

RUSKOLA, Teemu. 1996. "Minor Disregard: The Legal Construction of the Fantasy That Gay and Lesbian Youth Do Not Exist." *Yale Journal of Law and Feminism* 8: 269–329.

SCHULTZ, Vicki. 1992. "Women 'Before' the Law: Judicial Stories About Women, Work, and Sex Segregation on the Job." In Judith Butler and Joan W. Scott (eds), *Feminists Theorize the Political*. New York: Routledge, pp. 297–338.

SEATTLE TIMES. 1993. "Army Officer Says Spirits Rise When Gay Soldiers Ousted—Experts Say Permissive Allies Still Discriminate in Practice." 30 April, p. A5.

SEDGWICK, Eve Kosofsky. 1990. *Epistemology of the Closet*. Berkeley: University of California Press.

SHENON, Philip. 1997. "New Study Faults Pentagon's Gay Policy." *New York Times*. 26 February, p. A10.

TAYLOR, Joe. 1993. "Senators Get Sailors' View of Navy Gays." *Boston Globe*. 11 May, p. 3.

U.S. DEPARTMENT OF DEFENSE. 1993. Enlisted Administrative Separations: Standards and Procedures. Code of Federal Regulations, VOL. 41, PART 41 Appendix A.

Since Sigmund Freud, association has been a tool for self-knowledge. "Free" associations surprise us when, on analysis, they turn out to follow the logic of our psyches.

The Birth of Pleasure (2002) *proceeds by association as Carol Gilligan identifies themes that resonate across science, literature, clinical practice, and a scholar's field observations. Patricia Foster highlights the moments when Gilligan grounds her themes—when they flow like loose currents into Gilligan's body and biography. Foster calls these autobiographical moments "vertical drops." Stitching together the vertical drops that are scattered through* The Birth of Pleasure *and framing them with drops into her own biography, Foster replays in (at least) two intimate voices Gilligan's themes of open-hearted desire: desire blurred by dissociation and desire struggling against dissociation.*

Many years ago when I was twenty-four, I worked for three months at Neiman Marcus selling purses. Most of my hair had fallen out, and I wore a wig. To deflect from this reality, I dressed lavishly: layered outfits that required pantyhose and dangling earrings, square-toed shoes, and tiny silver bracelets. I thought of the "real me" as absent, departed, and thus the mask of clothes and wig was merely a mask over a mask: contrived beauty covering reckless emptiness. "Me" waited somewhere anxiously in the wings, hoping to be summoned, needed.

All day I did my gig: selling smart leather bags with straps that could be detached and folded neatly inside, tiny beaded evening bags with jeweled clasps the size of fifty-cent pieces, sleek calfskin envelopes a woman could slide like a letter under her arm. All around me women buzzed like honeybees, buying and selling, looking and touching. Ironically, I imagined myself the only loose wire, the only counterfeit persona in this fashion exchange.

And yet what I dreaded were the nights I left early, the nights I did not work until 9:00 p.m. Because I was new and had no friends in Atlanta and was terrified of meeting anyone outside of the terms of buying and selling, I went back to the room I rented, replaced the wig with a cloth bandanna, changed into jeans, heated up a chicken pot pie, and rushed to the movies. At the movies I sneaked in my pie and ate it quietly while the silver screen played out its pivotal plot. It was only here that I felt ashamed, only here, alone, wary, unobserved, that I knew I was lost. Only here, with popcorn splashed across the floor and the sticky sap of spilled coke beneath my feet, did I feel safe enough to recognize that I'd split apart. Darkness protected me. My warm chicken pot pie filled me. The movie distracted and sometimes captured my attention. A great sense of relief flowed through me, and behind it came the whammy of despair.

If I were writing that story, it would be those moments in the theater that would give me pause, those moments in the flickering darkness that would rise up to reveal how *not knowing* moves slowly toward *knowing*. It's here that I would try to discover what had been covered up, tamped down, inverted, because it was here that the first inklings of awareness arrived.

In nonfiction, there's sometimes a place called "vertical drop," where the narrator deepens the sense of intimacy in an essay or book. This is different from an epiphany in fiction, where there's often a moment of reversal, a sense of everything seen in a new light. In nonfiction, the drop is not necessarily a moment of resolution or recognition—the *a-ha!* moment of a short story—but rather a release to vulnerability, knowledge. A place where the narrator pushes away her own constraints and lets the reader in. A kind of clearing. It is here that the narrator often discovers on the page the story beneath the story: the story of what lies in the way, the story of gaps and repetitions, the story of loss and betrayal.

While reading *The Birth of Pleasure: A New Map of Love*, I found myself tendered toward these moments, moments where the writer drops beneath criticism and commentary, beneath analysis and observation, to the confessional heart of her own story. Perhaps this seems odd. After all, this is not an autobiography or memoir. This is a book that the writer herself calls "orchestral," a book of multiple melodies and many themes. In this book the formal structure repeats and deepens the story of Psyche and Cupid and the birth of Pleasure. And yet confession is part of its scope. Confession pulls me in. The "I" warms the page, sets the terms.

Carol Gilligan begins *The Birth of Pleasure* with both a tale and an *I*— an *I* who doesn't know why she's been drawn to maps of the desert with their hot dry winds and their unnatural stillness; an *I* who (still not knowing) decides to follow her curiosity to trace an ancient story about love told in North Africa in the second century through its pilgrimage to Europe, its impact "falling like rain into a tradition whose origins lie in the birth of tragedy" (ibid., 3). This story sweeps through the centuries, slow-moving, undulating, winding its way beneath the rich, dark earth, beneath insularity and predictability, beneath anxious grandmothers and opportunistic fathers, beneath tenacious bridegrooms and future brides, beneath the many idealized versions of what love must surely be. The story, the narrator tells us, leads to the birth of Pleasure.

What is the story? Who is this *I*?

The plot, the formal structure of the book, is the answer to the first question, a multilayered response to the articulation of this new map of love, a way of breaking the taboos on seeing and speaking that begins with the ancient myth of Psyche and Cupid, traverses epic poetry, Greek drama, sneaks into the underworld of Freudian psychology, unwraps the larger story of Anne Frank's *Diary* (1947), rereads novels and plays, and sets up shop with young boys at age five, young girls on the cusp of adolescence, and couples caught in the crisis of love.

But who is the *I*, and what are we to make of the confessional story Gilligan tells—the story not about myth, legend, case study, or literary criticism, but the story of a girl growing up in a thoughtful, prosperous family caught in something blurry, distorting—something that needs to be scratched at, something that's not above the surface, but hidden, secretive, trapped in the cracks like little pieces of salt mixed in with the dirt? Confession takes us not just into the narrator's mental landscape but also into the urgency of the book, the writer's own story of dissociation and return, of love, tragedy and its antidote: voice.

In confession, it's always the story beneath the story, the hidden text, that matters, the bruise beneath the wound. The reader waits breathlessly for the narrator to walk out of the expected plot, to turn the corner into the undisclosed. Without this progression—a shift from the articulated trauma to the thing with invisible trip wires—confession is a sham. As readers we want not just discovery; we want the mysterious and the incomprehensible to become more knowable. In *The Birth of Pleasure*, the narrative deepens when the author drops the role of critic and therapist and opens herself to her own autobiography. Who is this *I*? It's as if she's tearing away a scrim, saying, "me too! me too!" to the reader as she tells us her story of a break in relationship, a story when she too had the myth of safety ripped away, when she too felt scrambled, dislocated, surprised. She tells this not in one big gulp but in embedded moments planted throughout the text, moments that come not as a surprise but as a natural movement to intimacy.

The first instance comes after the narrator has discussed the startling (and oddly familiar) knowledge that teenage girls often give up on relationship in order to have relationships, then begin the dangerous slide into dissociation—*not knowing what you know.* " 'If I were to say what I was feeling and thinking, no one would want to be with me,' seventeen-year-old Iris says" (ibid., 10). Gilligan acknowledges how Iris's "pleasure in such relationships becomes compromised by her awareness of having silenced herself " (ibid., 10).

Here the narrator remembers her own silencing on the cusp of adolescence by her mother and her teachers; she remembers, as well, her own resistance to the "correction" of her high-spirited nature. Thinking about that time in her life, she's surprised by a dream in which she's wearing glasses over her contacts and "seeing double." In the dream, she's with a therapist who says to her, "I cannot offer you myself " (ibid., 11). This comment evokes shame for wanting so much, for exhibiting such hunger. But it's only when the narrator takes off her glasses that she is released from shame and the "endless wanting of what was being withheld." She recognizes that she doesn't want enmeshment or the therapist's capitulation: "I wanted what I had wanted with my mother and my women teachers, I wanted the woman in the dream to be herself" (ibid., 11–12). And being herself means being direct and open in relationship rather than being surreptitiously competitive. It is here that the narrator takes us to a symbolic place in her life where the terms are revealed: as a woman she's been asked to see double, to distort her own vision. She's been asked to do this by the women closest to her, the women who are her guides, her mentors to adulthood. To wear contact lenses is to correct vision for clarity. To "correct" clarity is to restrict and distort. But why the mother? I can't help but ask. Who is the mother competitive with? What does this mother want her to be?

The second time the narrator drops into the vulnerable place of her own life, she's been engaged in an intense discussion of the different editions of *The Diary of Anne Frank*. Gilligan focuses on the self-editing and the professional editing of the *Diary* and on the five newly discovered pages that reveal Anne's perceptions about her mother's sacrifice for love and the reasons for her coldness. Anne says she knows "a thing or two," knows that her father was deeply in love with another woman whose family rejected him, knows that her mother has never had first place in his heart. Anne abhors the idea of such a sacrifice and rejects it for herself. But it is her awareness of how the mother's back story impinges on the front story of *their* relationship that matters.

It is here that Gilligan reveals her own mother–daughter story and enters the landscape of her twelve-year-old self. This story begins with an unconditional love being swept away and new boundaries and artificial conditions being placed on relationship. The twelve-year-old narrator has just come back from camp to find that her beloved Popsy (her father's father) has been sent away from his room next to hers in their New York apartment; he is the one person who has loved her unconditionally and who has been the joy of her childhood. It's her mother who has done the sending, finding Popsy an apartment nearby because she thinks her daughter has reached the age where it's not wise for a young girl and an old man to share a bathroom. This is not the act of a wicked stepmother in fairy tales. It is merely the overly conscious mother of patriarchy who articulates the necessity of gender boundaries, who sees propriety in privacy. Adolescence is initiation into sexuality, and with it come restraints. And yet the narrator feels betrayed. Betrayed because such boundaries are being drawn without her consideration; betrayed because such boundaries make the narrator self-conscious about her actions and behaviors "where before they had been innocent"; betrayed because she's expected to concede (ibid., 111).

The narrator looks beneath this "wound" to reveal the story beneath the story: the mother–daughter plot, the power plot of authority versus desire, the bruise of broken relationship. The more vulnerable story of the mother's life, her back story, lies behind these actions. We are told that the mother had a twin who died at thirteen—near the age at which the narrator returns from camp. Such a loss would certainly ratchet up the anxiety about young womanhood, about protection and safety and the anxiety of separation. Such a loss might shadow judgment, nudge appropriation. We are also told that the mother lived, as an adult, two distinct personas. In one persona, she was Mabel Friedman, a beloved wife in an idealized marriage, a mother and career woman who became a "therapist helping emotionally disturbed children" (ibid., 117). In this role, she's the enforcer of patriarchal rules, subordinated to traditional cultural rites of courtship and marriage. In this role, she gives the narrator her lines ("[T]ell Aunt Bess that you loved her present"; "Say, 'My mother says I have to be home by midnight'" [ibid., 119]), nags her about food, sets a beautiful table for parties and dinners, sings around the piano, and is in love with her husband. Mabel Friedman is a wife and mother.

In the second persona, she is Mabel Caminez, the maiden name she used on her accounts when she worked as a decorator. In this role, the narrator remembers her mother as fun, spirited, magical; a woman whose intuitive sense of color and style flowed into her intuitive sense of play. In this role, she bicycles with her daughter, has eccentric painter friends, and is adored by her daughter.

This doubleness "riddled our relationship," the narrator says as she grapples with the eclipse of one woman by another, knowing that both set up templates for womanhood, templates for trust (ibid., 123). The narrator trusts Mabel Caminez; she doesn't trust Mabel Friedman. The narrator trusts play and intuition, pleasure and nonconformity and straightforward desire. She doesn't trust the patina of perfection or the hierarchy of form. More than that, doubleness is confusing. It's like wearing a pair of glasses over your contacts, a blurry distortion, a trope of confusion. Which mother will she wake up to? Which mother holds her hand? Which mother might sideswipe her with new decisions, new demands? How can she know her mother if her mother is, in effect, two personas tucked inside each other?

In a revelatory dream many years later, the narrator leaves the patriarchal matron behind, leaves Mabel Friedman in a birdcage, covered up, stiffened, trapped in fabrication, in doubleness. "*She* will go mad," the narrator says in the dream, but she can't find the connection to her mother's life until she remembers the father's injunction after a mother–daughter fight: "Don't ever speak about your mother that way. Don't ever call her 'she'" (ibid., 125). Only then does the narrator know she's undoing "the prohibition" not to see and speak. The narrator in the dream is waking up, separating the two mothers. She's seeing, as Anne Frank had seen, why she distrusted Mabel Friedman and why the distrust was difficult to voice. She's seeing that something of her mother was being sacrificed, something of the spirit, something that could make a woman go mad, something that could be passed down, a kind of cultural legacy, from mother to daughter. And she understands how the doubling blurred the seeing, because right inside Mabel Friedman, the difficult and appropriating mother, was Mabel Caminez, the loving woman who was bright and intuitive, the woman who said to her daughter, "Darling, you know" (ibid., 110).

In the final section of the book, the narrator confesses she's felt as if she's lived most of her life underwater because of losses that were so shocking that she could not speak of them at the time. And the loss, the reader understands, is the intimacy of relationship with the mother. "Later in the 'In Our Own Voices' workshops," the narrator tells us, "when I drew the river of my life and placed stepping stones in it, I saw that the stepping stones in my life were places where I had surfaced" (ibid., 163–64), including when she fell in love, when she fell into work that was all-encompassing, when she experienced nature and bodily pleasure. When she stayed in relationship with her sense of pleasure and knowledge, she had both powerful connections and powerful conflicts. And what the narrator comes back to is the ecstasy of pleasure she felt with Popsy, a man of relationship.

To end the sequence, the narrator brings her parents back to her in another dream, one in which they enter *her* world, become part of her sense of pleasure and work. In this dream, they come willingly and sit with her while she works because "[t]here is room. . . . Plenty of room for you to stay" (ibid., 234). Plenty of room because this is the narrator's territory, the narrator's comfort zone, the narrator's place of creation and intent. Her intent now is to share the world she's made, to build a bridge between two different paths, two generations, to repair what was broken by inviting them to see who, what she has become.

What the narrator has given us in these autobiographical fragments is a personal stake, a rite of passage in her development, that parallels the stories of characters in novels, diaries, and plays, clients in psychotherapy, and girls and boys going through crisis. The crisis of relationship, we understand, is always an autobiographical crisis refracted through a cultural lens, a buried knowing struggling for breath.

After reading *The Birth of Pleasure*, I see now that those nights I sat in the movies alone were a central part of the drama I was living. I managed a doubleness: in one mode I was a public female wearing a disguise of femininity in the mecca of commerce. The role required that I be social, subordinate, useful, and engaging. At night, I took off the disguise and became a private female: alone, lonely, autonomous, and curious. This self was shattered but real, a woman at the movies feeding herself and keeping her eyes open.

Yet there was little pleasure in either mode. Pleasure, I slowly began to see, required an open-eyed casting off of roles. Pleasure came from immersion in the moment, a dropping into immediacy and intimacy—a kind of vertical drop, a lifting of restraint. I wish I could go back to my former self and blow a sweet breath of advice: "Go there," I would say. "Follow curiosity." I wish the actual progression toward pleasure did not require such a difficult unraveling. But it does. For most of us, it does.

Reference

GILLIGAN, Carol. 2002. *The Birth of Pleasure: A New Map of Love*. New York: Alfred A. Knopf.

The Politics of Pleasure

Carol Gilligan looks to postcolonial and African–American literature for evidence that people naturally resist a social order marked by hierarchy and the suppression of love.

It is not surprising that this resistance is found in the work of subordinated people. As Gilligan shows in the novels of Arundhati Roy and Michael Ondaatje, straddling and blending the culture of the colonizer and the culture of the colonized produces a double consciousness that enables critical thought. So does straddling and blending the culture of a dominant majority and the culture of a minority. In a state of double consciousness, the bonds of cultural scripts and naturalized social orders are loosened. Double consciousness allows us to imagine that things might be other than they overwhelmingly are.

When a group of artists and scholars—many of whom are contributors to this volume—gathered to study and respond to Gilligan's The Birth of Pleasure *(2002),* Toni Morrison *talked about postcolonial and African–American fiction and the themes of love and liberation in her own work. This is what she said.*

Love and Pleasure as Political Liberation
TONI MORRISON

I want to add something to the conversation.

African–Americans are not understood to be postcolonial in the classic sense. However, there was a long history of sharing some of the characteristics of other colonial cultures and societies. And it is because of that that I want to make a brief for the exceptionalism, perhaps, of African–American literature vis-à-vis this love and liberation discussion you are having. At least my share in it. For I have been very careful and very deliberate to reflect what had always seemed to me to be the case: that in love and pleasure there is liberation—political liberation.

When people migrate from Virginia north in *Jazz* [1992], what they hear in the music is this incredible idea of personal choice. The lyrics of jazz and blues are exuberant, because for the first time you get to choose whom to love. And that releases all sorts of passion, some of which is fruitful, some of which is not. But it is intense, and it is personal freedom. And it also can activate political freedom.

Early in *Beloved*, you have a woman standing in the middle of the forest preaching resistance to slavery:

Here . . . in this here place, we flesh; flesh that weeps, laughs; flesh that dances on bare feet in grass. Love it. Love it hard. Yonder they do not love your flesh. They despise it. They don't love your eyes; they's just as soon pick 'em out. No more do they love the skin on your back. Yonder they flay it. And O my people they do not love your hands. Those they only use, tie, bind, chop off and leave empty. Love your hands! Love them. Raise them up and kiss them. Touch others with them, pat them together, stroke them on your face 'cause they don't love that either. *You* got to love it, *you*! And no, they ain't in love with your mouth. Yonder, out there, they will see it broken and break it again. What you say out of it they will not heed. What you scream from it they do not hear. What you put into it to nourish your body they will snatch away and give you leavins instead. No, they don't love your mouth. *You* got to love it. This is flesh I'm talking about here. Flesh that needs to be loved. Feet that need to rest and to dance; backs that need support; shoulders that need arms, strong arms I'm telling you. And O my people, out yonder, hear me, they do not love your neck unnoosed and straight. So love your neck; put a hand on it, grace it, stroke it and hold it up. And all your inside parts that they just as soon slop for hogs, you got to love them. The dark, dark liver,—love it, love it, and the beat and beating heart, love that too. More than eyes or feet. More than lungs that have yet to draw free air. More than your life-holding womb and your life-giving private parts, hear me now, love your heart. For this is the prize (1987, 88–9).

That is the first political act—enshrining and developing love for one's self. The characters lived in the most classic patriarchal system. And they replicated it a bit within their own families. But the conclusion of that book, and of *Paradise* (1997) as well, is how people are politically enabled by passion, pleasure, and love. So that when Paul D says, "You are your best thing," Sethe can move, if she chooses, from being the mother who sacrifices everything and who murders the children, because she has the best political solution to slavery that ever came, which is that we can't—no one can—put up with it. He says, you know, "You—you are—you are you. And you are your best thing. Don't mourn. Organize" (1987, 335). That kind of thing.

There is the same implication of a resurrection that is beyond death in *Paradise*, in which self-love—as well as community love and the recollection of deep sexual pleasure—is part of the enabling process as opposed to the tragedy.

References

MORRISON, Toni. 1987. *Beloved*. New York: Alfred A. Knopf.

———. 1992. *Jazz*. New York: Alfred A. Knopf.

———. 1997. *Paradise*. New York: Alfred A. Knopf.

Carmen Gillespie follows through Toni Morrison's novels the thought that being loved is a necessary condition for survival and for personal and political freedom. Allowing herself to be drawn unblinkingly by the heat of Morrison's characters' desire, Gillespie sees souls destroyed for want of resonance. But she also sees souls enabled by individual and collective self-regard to shed the burden of what post-colonial novelist Arundhati Roy has called "love laws"—the rules of hierarchy that say who is to be loved and how much.

Toni Morrison and the Politics of Desire
CARMEN GILLESPIE

The last line of Toni Morrison's Nobel Lecture, "Look. How lovely it is, this thing that we have done—together" (1993) is not merely a conclusion to a speech but a reference to the participatory, interactive, and dynamic experience between reader and language that is the foundation for all of Morrison's fiction. This intimate caress between book and reader references a foundational question that Morrison invites readers to engage with her: What does it mean to be loved?

In *The Birth of Pleasure*: *A New Map of Love* (2002), Carol Gilligan considers this same question and looks specifically at how the answers are constrained, perhaps even deformed, by the narrative foundations of Western culture—a culture that defines love, pleasure, and desire as experientially inseparable from trauma and violence. As Gilligan notes, "Perhaps patriarchy, by establishing hierarchy in the heart of intimacy, is inherently tragic, and like all trauma survivors, we keep telling the story we need to listen to and understand" (ibid., 5). This quest for understanding forms the philosophical core of Gilligan's *The Birth of Pleasure* and has always been the heart of Morrison's narrative universe. Both Gilligan and Morrison tell and retell patriarchy's stories of tragic love, not only to understand them but also to find or create possibilities beyond the oppressions of hierarchy. In her response to *The Birth of Pleasure*, Morrison remarked that she has attempted to create literature in which "love and pleasure" are understood as "political liberation." A brief examination of her novels *The Bluest Eye* (1970) and *Paradise* (1997) confirms her observation as well as Gilligan's assertion that

> freeing love means freeing the voice. . . . [I]t imposes psychic equality in the sense of everyone's having a voice and feeling free to speak. To say this is to see the affinity between love and democracy; to see that love is the psychic grounding for a democratic society—not an idealized love, but the actual gritty pleasure of living in relationship (2002, 208).

Morrison's first novel, *The Bluest Eye*, depicts the coming of age of Pecola Breedlove, an African–American girl who is the polar opposite of America's Dick-and-Jane image of the beloved offspring, and who seems—and feels—utterly unloved. Morrison evokes Pecola's circumstances and her ultimate psychic breakdown by positioning her within the complexities of desire.

The work of cultural studies theorist Paul Miers (1999) shows why an examination of Pecola's desire exposes the logic of the culture that breaks her spirit. Human desire, Miers argues, is governed by the laws and expectations of the culture in which it arises. The norms or grammar of a culture influence and inform the interactions of its members and determine the power relationships between them (ibid., 1078–92). This grammar is internalized and affects all aspects of behavior and interaction. As Gilligan notes, pointing to the way authentic voice can be silenced by cultural grammar, the psyche is "a voice often hidden in the structure of a sentence" (2002, 8). Cultural grammar includes internalized norms regarding race, gender, class, and heteronormativity. It also defines love and sex, the central symbolic and physical manifestations of desire and pleasure between human beings. Gilligan and Morrison both demonstrate that in fiction pleasure can be a site for the reinscription of or challenge to cultural grammar—to the hierarchies of patriarchy.

Throughout her fiction, Morrison uses sex and sexuality, as well as more abstract conceptions of pleasure, to expose both the constraints of patriarchy and the possibilities for reimagining the laws that govern all interactions within it. Although Pecola Breedlove, the most poignant of *The Bluest Eye*'s child subjects, is not equipped to reimagine cultural norms that poison her sense of self, her helplessness stands as an eloquent challenge to those norms. Morrison manifests this challenge through myriad and multilayered sexual references. She reveals both the destructive and the reproductive potential of desire and sexuality expressed in a patriarchal context. Morrison suggests that the ability to synthesize, cohabit, and redefine the contradictory roles of oppression and agency enables a pragmatic, often graceful, and artful survival that the child, Pecola, does not have the resources to achieve. The sanctuary that eludes Pecola is cousin to the triumphant survival of blues songs. It is a technique that transforms trouble by generating original and dynamic meaning at the intersection of subjugation and resistance, an intersection Morrison often represents as sexual encounter.

Describing the resilient women of the rural South who helped rear Pecola's father, Cholly Breedlove, Morrison writes, "They plowed all day and came home to nestle like plums under the limbs of their men. The legs that straddled a mules' back were the same ones that straddled their men's hips. And the difference was all the difference there was" (1970, 138).

This suggestive language foreshadows the theoretical matrix that Morrison initiates and develops in this novel and throughout her canon. Recalling Zora Neale Hurston's critique in *Their Eyes Were Watching God* (1937) of cultural associations between black women and mules, Morrison illustrates the dilemma of the simultaneous representations of black women as beasts of burden and as sexual dominatrices—the stereotypical polarities African–American women have had to negotiate since slavery. Morrison's phrasing illuminates the dichotomous artificiality, yet central-ity, of the *difference* between these identities. The ability of the women Morrison describes to inhabit these seemingly contradictory positions—as mule and as lover—points to their rejection of definitions imposed by oth-ers and their bold act of claiming self-definition. This capacity to reject designation as mule or lover in favor of a more complex identity marks the difference between life as a dynamic subject and existence as a dichotomized object. The fluidity of the women's self-enactments is a generative response to the oxymoronic relationship between domination and victimization, desire and repugnance. "Metamorphosis—changing the shape, overcoming the form—is the essence of creativity. It is by its very nature improvisational, taking off from the familiar and heading into the unknown" (Gilligan 2002, 231). The ease of the women's transforma-tion suggests an empowering rewriting of representation and an ability to shape-shift—to generate new and organic self-definitions.

Gilligan's ruminations on the need for an escape from relationships defined by patriarchy, for the creation of narrative challenges to the hier-archy of man over woman, are theoretically related to the possibilities suggested by Morrison's phrase, "the difference was all the difference there was." Morrison's phrase focuses the reader on the space imagined by the women's invented subjectivities. Morrison's conflation of the polar-ities that often govern patriarchal grammars both forces a conceptual collapse and generates an opening for new linguistic and cognitive possi-bilities. As Gilligan said of the daughter born to Psyche and Cupid, there awaiting fulfillment is "the promise of transformation[;] . . . pleasure lies at its center" (ibid., 207).

Morrison's conjoining of seemingly oppositional constructs creates the tension in *The Bluest Eye*'s opening line, "Nuns go by quiet as lust," and in her narrator's statement near the end of the text describing the incestuous rape of Pecola by her father, "He wanted to fuck her—tenderly" (1970, 128). By conjoining jarringly polarized and overtly sexualized language, Morrison points to the violent dichotomies that traditionally characterize human desire, aggression, submission, and symbiosis.

Morrison's artful language defies these simplistic categorizations and compartmentalizations. Her phrases expose the complexity and primacy of desire and its inextricable connection to the fundamental conundrums of oppression.

When Cholly Breedlove is a child, Aunt Jimmy, his principal caregiver, falls ill, and the community healer, M'Dear, is summoned to her bedside: "M'Dear loomed taller than the preacher who accompanied her . . . Four big white knots of hair gave power and authority to her soft black face. Standing straight as a poker, she seemed to need her hickory stick not for support but for communication" (ibid., 106). The night before his Aunt Jimmy dies following a brief illness, Cholly has a sexual dream about M'Dear: "He was aware, in his sleep, of being curled up in a chair, his hands tucked between his thighs. In a dream his penis changed into a long hickory stick, and the hands caressing it were the hands of M'Dear" (ibid., 109).

This startling dream is another example of Morrison's attempt to force her reader to confront the contoured edges of meaning and to reintegrate them into an expansive and newly imagined whole. Once again, sexuality is the terrain of the intersection of oppositions. M'Dear as healer, nurturer, and community mother, like the nuns, is the traditional antithesis of a sexual woman. Cholly's dream enacts what literary theorist Wahneema Lubiano (1995) would call a textual interruption in the expected definitions of the language. The familiar signifiers are disrupted and therefore destabilize the reading and discernment of meaning. Cholly's dream would typically be labeled as inappropriate and taboo; however, it is possible to redefine the signifiers in this passage so that new meanings emerge from their intersection. Looking beyond a presumed polarity between childhood and eroticism, a reader can understand Cholly's dream not merely as sexual fantasy but further as a yearning for the pleasure of maternal nurturing.

Morrison's interrogation of pleasure is not, of course, limited to sexual pleasure. In her quest to create new possibilities for realizing individual and communal well-being, Morrison explores the full range of the human hunger for pleasure. Through a deft use of words and constructs that have generally uncontested and simplistic definitions, Morrison proposes new understandings that more accurately reflect the chaos and disorder of human experiential realities. Throughout Morrison's efforts at ideological dismantling, the quest for pleasure remains at the center.

At the beginning of *The Bluest Eye*, Claudia as narrator reflects upon the events that form the plot of the novel, saying, "But since *why* is difficult to handle, one must take refuge in *how*" (1970, 3). By redefining language and reaching toward new definitional possibilities, the "how" of the often horrific and traumatic events that characterize human behavior can be examined from an alternative vantage.

This reinvented language inhabits the space between meanings and relies on the principle that "the difference was all the difference there was." Difference, so understood, may allow for liberatory or at least honest possibilities that conformity to the "normalcy" of patriarchy could never allow. In forcing the intersection of polarized concepts, Morrison initiates a complex theorization that emerges from the inside out. If this endeavor is successful, it forces the reader to embrace and take responsibility, both for Pecola, Morrison's personification of difference, and for the creation of a definitional experience unbound from the polarizing constructs of subordination:

> [P]icking and plucking her way between the tire rims and the sunflowers, between Coke bottles and milkweed, among all the waste and beauty of the world—*which is what she herself was*. All of our waste which we dumped on her and which she absorbed. And all of our beauty, which was hers first and which she gave to us. . . . We were so beautiful when we stood astride her ugliness (ibid., 162–3; emphasis added).

At the end of *The Bluest Eye*, Pecola is destroyed, and the reader is left in the rubble of collapsed categories and dismantled notions of contradiction and difference—of black versus white, male versus female, good versus evil, sexual versus chaste, rich versus poor. These oppositions construct the structural pillars and hierarchies of meaning that allow us to isolate and separate Pecola's subjectivity and humanity from our own.

Pecola's psychic disintegration stems from the brutality she has experienced, but more fundamentally, it has roots in the absence of relationship—with self, with family, with community—and in the absence of "the pleasure of being a soul in a body living in connection with others" (Gilligan 2002, 10). The destructive absence of pleasure in Pecola Breedlove's life contrasts with the salvation that the discovery of pleasure brings to the Convent women in Morrison's novel, *Paradise*. The Convent women discover pleasure—paradise—in that same metaphorical and psychic space that was so destructive for Pecola by claiming the power of self-definition and by rewriting their narratives with nonjudgmental compassion. In Morrison's own words, for the women in *Paradise*, "self- love, as well as community love, as well as the recollection of deep sexual pleasure is part of the enabling process as opposed to the tragedy." (See pp. 186–7 of this volume.)

In *Paradise*, Morrison uses the herb wintergreen as a symbol for the ritual discovery of pleasure the Convent women experience—a psychic (re)membering denied to Pecola. Wintergreen is purported to be a curative for both internal and external wounds and is described as having a creeping root that proliferates in forested mountains and valleys. The word "wintergreen" only appears four times in all of Morrison's novels: once in *The Bluest Eye* and three times in *Paradise*. It seems intentional that Morrison refers to wintergreen only in these novels, concerned as they are with the dangerous spaces women occupy and with the often urgent need for repair of our bodies and spirits. She references the herb in both instances as a trace, a nearly imperceptible yet essential element in a healing ritual in the laying on of hands.

In *The Bluest Eye*, the protagonist–narrator Claudia recalls the abrasive quality of her mother's hands as the overworked woman anxiously applies balm to her ailing daughter. "[I]t was a productive and fructifying pain. Love, thick and dark as Alaga syrup, eased into that cracked window. I could smell it—taste it—sweet, musty, with an edge of wintergreen in its base—everywhere in that house" (1970, 7). Although the experience is painful, Claudia, whose determined resilience stands in stark contrast to Pecola's desolation, recognizes that the discomfort her mother's efforts engender is rooted in a sincere urgency and a zealous, if hasty and abrasive, compassion. Claudia, the adolescent, dreams of simple sensual pleasures: "she wanted pleasure, all her senses engaged and the experience of relationship that comes with the awareness of being seen, being offered what gives her pleasure, being known, being loved" (Gilligan 2002, 115). Claudia's desires are a child's version of those held by the Convent women in *Paradise*, and they, as adult women with agency, are able to achieve their quests for pleasure. But, as Gilligan reveals in her reading of the myth of Psyche, the women must confront patriarchy and its fear and the policing of female pleasure in order to achieve freedom.

The brutality of patriarchy manifests in *Paradise* as the men of Ruby invade the Convent and attempt to disrupt the restorative experiences of the women who have found solace—home—within its cool, dark sanctuary. The men of Ruby who convene at the Convent door cannot abide the resistant rejuvenation they sense within.

Within that door, Consolata ("Connie") offers the women sanctuary and love. " 'If you have a place,' she [says,] 'that you should be in and somebody who loves you waiting there, then go. If not stay here and follow me' " (Morrison 1997, 262). The women's redemption comes in experiences of what Gilligan describes as resonance. It emerges from the telling of their collective narratives and their communion with each other, generated by the empathetic catalyst of Connie's careful consolation.

> Six yellow apples, wrinkled from winter storage, are cored and floating in water. Raisins are heating in a saucepan of wine. Consolata fills the hollow of each apple with a creamy mixture of egg yolks, honey, pecans and butter, to which she adds, one by one, the wine-swollen raisins. She pours the flavored wine into a pan and plops the apples down in. The sweet, warm fluid moves (ibid., 260).

It is this sweet, warm fluid and all that it represents that both attracts and repels the men of Ruby. Their incompatible and competing desires are particularly evident in the next reference to wintergreen. As the men invade the Convent, one of them, we are not told which one, stops and "lifts the pitcher of milk. He sniffs it first and then, the pistol in his right hand, he uses his left to raise the pitcher to his mouth, taking such long, measured swallows the milk is half gone by the time he smells the wintergreen" (ibid., 7). The destructive, phallic power of the gun must be set aside, albeit temporarily, in order to consume the sustenance, the women's milk. It is the wintergreen that signifies the restoration the women experience in the Convent and that is available to the men if they were open, rather than violently closed, to its possibilities.

Shortly before the men arrive at the Convent with murderous intentions, the women participate in a spontaneous ritual celebrating the arrival of long-awaited rain as well as their new-found self-awareness:

> There are great rivers in the world and on their banks and the edges of oceans children thrill to water. In places where rain is light, the thrill is almost erotic. But those sensations bow to the rapture of holy women dancing in hot sweet rain. They would have laughed, had enchantment not been so deep. . . . Tired from their night dance but happy, the women return to the house. Drying themselves, they ask Consolata to tell them again about Piedade, while they oil their bodies with wintergreen (ibid., 283–84).

The rain, the wintergreen, and the women's self-affirming sensual pleasure are physical manifestations of the balm of their narrative community, the balm that will allow them to recover from injury and perhaps, as the ending of *Paradise* suggests, even to transcend death. As Gilligan affirms,

> the symptoms of dissociation (loss of voice, difficulty in seeing or saying what one knows, . . . not really living one's life) are so often

revealed through the body because the body is our strongest barometer of our consonance with or dissonance from the world around us. Through the experience of sensual pleasure, we come into associative relationship with ourselves (2002, 161).

The Convent women's baptism in the rain is a ritual reclamation of voice, self-definition, and sensuality, and it accomplishes what Claudia and Pecola could only wish for, an open embrace of pleasure.

The women's wintergreen smell, consumed through the milk, sends the hunter back to envisioning the Convent residents as prey; however, he fails to realize the irony of his consumption of sustenance, milk, which derives from the very source he seeks to destroy. The milk evokes a memory of pleasure that the hunter cannot or will not allow himself to acknowledge. He becomes the archetype of patriarchy and illustrates its limitations, its hunger, and its self-destructiveness.

Morrison's language engenders meanings that do not rest upon the hierarchies that are the skeleton of patriarchy. In the collapse of patriarchy's dichotomous frameworks, there is the possibility of imagining new narrative foundations in which "we see through the categories that have blinded our vision . . . [and] step out of a frame" (ibid., 207). Through their work uncovering the narrative foundations of patriarchy, both Morrison and Gilligan help move us toward a reconsideration of voice, love, sexuality, self, other, freedom, and pleasure—one that does not eke out sustenance from the trauma and violence of patriarchy but that is rooted in the interactive cocreation of invented and original terrains of understanding. Morrison and Gilligan ask us to imagine new narratives that will "arc to the place where meaning *may* lie" (Morrison 1993) and that will lead us, individually and collectively, to cultivate the birth of pleasure.

References

GILLIGAN, Carol. 2002. *The Birth of Pleasure: A New Map of Love*. New York: Alfred A. Knopf.

HURSTON, Zora Neale. 1937. *Their Eyes Were Watching God*. Philadelphia: J. B. Lippincott.

LUBIANO, Wahneema. 1995. "The Postmodernist Rag: Political Identity and the Vernacular in *Song of Solomon*." In Valerie Smith (ed.), *New Essays on Song of Solomon*. Cambridge: Cambridge University Press, pp. 93–115.

MIERS, Paul. 1999. "Language and the Structure of Desire." *Modern Language Notes* 114 (December): 1078–92.

MORRISON, Toni. 1970. *The Bluest Eye*. New York: Holt, Rinehart and Winston.

———. "Nobel Lecture." 1993. Lecture presented at the Nobel Prize Award Week, Stockholm, Sweden, December 7. Available at: www.nobel-prize.org/literature/laureates/1993/morrison-lecture.html

———. 1997. *Paradise*. New York: Alfred A. Knopf.

If holding on to the relational instinct is key to the happiness of individuals and families, perhaps it is also key to the health of a society. Peggy Cooper Davis explores this possibility as she considers how, in post-slavery United States, in post-Nazi Germany, and in post-apartheid South Africa, the memory of atrocity rouses fellow-feeling and reminds us to stay alive to "outsider" voices.

Love, Law, and Politics
PEGGY COOPER DAVIS

The claim of this chapter is that law and politics should be grounded in love. This love is quieter than—although just as elusive as—the open-eyed passion of Carol Gilligan's Psyche. It is the fellow-feeling that leads us to presume connection rather than detachment and to respect the value and voice of each human subject. Like a healthy romantic passion, it requires the courage to face the sometimes stormy weather of relationship. And like a healthy romantic passion, it offers an alternative to tragedy.

In what follows, I will explain this radical-sounding claim and then speculate about the kind of culture in which it might find traction. The claim, I will argue, is a lesson of history, and it takes hold when people are able to do two things: to think relationally in public spheres and to avoid the suppression of subordinate voices.

WHAT HISTORY TEACHES

When law and politics are not grounded in love, we risk atrocity. That is the lesson of the Holocaust, of apartheid, and of chattel slavery. To leave people outside our circle of fellow-feeling is to license their abuse. This lesson is hard learned and easily forgotten, so it is important to mark its endurance. It endures in the constitution of post-Nazi Germany. It endures conspicuously in the constitution by which the new South Africa explicitly repudiated its apartheid past. And it endures more subtly in the constitution by which the United States was reformed after the Civil War ended slavery within its borders. There is special wisdom in what South African jurists and legal scholars describe as a constitutional tradition that is constructively "reactive" to a history of oppression.

The German and South African Constitutions embody the lesson of love in requirements of respect for human dignity. But what does it mean to respect human dignity? It means nothing more than to maintain the sense of fellow-feeling that stays the hand of abuse and counsels attention to human need. The histories of Germany, South Africa, and the United States suggest that this sense of fellow-feeling is best understood in the process of contemplating its lack. Certain constraints on people and certain ways of relating to people strike us as deeply inconsistent with the respect they are due. As failures of the love they are owed. As abusive or unmindful of basic human needs. We then reason back to discover what counts for us as abusive or inadequately mindful of the needs of our fellow-beings. The process involves more than abstract reason. It involves empathy. It involves tapping and assessing relational feelings and exercising judgment in light of those feelings.

When we contemplate torture or murder or indifference to severe deprivation, our sense of dissonance may reflect identification and faith that our own kind is precious. And identification may encompass a collective perspective such that the suffering or death of one is felt as a direct loss to all.[1] It may also reflect an understanding of what it means to be human—a belief that human beings are self-aware in ways that add dimensions to experiencing deprivation or abuse.

When we contemplate more subtle forms of abuse or indifference, additional considerations come (or come more conspicuously) into play. Coercion or constraint with respect to such things as political voice, religious observance, liberty of conscience, family formation, or reproductive choice are tested not only in terms of identification, collective perspective, and human self-awareness, but also in terms of our understandings of human capacity and human desire. How, we ask, is it right to treat a reasoning being who has moral consciousness and ambitions about the construction of a life? Then, respect for human dignity involves more, than the avoidance of suffering; it involves giving reasonable reign to our expressive capacities and desires (Cornell 2008, 110–201).

The Constitution that reconstructed the United States after secession and the Civil War does not specifically embody a concept of human dignity, but it is similarly responsive to the lesson of love. It was conceived in accordance with principles that were explicitly described in the halls of Congress and elsewhere as antislavery principles. These principles required more than the simple abolition of slavery. They required making all persons born or naturalized in the United States free citizens. And they required redefining the attributes of citizenship.

It was in redefining the attributes of citizenship that the drafters of the reconstructed United States Constitution conferred what amounts to a right to respect for human dignity. Free citizenship was defined in negative reference to chattel slavery; it was chattel slavery's opposite. As the term "chattel" implies, and as anti-slavery advocates repeatedly said, enslaved people in the United States were treated instrumentally—as if they were beasts rather than women and men. They were the property of masters rather than members of families or of the larger political, economic, and social community. As such, they were denied the rights to marry, to maintain parental ties, to inherit or pass on property, to control or profit from their work, or to function as members of—and thereby to participate in constructing—the political communities in which they were forced to reside. Outrage against slavery was related to its violence and to its effects on free labor. But it was as directly related to the dissonance between the constraints and coercions of chattel slavery and the capacities and desires of enslaved human beings—the uniquely human capacity for self-reflection and reason and the desire to assume and to shape one's life and to participate in constructing one's community in terms of relational and aesthetic standards. To be a free citizen in the postbellum United States was not just to be protected against the violence of enslavement. It was to be at liberty to form and pursue a life plan and to have a voice in the political community. It was to have one's human dignity respected.

Among Germany, South Africa, and the United States, South Africa has embraced reactive constitutionalism most wholeheartedly; the project of forming an anti-apartheid state seems to be a national mission in what is popularly known as "the new South Africa." Although anti-Nazism is not as central to Germany's contemporary identity as reaction against apartheid is to the contemporary identity of South Africa, Germany also acknowledges its Constitution as reactive to the Holocaust. By contrast, there is little recognition in the United States that its reconstructed Constitution is reactive to slavery. There is instruction in considering further the extreme cases of South Africa and the United States.

The South African Constitution is, to be sure, more explicit in requiring respect for human dignity and in drawing the implications of that requirement. It provides explicitly that "[e]veryone has inherent dignity and the right to have their dignity respected and protected."[2] Moreover, the South African Constitution sets out in no fewer than nineteen sections the civil rights implications of that pronouncement.[3]

The South African Constitutional Court is inspiring for its fealty to the principle of respect for human dignity. In the first case argued before it, the Court declared the death penalty inconsistent with the respect that is mandated by the South African Constitution. It has scrutinized criminal and other investigative procedures in terms of their respectfulness of human dignity. And it has held that the prohibition of same-sex marriage would unconstitutionally affront the dignity of gay and lesbian people.

By contrast, the Supreme Court of the United States has, since the end of the Reconstruction era, used the principle of anti-slavery to limit rather than enrich its definitions of protected civil rights, arguing at times that Reconstruction's great declarations of civil rights should be construed narrowly in cases that did not concern the rights of former slaves or their descendants. Moreover, the United States Court has avoided making judgments about what respect for human dignity might require, preferring instead to assess such things as the cruelty of a punishment or the justifiability of restrictions on liberty in terms of tradition, legislative judgments, and popular acceptance. Thus, the death penalty has withstood constitutional challenge, and same-sex marriage continues to be prohibited.[4]

Opinions of the United States Supreme Court guaranteeing or compromising the rights to marriage, procreative choice, parenthood, sexual intimacy, procedural fairness, protection against extreme punishments, or control over the manner of one's death do not tell the story of a nation setting itself against the ideologies of slavery. They are therefore uninformed by an account of how and why our Constitution should protect such things. The Supreme Court of the United States came closest to recognizing a constitutional principle of respect for human dignity when it announced, in a case affirming (but limiting) the right of a pregnant women to choose abortion, that:[5] "At the heart of liberty is the right to define one's own concept of existence, of meaning, of the universe, and of the mystery of human life. Beliefs about these matters could not define the attributes of personhood were they formed under compulsion of the State."[6] This statement, woefully lacking support on the current Court was derided by Justice Scalia as "sweet mystery of life dictum".[7]

The Court might have related this idea about human dignity and human rights to a national history of slavery, emancipation, and constitutional reconstruction. But it did not.

The importance of a reactive constitutionalism is manifest in the United States's and South Africa's highest courts's opinions concerning the constitutionality of laws criminalizing consensual, homosexual sodomy.[8] At the heart of the United States Court's opinion, in *Lawrence v. Texas*, is a conclusion that distills and relies on the "sweet mystery" passage: "Liberty presumes an autonomy of self that includes freedom of thought, belief, expression, and certain intimate conduct."[9] But there is nothing in the opinion that tells us *why* liberty presumes this kind of autonomy or why the people of the United States might have chosen to define liberty in this way. The statement is made in absolute terms, admitting of no dispute. It must be accepted, if it is accepted, as indisputably implied by our Constitution's language or as indisputably "true."

The opinion of South Africa's Court of course relied on the South African Constitution's more explicit terms, not only in its requirement of respect for human dignity, but also in its guarantees against discrimination. But the power and clarity of the South African Court's opinion come equally from its commitment to constructing constitutional rights, liberties, and obligations in a way that reflects the lessons of apartheid and the principles embodied in the struggle against it. Justice Lourens Ackerman spoke not in terms of naked absolutes but in terms unhesitatingly informed by conscientious analysis of the history of South Africa and that of other nations. When he said that "the experience of subordination—of personal subordination, above all—lies behind the vision of equality,"[10] he appealed to both logic and experience. And when he said that anti-sodomy legislation built "insecurity and vulnerability into the daily lives of gay men," just as apartheid once built insecurity and vulnerability into the daily lives of people of color,[11] his words had special—and potentially transformative—resonance for all who had lived or known apartheid and other forms of human oppression.

One cannot compare post-apartheid South Africa and post-slavery United States without noting three conspicuous and important differences. Apartheid was the instrument of a colonial power against an indigenous people; slavery was not. The subjects of apartheid's oppressions were a majority of the nation's population; the enslaved in the United States were a minority. Finally, the new South Africa was born of a struggle against apartheid. The Reconstruction of the United States was the aftermath of a war fought primarily to end Confederate secession. Ending slavery was the primary goal of African–American combatants but not of the Union. These are important differences, to be sure. But they do not tell the whole story of why the people of the United States have learned less well from slavery than the people of South Africa have learned from apartheid. To get at the full story, we must consider the United States's and South Africa's respective abilities to think relationally about legal and political issues and to give resonance to a diversity of political voices. Gilligan's work illuminates these issues of relationship and voice. It helps us to understand why relational reasoning and openness to multiple voices are important to the character of a democratic society and why they are so exceedingly difficult to sustain.

THINKING RELATIONALLY ABOUT LAW AND POLITICS

It is important in law and politics, but relatively easy, to avoid fallacious reasoning. The difficult and often more consequential moves are made in the construction of premises rather than in reasoning from them. And a great deal turns on whether those premises are chosen from a relational stance or from a stance of detachment.

Consider, for example, how one might analyze the equity or constitutional legitimacy of requiring that a government guarantee its citizens a measure of social and economic security. May I be taxed so that this requirement can be enforced? This is not a question of logic but a question of valuation. The answer depends on how I identify and monetize the value to me of what my tax dollars will buy. To the extent that my tax dollars buy roads, power lines, streetlights, sanitation services, and police protection that I use, then I have made an investment rather than a sacrifice. If my tax dollars provide these basic services or provide food, shelter, or medical care for others, I can regard the expenditure as an unfair sacrifice. But if I share a bond of community with those who benefit from my tax dollars, and if I value our collective well-being, then, once again, I can feel that I have made an investment rather than a sacrifice.

A similar analysis could be made with respect to any number of legal or political questions. Affirmative action can be thought of as an inequity or as a social good. Restraints on police interrogations or limitations on criminal punishments can be thought risky for or respectful of human rights. Why might the idea of sacrifice or inequity or risk spring more readily to mind than the idea of investment or collective well-being or respect for human rights? The causes are many, but important among them is that, as Gilligan has shown, we are developmentally primed to reject relational thinking about public matters and to reason instead from a position of detachment.

In encouraging a feminist project of re-metaphorization, Drucilla Cornell (2008) points usefully to the constructedness and the social power of metaphors. There is much to be learned from examining the metaphors by which we understand ourselves and our cultures. When Gilligan (2002) dissects the Oedipal myth that stands in so many cultures as metaphor for human development, she is able to show how it is that we come to fear and avoid relational thinking in public life.

According to the Oedipal story of development, male children must suppress their sexual longing for the mother and internalize the law of the father. Overcompensation in this charged, emotional context leads to rejection and debasement of the feminine and the relational pleasure that mothering recalls and represents. Gilligan calls attention to how this story of debasing the feminine and internalizing paternal law supports and reinforces patriarchy. Growing up in a patriarchal environment and under the sway of the Oedipal story of development (or a comparable story), boys are led from about the age of five to view separation and detachment as central developmental goals. They often learn to fear relationship as a prelude to tragedy. And they often learn to valorize detachment and demean the relational.

Drawing on infant research and her own interviews and observations of little boys and their parents, Gilligan also tells us that this rejection of the relational goes against a natural, pleasurable, and adaptive intersubjectivity. We are, she argues, wired to take pleasure in human relationships. Moreover—and, Gilligan would argue, happily—we thrive through cooperation.

What about women and girls in this story? Not surprisingly, Gilligan finds Freudian accounts of girls' development deeply inadequate. She draws on evidence of differently timed developmental crises in boys and girls and on her own research with very young boys and adolescent girls to argue that for girls the invocation to reject the relational is delayed and differently experienced. Girls are likely to be called upon to hold to relational values in domestic and other caregiving contexts but, starting at about the time of puberty, they are simultaneously called upon to suppress relational intelligence and passion *for the sake of relating* in a male-dominated culture of detachment. I will return presently to this female predicament and its consequences for the development of voice in a democratic society. What is relevant here is that in public spheres both women and men are motivated to avoid relational thinking. The resultant culture of detachment has an effect on the construction and interpretation of legal and political concepts like socioeconomic justice or equality or civil liberties. Relational, collective constructs are suppressed because they are associated with the domestic and the maternal; and detached, individualistic constructs are embraced and associated with the law of the father. If this is true, then the character of our constitutionalism will depend in important respects on whether or not we come to terms with our fear of the "feminine."

Perspective and Voice

I have attempted to show through Gilligan's work that the patriarchal developmental story predisposes us against thinking relationally about the meaning of constitutional principles. But this developmental story erects a second, complementary obstacle to the development of a relational constitutionalism by enshrining a superordinate perspective and silencing the voices of the subordinate. To elaborate this point, I turn again to a story of slavery and anti-slavery in the United States.

The black physician James McCune Smith and the white patrician William Garret Smith were friends and colleagues in the abolitionist movement. In an essay written in 1861, Garret Smith wrote that the president of the Southern rebel Confederacy was "cheered and strengthened by the entire devotion . . . to his cause of all around him." McCune Smith pointed out in a letter to his friend that this single phrase showed a failure to appreciate the situation in the rebel South: "Is this true?" he wrote. "Is it not virtually ignoring one-half of those around Jeff Davis (I mean the Slaves)?" (Quoted in Ripley 1985, 113–14.) A substantial proportion of the people living in the Confederate states were slaves, free blacks, or native Americans. Yet, as McCune Smith understood, when most people in the United States during the Civil War imagined the Confederate community—when they imagined the political and social entity that the South had become—they instinctively imagined it in terms of its superordinate members. They erased slaves, native Americans, and free blacks and imagined a white community.

Of course, I do not tell this story to suggest that anyone imagines the new South Africa as a white community. Nor do I tell it to malign white abolitionists in the United States. I tell it for two reasons. The first is to show how easy it is, even for people with the most egalitarian intentions, to slip into imagining a political institution or community in terms of its more affluent and powerful sectors.

This tendency to see an issue from a perspective of power is, like the tendency to think in detached rather than relational terms, reinforced by the Oedipal story of development. To say that the Oedipal story of development enshrines patriarchy is to say that it enshrines a hierarchical order. As I will explain presently, hierarchical orders depend on silencing those on the bottom rungs. The subordinated are silenced to promote and protect the perspectives of the dominant. Under patriarchy, the detached perspective associated with the law of the father is privileged in public life, and the relational knowledge and desires of women and children are debased and suppressed. In this hierarchical, psychological environment, it is not surprising to find a tendency to assume the superordinate perspective in public discourse.

Assumption of a superordinate perspective is consequential. To focus on a tension between socioeconomic justice and sacrifice is to imagine the issue from a superordinate perspective. From a perspective of power. This is a perfectly legitimate perspective, but it is a perspective. If we think through the issue from a different perspective, we might see it differently. Instead of asking, "How is it fair to tax some to benefit others?" we might ask, "How do we build a society in which my children and I can be full participants?" And we might also ask, "How should the fruits of my nation's natural resources and my people's labor be shared?"

Our tendency to think of public issues from a superordinate perspective is heightened because subordinate voices are largely absent in public discourse. So, the second reason I tell the story of the two Smiths is to call attention to McCune Smith's assertion of a subordinate voice, and to invite you to think about why it may be hard in public discourse to not only appreciate subordinate perspectives but to also voice the perspectives of women, or people of color, or queer people, or any people who have been colonized. To explore this question, I return to Gilligan's account of male and female psychosocial development and connect it to her emerging theories of democratic voice.

Although Gilligan is perhaps best known for calling attention to a feminine ethic of care, her work cannot be fully understood in those terms. We must read *In a Different Voice: Psychological Theory and Women's Development* (1982) beyond Amy's and Jake's resolutions of a moral dilemma and through Gilligan's interviews with young girls and with women confronting unplanned pregnancies. And we must read her later work. When we do so, we realize that postpubescent loss of voice—and the struggle to resist that loss—are more central than an ethic of care to Gilligan's account of women's development. And we realize that within the terms of Gilligan's theory, staying authentically in relationship—in her words, bearing "the weather of relationship"—supplants the other-focused notion of care. For, as Gilligan shows, selfless care and authentic relationship are mutually inconsistent; maintaining the voice of the "I" is necessary to the health of the "we."

Why might it be hard to maintain the voice of the "I"? I have said that in Gilligan's view boys are led from their preschool years to fear, suppress, and denigrate the relational and the feminine. They are more encouraged to take on a paternal voice of detachment—to think and speak in terms that are abstract and rule bound rather than personalized and contextual. I have also said that in Gilligan's view postpubescent girls are, paradoxically, led to suppress their relational intelligence and desire *for the sake of relating* in a culture of detachment. But they are not likely to be encouraged, as boys are, to take on the stereotypically masculine voice of detachment. Nor are they encouraged to give voice to the relational in public spheres. Thus, especially in public spheres, boys are at risk of being limited by a voice that masks their relational insights and instincts, and girls are at risk of being left voiceless.

I believe that this silencing pattern of denigration and deference is replicated in forms of subordination other than patriarchy. And, of course, many of us who are subordinated and silenced on other grounds are also subordinated and silenced as women. We too easily lose the "I" in a relationship. Hence, we are at risk of too easily accepting the conceptualization of distributive or compensatory or procedural justice in terms of sacrifice or inequity or risk and neglecting both our own perspectives and the more relational conceptualizations that would strengthen us as they strengthened our polities.

Gilligan's concept of voice helps us to see, then, that the tendency to neglect the perspectives of the powerless is triple-barreled. Its force comes, as I have said, from the inhibition of relational logics that tolerate competing perspectives and from the salience of superordinate perspectives. But it also comes from the fact that the voices of subordinated people are especially inhibited.

THE LANGUAGE OF A RELATIONAL AND MULTIVOICED CONSTITUTIONALISM

I return briefly to a comparison of the United States and South African courts' treatment of the criminalization of homosexual sodomy, for these cases shed light not only on the value of a reactive constitutionalism but also on the value of relational constitutionalism that is alive to history, to context, and to the range of constituent voices.

Bowers v. Hardwick, the United States Court's opinion that *Lawrence* overruled, is written in terms that are painfully disrespectful of the sensibilities and likely perspectives of queer people. If the majority justices had imagined their words being heard or read by anyone who was not heterosexual, it is hard to believe that these otherwise humane people would have spoken as they did. The majority described Hardwick's claim—that under the Court's precedents criminal proscriptions against homosexual sodomy unconstitutionally infringed his liberty—as "at best, facetious."[12] Chief Justice Warren E. Burger found it necessary in his concurrence to quote Sir William Blackstone to the effect that homosexual sodomy was an "infamous *crime against nature*," an offense of "deeper malignity" than rape, a heinous act "the very mention of which is a disgrace to human nature," and "a crime not fit to be named." He then added, without the cover of an attribution, that "[t]o hold that the act of homosexual sodomy is somehow protected as a fundamental right would be to cast aside millennia of moral teaching."[13] Neither opinion contained a word that referenced the perspectives of homosexual people.

When the United States Court overruled *Hardwick*, the majority opinion challenged the *Hardwick* majority's narrow characterization of the right at stake as a right to commit homosexual sodomy; it addressed the stigma that the anti-sodomy laws attach to homosexual people; and it disputed the *Hardwick* majority's assertions that proscriptions against homosexual intimacy were sustained throughout Judeo-Christian cultures. But, like the *Hardwick* Court, the *Lawrence* Court never spoke from or about the perspective of homosexual people. Even in *Lawrence*, the queer were voiceless.

Justice Bruce A. Ackerman's opinion for South Africa's Court stands in admirable contrast. In considering whether the sodomy laws' discrimination against homosexual people was unfair, he was required under the Court's precedents to focus "on the impact of the discrimination on the complainant and others in his or her situation."[14] He did this not from a position of detachment but from a considered position of empathy. After his observation that the experience of subordination lies behind the vision of equality, he said, "To understand 'the other' one must try, as far as is humanly possible, to place oneself in the position of 'the other.'"[15] Attempting to understand the constitutional question before him from all relevant perspectives, Justice Ackerman was able to weigh the full range of the government's justifications for the discrimination against a fuller range of its personal and social effects. A reactive constitutionalism became, then, a more richly democratic constitutionalism.

CONCLUSION

I do not know whether patriarchal developmental influences have comparable force in South Africa and in the United States, but I suspect that they do. If that is so, why might South Africa have succeeded where we have failed in the United States to develop a relational constitutionalism? It seems clear that the answer lies in part in South Africa's determination to face and learn from the failures of empathy and voice that were both causes and effects of apartheid. But perhaps it is also because an appreciation of *ubuntu*, understood as consciousness that the self is necessarily constructed in relation to others, stands in South Africa as a counterweight to patriarchal pulls toward detachment. Perhaps the philosophical principle of *ubuntu* in South African culture is like the artistic vision of improvisation in American jazz music: it enables harmonious liberation of the "I" within the embrace of a loving and swinging "we."

Notes

1 Drucilla Cornell explains that the concepts of *ubuntu* and *seriti* stand for such an interconnectedness that harming one member of a community harms all members (2008, 107–19).

2 South African Constitution, CHAPTER 2, SECTION 10, 1996.

3 Ibid., SECTIONS 11–39, 1996.

4 In contrast, some state courts have been more specific as to what respect for human dignity would require under state Constitutions (see, e.g., *Goodridge v. Dep't of Pub. Health*, 440 Mass. 309, 312 [2003] ["The Massachusetts Constitution affirms the dignity and equality of all individuals and thus cannot prohibit same-sex marriage"]; In remarriage Cases, 43 Cal. 4th 757, 823 [2008] [The Constitution of California demands "equal dignity and respect . . . without regard to their sexual orientation" for all persons]).

5 *Planned Parenthood v. Casey*, 505 U.S. 833 (1992).

6 *Planned Parenthood*, 505 U.S. at 851.

7 *Lawrence v. Texas*, 539 U.S. 558, 588 (2003) (Scalia, J., dissenting).

8 *Lawrence*, 539 U.S. 558; *Nat'l Coal. for Gay & Lesbian Equality v. Minister of Justice* 1998 (12) BCLR 1517 (CC) (S. Afr.). Available at www.saflii.org/za/-cases/ZACC/1998/15.pdf

9 *Lawrence*, 539 U.S. at 562.

10 *Nat'l Coalition*, (12) BCLR at para. 22 quoting Michael Waltzer, 1983.

11 *Nat'l Coalition*, (12) BCLR at para. 28.

12 *Bowers v. Hardwick*, 478 U.S. 186, 194 (1986).

13 *Bowers*, 478 U.S. at 197.

14 *Nat'l Coalition*, (12) BCLR at para. 17 (quoting *Harksen v. Lane* 1998 [1] SA 300 [CC] [S. Afr.]).

15 *Nat'l Coalition*, (12) BCLR at para. 22.

References

CORNELL, Drucilla. 2008. "A Call for a Nuanced Constitutional Jurisprudence: South Africa, Ubuntu, Dignity, and Reconciliation." In Sanja Bahun-Radunović and V. G. Julie Ragan (eds), *Violence and Gender in the Globalized World*. New York: Ashgate, pp. 107–19.

GILLIGAN, Carol. 2002. *The Birth of Pleasure: A New Map of Love*. New York: Alfred A. Knopf.

——. 1982. *In a Different Voice: Psychological Theory and Women's Development*. Cambridge, MA: Harvard University Press.

RIPLEY, C. Peter (ed.). 1985. *The Black Abolitionist Papers. Volume 5: The United States, 1859–1865*. Chapel Hill: University of North Carolina Press.

WALZER, Michael. 1983. *Spheres of Justice: A Defense of Pluralism and Equality*. New York: Basic Books.

In postcolonial and African–American fiction Carol Gilligan found characters who struggle against dissociation and suppression of voice to speak out against hierarchy. Toni Morrison and Carmen Gillespie elaborated on this finding to describe how desiring, being loved, and being capable of self-love make it possible for Morrison's characters to exploit the liberating potential of double consciousness and exercise political voice. They also examined the other side of this message to see how lovelessness and self-loathing silence and subordinate Morrison's characters.

Robin D. G. Kelley looks to social and artistic movements rather than to the fiction of subordinated people, but he, too, discovers liberating potential in the position of the cultural outsider. His focus is on black feminism and surrealism. Kelley finds in black feminism a critique of patriarchy's racialized suppression of love. He defines surrealism to include African–American and postcolonial thinkers who were ignored in previous accounts of the surrealist movement. On this view, black feminism and surrealism are partially—and revealingly—overlapping categories. In both, he finds the daring and self-preserving need to imagine one's self out of engrained cultural patterns and to speak in a different political voice. Then, in an example of what Patricia Foster describes as a "vertical drop," Kelley associates his readings of social movements to formative childhood memories: rejecting the patriarchal wisdom that manhood is found in separation from the maternal, he takes lessons about love and democratic voice from a surrealist, radical, black feminist mother.

For me, *The Birth of Pleasure*: *A New Map of Love* (2002) opened up the question of love's relationship to the "politics of liberation" in profound ways. I was introduced to the book at a particularly vulnerable moment in my own work. I had just published a book called *Freedom Dreams*: *The Black Radical Imagination* (2002), which examines social movements in order to recover the dreams of a new world that have yet to be realized. It begins with the premise that the catalyst for political engagement has never been misery, poverty, and oppression. It has been hope—the promise of constructing a world radically different from the one we've inherited.

It was not until I nearly completed *Freedom Dreams* that I realized the degree to which a vision of love lay at the foundation of the radical social movements I had studied. In the introduction, I wrote the following, more as a confession than as a thesis:

> Freedom and love may be the most revolutionary ideas available to us, and yet as intellectuals we have failed miserably to grapple with their political and analytical importance. Despite having spent a decade and a half writing about radical social movements, I am only just beginning to see what animated, motivated, and knitted together these gatherings of aggrieved folks. I have come to realize that once we strip radical social movements down to their bare essence and understand the collective desires of people in motion, freedom and love lie at the very heart of the matter (ibid., 12).

By love, I was not necessarily talking about what gets called romantic love, but neither is Carol Gilligan. At the heart of love's tragic story of loss is patriarchy: a masculinity that doesn't allow for intimacy and emotional freedom, a fear of vulnerability, a silencing of women who speak about love and desire and who refuse to be mere objects. The roots of these failures are manifest in families—in relationships between fathers and sons, mothers and daughters, husbands and wives. But the consequences of these failures permeate and shape an entire culture. Ultimately, the overturning of patriarchy—the casting off of traditional gender roles that silence women and harden men—would yield a culture based on trust, mutuality, and love. This would be the birth of pleasure—and, to take it one step further, the birth of freedom.

Clearly, Gilligan is not just interested in couples. Toward the end of her book, she reflects on "the connection between love and democracy, the intimate joining of private and public life" (2002, 232). I think there is a connection between Gilligan's revolutionary conception of love and that of Dr. Martin Luther King Jr., who understood love as a constant struggle to build and rebuild community. Making community requires a kind of nakedness: leaving one's armor at the door, opening oneself up to others and giving freely, being vulnerable, speaking truth while allowing others their voice. Love, in other words, is not a thing you adopt or embrace; it's a process of making community by nourishing relationships and at the same time remaking yourself over and over again.

In what follows, I will briefly explore black feminism and surrealism, two movements that have offered new visions of democracy rooted in love, in the "intimate joining of private and public life."

Feminists have obviously been thinking about these issues for some time, but radical black feminists have had special insight about the relationship between love and politics. They remind us that family relationships and love were—and are—experienced through a context of white supremacy. The most severe instance, of course, is slavery, where the ultimate patriarch was the owner and where "loss" could mean having one's child or lover sold away. Indeed, as Peggy Cooper Davis demonstrates in her path-breaking book, *Neglected Stories: The Constitution and Family Values* (1997), the antislavery struggle for the Fourteenth Amendment defined citizenship not just as a right to life and to participation but literally as the right to love: the right to create families.

Even under so-called freedom, black women were cast by white citizens and the state as sexually available and promiscuous, and black men were cast as potential rapists. Entire communities were rendered unintelligent, incapable of "love," sites of raw animal desire. Moreover, black feminist thinkers showed how racism affected not only black people but everyone, including the white folk. Their work exposes the misleading artificiality of the wall erected between public and private, especially given the importance of the labor of women of color in the maintenance of white households and in child rearing, as well as the critical role of sexual violence and lynching in upholding race and gender hierarchies (Kelley 2002, 135–56).

One might say this is all history, all behind us, but it is not. Just consider how the fear of loss as the outcome of love may have profoundly different meanings for poor and working-class black women who lose their sons and lovers to a burgeoning prison system, a police officer's bullet, or gang violence. Or consider the stifling black nationalist patriarchy that demands subordination and reproduction for the maintenance of an embattled race. This context makes the road to pleasure a stony one indeed.

The amazing story, for me at least, is that black people continue to pursue love. Much of black feminist theorizing anticipates Gilligan's profound insights in *The Birth of Pleasure* as well as their political importance. Groups like the Combahee River Collective and the Third World Women's Alliance and activist-intellectuals like Barbara Smith, Pat Robinson, Patricia Haden, Donna Middleton, and Audre Lorde consistently pointed to the damage patriarchy inflicted on everyone—women, children, and men (Lorde 1995, 283–92; Robinson et al. 1995, 175–84; Smith 1999; Robinson and Black Sisters 2000, 135). They insisted that nothing short of revolution could bring about real freedom, and that revolution must begin with ourselves, with our relationships with one another, with how we love, speak, and handle pain.

Some black feminists have linked the struggle for self-transformation and love to the overthrow of compulsory heterosexuality. For Cheryl Clarke (1995, 241–52) and the late June Jordan (1995), achieving sexual freedom was foundational to all other struggles for freedom. These thinkers saw early on what has become apparent to many of us today: they saw that lesbian, gay, bisexual, transgendered, and transsexual movements contribute to the freedom of all by challenging all claims of normativity. Indeed, the movement against compulsory heterosexuality may be the only conceptual space we have to construct a politics of desire and to open our imagination to new ways of living and seeing.

I argue in *Freedom Dreams* that surrealism is also a source of emancipatory visions of love.[1] According to the Chicago Surrealist Group,

> Surrealism is the exaltation of freedom, revolt, imagination and love. . . . Its basic aim is to lessen and eventually to completely resolve the contradiction between everyday life and our wildest dreams. By definition subversive, surrealist thought and action are intended not only to discredit and destroy the forces of repression, but also to emancipate desire and supply it with new poetic weapons (quoted in Kelley 2002, 158).

We know that the more famous relationships in the Paris Surrealist Group and elsewhere were replete with episodes of misogyny and patriarchal order, but the vision that surrealism promoted nevertheless has all kinds of revolutionary possibilities. Surrealist women in Europe and the

United States such as Toyen, Valentine Penrose, Leonora Carrington, Meret Oppenheim, Claude Cahun, and Mary Low proposed a more revolutionary sexuality and resisted the subjugation of women to men's desires (Kelley 2002, 164). Just as Gilligan draws on the moving story of Psyche and Cupid, contemporary American surrealists turn to the narratives of women's blues singers for illuminating myths and signs of possibility. Along with black feminist thinkers like Angela Y. Davis (1998) and Hazel Carby (2000), they have found in the songs of Bessie Smith, Ma Rainey, Alberta Hunter, Memphis Minnie, Lucille Bogan, and Ida Cox a poetics of sexual freedom and power—a poetics to articulate desire, as well as pain, loss, alienation, and dislocation.

In the tradition of the great blues singers from whom she descends, surrealist poet Jayne Cortez understands and embraces the transformative, magical quality of the erotic. More importantly, she calls for disarmament and real nakedness, a bold act of vulnerability and exposure that is prelude to the kind of uncensored voicing of desire that Gilligan says we need. Consider "Say It":

> Say it
> and peel off that gray iguana skin mask
> Say it
> and clean out your cockpit of intoxicated spiders
> Tear the sexual leaves of grief from your heart
> Pluck the feathers of nostalgia from your nipples
> Push the slow-moving masochistic mudslide
> of contralto voices
> from your afternoon skull of anxiety
> Say it
> and let the tooth chips fall from
> your hole of rebellious itches. . . .
>
> (Quoted in Kelley 2002, 189–90.)

In the end, choosing a politics of love, finding the voice to boldly "Say It" in a world where gender roles—and class and race—silence men and women, is risky business. As Gilligan reminds us, it requires holding onto the relational voice of childhood. It requires relinquishing power and control, building a new world from our imagination, and believing that we are capable of making it real: "Hope is the most dangerous emotion: it invites us to imagine an escape from tragedy, it tempts what we have come to think of as fate. The hope of the new, the nakedness of standing without a frame, heightens our awareness of vulnerability and, with it, the temptation to return at whatever cost to the known" (2002, 233).

I know that a world of pleasure, a world without patriarchy, is possible, not from my academic studies but from my mother. You see, I'm one of the lucky ones. My mother suffered loss, but she never lost her spirit of rebellion or that dusty, ragged map of love that Gilligan searches for in *The Birth of Pleasure*. Paradise for us was a little rat- and roach-infested tenement apartment on 157th and Amsterdam, where my mother alone, a high school dropout, taught us about figures like Shiva, the god who is half-man, half-woman. She explained that God was neither male nor female but a force within all living things. When I was seven she taught my sister and me about sex, not about sin or fornication. Sex was a beautiful thing, she explained, an expression of love and equality where people communicate their love with their bodies and create a living art. She showed us how to meditate, to embrace the comfort of darkness and silence, to see a world of possibility through our Third Eye. She showed us that the Marvelous was free—in the patterns of a stray bird feather, in a Hudson River sunset, in the view from our fire escape, in the stories she told us or the way she sang Gershwin's "Summertime," in a curbside rainbow created by the alchemy of motor oil and water from an open hydrant. She wanted to raise free spirits, revolutionaries who understood that freedom is not what the majority thinks. She wanted to raise feminists, critics of patriarchy who believe gender and sexual relations can be reconstructed. She wanted to raise poets, spiritual surrealists who can see the poetic and prophetic in the richness of our daily lives. She wanted to show us a more expansive, fluid, "cosmos-politan" definition of blackness, to teach us that we are not merely inheritors of a culture but its makers.

I am who I am because of my mother's intellect and my mother's love. She did not need a high school diploma or a husband or a switch to raise a black male intellectual committed to feminism, social justice, poetry, love, and something even more visionary than socialism. She taught me how to be a man by rejecting manhood altogether. She taught me that I did not have to model myself after my father or any man, for the beauty of humanity is in its potential for transformation, in its ability to transcend the categories that define and constrict us.

Note

1 For more on Surrealism, see Kelley (2002, 157–94).

References

CARBY, Hazel. 2000. *Cultures of Babylon*. London: Verso.

CLARKE, Cheryl. 1995. "Lesbianism: An Act of Resistance." In Beverly Guy-Sheftall (ed.), *Words of Fire: An Anthology of African–American Feminist Thought*. New York: New Press, pp. 212–51.

DAVIS, Angela Y. 1998. *Blues Legacies and Black Feminism: Gertrude "Ma" Rainey, Bessie Smith, and Billie Holliday*. New York: Pantheon.

DAVIS, Peggy Cooper. 1997. *Neglected Stories: The Constitution and Family Values*. New York: Hill and Wang.

GILLIGAN, Carol. 2002. *The Birth of Pleasure: A New Map of Love*. New York: Alfred A. Knopf.

GUY-SHEFTALL, Beverly (ed.). 1995. *Words of Fire: An Anthology of African–American Feminist Thought*. New York: New Press.

JORDAN, June. 1995. "A New Politics of Sexuality." In Beverly Guy-Sheftall (ed.), *Words of Fire: An Anthology of African–American Feminist Thought*. New York: New Press, pp. 407–11.

KELLEY, Robin D. G. 2002. *Freedom Dreams: The Black Radical Imagination*. Boston: Beacon Press.

LORDE, Audrey. 1995. "Age, Race, Class, and Sex: Women Redefining Difference." In Beverly Guy-Sheftall (ed.), *Words of Fire: An Anthology of African–American Feminist Thought*. New York: New Press, pp. 283–92.

ROBINSON, Patricia and Black Sisters. 2000. "Poor Black Women." In Rosalyn Baxandall and Linda Gordan (eds), *Dear Sisters: Dispatches from the Women's Liberation Movement*. New York: Basic Books, p. 135.

———, Patricia Haden, and Donna Middleton. 1995. "A Historical and Critical Essay for Black Women." In Beverly Guy-Sheftall (ed.), *Words of Fire: An Anthology of African–American Feminist Thought*. New York: New Press, pp. 175–84.

SMITH, Barbara. 1999. *The Truth that Never Hurts: Writings on Race, Gender, and Freedom*. New York: Routledge.

Constitutional scholar David A. J. Richards, a student of resistance movements, has had a long intellectual friendship with Carol Gilligan. In The Deepening Darkness *(2008), Gilligan and Richards trace contemporary resistance to patriarchy to artists and thinkers of classical Rome (Augustine, Vergil, and Apuleius). Here, Richards explores the psychological and literary dimensions of political life that the Gilligan–Richards collaboration has illuminated. In doing so, he speaks to the tension between patriarchal conceptions of manhood and conceptions of democracy informed by relational feminist theory. Moreover, in a vertical drop to the personal, he gives special life to the interplay among love, scholarly and political work, and pleasure.*

Love, Manhood, and Democracy

DAVID A. J. RICHARDS

Carol Gilligan and I met some eight years ago, in 2002, when we began, with Jerome Bruner, to co-teach a seminar on gender issues in democratic societies at the New York University School of Law. Since that time, Gilligan and I have co-taught the seminar successfully in various one- and two-semester formats every academic year. We probably will continue, as I tell Gilligan, until death do us part. Our teaching collaboration drew its power and appeal for each of us from our discovery of a remarkably fruitful intersection of our research and writing interests. When we began to teach together, I had just finished and published my long study of various American resistance movements in *Women, Gays, and the Constitution*: *The Grounds for Feminism and Gay Rights in Culture and Law* (1998), and Gilligan was beginning work on *The Birth of Pleasure*: *A New Map of Love* (2002). Neither Gilligan nor I had previously known each other or each other's work. We were astonished at the complementarity of our interests, as we used my recently published book and Gilligan's past books, articles, and ongoing work on *The Birth of Pleasure* as the basis for our co-teaching. Gilligan discovered in my work a history of American social movements in which gender-subversive, resisting voices (explicit and implicit in all her work) were central to the recognition of basic human rights under American constitutional law. I found in Gilligan's work a personal and political psychology that clarified the motivations for these movements—the psychological grounds for resistance to deep structural injustices.

My training is in moral and political philosophy and law, and my books over the years had always been multidisciplinary, drawing not only on political philosophy and law but also, increasingly, on history. Conversations with Gilligan suggested to me that I needed to be even more multidisciplinary, not only taking on developmental psychology but also using works of art as a way of exploring and understanding what holds patriarchy in place and what motivates resistance to it. Conversations with Gilligan led to my writing three books, *Tragic Manhood and Democracy*: *Verdi's Voice and the Power of Musical Art* (2004), *The Case for Gay Rights: From* Bowers *to* Lawrence *and Beyond* (2005a), and *Disarming*

Manhood: Roots of Ethical Resistance (2005b), all of which I wrote for Gilligan's eye and ear and first presented in our seminar ("Gender Issues in the Culture and Psychology of Democratic Societies." New York University School of Law, New York, Spring 2002). Both the subject matter and the method of these works developed from the closer study of resistance movements in light of my collaborative discussions with Gilligan. In what follows, I describe how engagement with Gilligan's ideas deepened my understanding of the social movements described in *Women, Gays, and the Constitution* and the conceptions of manhood and democracy that I developed in the more recent work.

THE PSYCHOLOGY OF REPRESSION AND RESISTANCE

Women, Gays, and the Constitution developed multidisciplinary arguments of interpretive history, political philosophy, and law to explain the important impact on American constitutional law of four social movements: antebellum radical abolitionism (including abolitionist feminism), free-love feminism of the Gilded Age, second-wave feminism arising in the wake of the civil rights and anti-war movements of the 1960s, and the more recent gay and lesbian struggle for recognition under law of their basic human rights. Closer study of all these movements, collaboratively with Gilligan (as she worked on *The Birth of Pleasure*), led to a stunning recognition of a personal and political psychology that, at once, explained the impetus for resistance to structural injustice in all these movements and the forms of cultural and legal repression aggressively directed against them.

I start with the gendered psychology of repression, and then I turn to the psychology of resistance. My account of structural injustice, or "moral slavery" as I called it in *Women, Gays, and the Constitution*, had explained such evils as extreme religious intolerance (anti-Semitism), racism, sexism, and homophobia as resting on dehumanizing stereotypes that rationalized abridgement of the human rights of whole classes of persons—stereotypes that drew their power from the unjust repression of the voices that would reasonably challenge their dehumanizing assumptions. Gilligan's psychology of the differential development of voice in boys and girls (and men and women) made clear that the structural injustices I had described as "moral slavery" were held in place by the violent suppression of free and equal sexual voice. The radical abolitionists in the antebellum period saw this as they identified the atrocity of American slavery and its rationale—racism—in terms of its injury to African–American intimate life as the relations of family life (the relations of love between spouses, of parents and grandparents to children, of children to parents and to one another) were brutally disrupted to serve the economic exigencies of slave owners. The brilliance of Harriet Jacobs's slave narrative, *Incidents in the Life of a Slave Girl, Written by Herself* (1861), which Gilligan and I studied closely in our seminar, is its cogent description of how the racialized binary of pure, asexual, white wife-women and impure, sexual, black slave-women wreaked havoc on black intimate life, divided white and black women from one another, and precluded for men and women of both races anything like an honest relationship of equal sexual voice. Nineteenth-century abolitionist feminists extended this insight into a critique of both racism and sexism as resting on the perpetuation of mythological stereotypes that draw their power from the repression of resisting voices.

Gilligan's psychology explained that the power of these mythological stereotypes rests on the traumatic breaking of sexual voice in relationship. The strength of cultural taboos against expression of women's sexual voice was shown dramatically in the repressive forces directed against the free-love feminists of the Gilded Age (Victoria Woodhull, Emma Goldman, Margaret Sanger) who demanded, among other things, access to contraception as a means of controlling their relationships as lovers, wives, and parents. Second-wave feminism understandably takes up its stance on the grounds of an insistence on equal sexual voice and leads to the similar claims of gays and lesbians today to a sexual voice free from unjust gender stereotypes. And both movements are met by a repressive politics that centers on the repression of sexual voice: "Don't ask, don't tell" and movements for the constitutional prohibition, at the state and federal levels, of abortion and same-sex marriage. Gender hierarchy renders racism only more intractable, as the achievements of a nonviolent movement like that of Dr. Martin Luther King Jr. are shortly followed by a patriarchal appeal to male honor and violence.

The great power of Gilligan's developmental psychology is not only in explaining the forms of repression that support structural injustice but also in clarifying the psychology of resistance. The psychology of resistance is central to Gilligan's interpretation of Nathaniel Hawthorne's *The Scarlet Letter* (1850).[1] Hester Prynne has been criminally condemned by her Puritan community and forced to wear a scarlet *A* for committing adultery and having a child out of wedlock. Prynne refuses to identify the father as Arthur Dimmesdale, the Puritan minister, bearing her punishment and shame alone, a fact that infuriates Prynne's husband Roger Chillingworth when he returns to the community after several years' absence. Chillingworth determines to inflict psychological punishment on Dimmesdale when he correctly identifies the minister as the father of Prynne's beloved child Pearl. In a play based on the novel, Gilligan high-

lights Prynne's resistance to patriarchal demands and her desire for a free
sexual voice in a relationship to Dimmesdale, the man she loves despite
his inability to break social taboos and voice his love for her. Why, Gilligan
asks, does Hester resist when her resistance costs her so much? In light of
Gilligan's work, I increasingly raised the same questions about the people
in the social movements I had studied. Why, I asked myself, have the
women and men I describe in *Women, Gays, and the Constitution*—whose
claims were denigrated and opposed, even by homicidal terror—been willing to pay such a high price for resistance?

Resistance to this kind of repressive injustice is, for Gilligan, necessary
for the integrated health of our bodies and minds. Hester is healthy in a
way that Dimmesdale is not because she holds to the truth of a loving
sexual voice. Her resistance preserves a truth in relationship that she will
permit no one to break traumatically, not patriarchal man or patriarchal
God. Traumatic breaks in relationship have, Gilligan argues, been culturally rationalized as the nature of things, a tragic price required by a conception of democratic manhood and womanhood enraptured by tragic
stories of love. Like Prynne, members of the social movements I describe
have suffered the trauma of broken personal and social relationships.
They, too, demand a free and equal sexual voice and associations with
lovers and friends as a way of finding their way out of the dissociation this
trauma has imposed on them.

MANHOOD IN A PATRIARCHAL ORDER

Gilligan's work has demonstrated that women enjoy a developmental
advantage over men in terms of the psychology of resistance, because traumatic breaks in relationship come earlier for boys than girls, leaving intact
relational sources of psychic health in young women that are less intact in
young men. Some men, through their relationships to women, may, however, discover resources of resistance to patriarchal manhood not otherwise available, including forms of artistic voice that express what for men
would otherwise be unspeakable: the emotional desolation that patriarchy
inflicts on them.

This point was dramatically brought home to me when I reconsidered
Verdi's music dramas, which had long compelled and moved me. Early in
our collaboration, Gilligan and I went together to see Verdi's *Luisa Miller*
at the Metropolitan Opera. We both were moved to tears by its vision of
two tragically oppositional fathers, one patriarchal and the other democratic. My study of Verdi's music dramas in *Tragic Manhood and Democracy*
examines how one great artist came to this vision through his relationships

with women. The multidisciplinary method of *Tragic Manhood* triangulates a political theory of structural injustice resting on the suppression of voice, Gilligan's developmental psychology of gender, and an interpretive reading of musical drama. I attribute the contemporary appeal of opera in general and Verdi's operas in particular to the way it speaks to democratic culture about traumatic breaks in relationship resulting from patriarchy's armored definition of manhood. The marks of trauma are dissociation and loss of voice and memory. Tragic art in all its forms has been important to democratic cultures because it exposes truths that are otherwise unspeakable, and music has a special capacity to tap suppressed voices and memories.

The tragic impact of patriarchy on democratic voice is, in my analysis, the central subject of Verdi's work. At its core is a complex psychic geography of the impact of patriarchal practices on a range of personal and political relationships—parents to children, siblings to one another, and adult men to women. This geography speaks more truthfully about the perils of conventional manhood than the patriarchal pieties do about us. For Verdi, the code of honor was fundamental to family, politics, and religion. It demanded of men emotional distance, conformity to hierarchical order, and combat readiness. These demands were developmentally inscribed by traumatic separations that suppressed the voice of relationship by rejection of the feminine as a siren song of the relational and by identification with male stereotypes understood as the embodiment of honor. The tragedy of patriarchy of which Verdi's tragic musical drama speaks is, then, the tragedy of a divided psychology that lives in the tension between hierarchical practices and democratic principles of equality, interconnectedness, and mutual regard.

MANHOOD REDEFINED

Verdi's understanding of the psychology of patriarchy was a direct result of his empathy for and his relationships with women. *Disarming Manhood* explores how empathetic relationships with women explain the sometimes remarkable capacity of men who are moral and political leaders to resist the violence of patriarchal manhood. The inquiry arises within the context of our growing historical understanding of the linkages between violence, including war and terrorism and appeals to manhood (see Braude 2003). My interest is in countertraditions that arise from resistance to these linkages. More specifically, I am interested in how men acquire an ethical voice that challenges the instinct of an insulted patriarchal manhood directed to meet any challenge to its authority with brute force. I focus, in particular, on the thought and psychology of five notable men who resisted dominant conceptions of violent manhood. Four of them, William Lloyd Garrison, Leo Tolstoy, Mohandas Karamchand Gandhi, and Martin Luther King Jr., form a tradition of thought, each earlier figure influential on later figures. All of them found their ethical voice of resistance through advocacy of forms of nonviolence. But, the fifth man I study, Winston Churchill, found his voice in arguing that the dominant pacifism of Britain in the interwar period failed appropriately to resist and thus encouraged violent forms of totalitarian manhood. Nonetheless, on the same basis of thought and psychology as the others, Churchill recognized and called for resistance against fascist dictatorships in Italy and Germany, prophetically urging some measure of deterrent force before the violence escalated to the catastrophic levels of World War II. While some of these men famously disagreed (Churchill and Gandhi, for example, on the independence of India from British colonialism), they all shared something extraordinary among men of their periods: a capacity to understand and resist violent injustice and to mobilize and lead remarkably successful, and sometimes nonviolent, movements of public resistance.

I am gripped, as many contemporary men are, by admiration for these men. When so much in the conception of manhood about them pulled them in more conventionally violent directions, they not only resisted but also disarmed of the role violence traditionally played in a man's sense of vindicating insults to his honor, these men also spoke in a more truthful voice about injustice, and they experimented in new arts of voice and reasonable persuasion, including literature (Tolstoy) and interpretive history (Churchill). Their experiments encouraged—not just in themselves but in others (often women)—a new kind of personal and political imagination that empowered creative forms of moral and political agency (for example, public civil disobedience). In each case, the resistance of these great men arises in their associations and experiences with women, and for each the sharp psychological lines traditionally drawn between manhood and womanhood were blurred.

Tolstoy and Churchill are a fascinating contrast—the one a life of ascetism and tragedy, the other a life of pleasure and relationship. Both were aristocrats, and both were courageous young soldiers in the wars of their respective imperial states. Both found their voices in writing: Tolstoy in literature, Churchill in journalism and histories and in his remarkable speeches. The thought and psychology of both men arose in unusual relationships to women as mothers or maternal caretakers and as wives. Neither of them was too different in their attitudes toward the women in their lives: Tolstoy was tormented by an idealization of women that inspired his pacifism but also led to marital misery and celibacy. Churchill found his voice in an honest relationship with a mother with a vibrant sexual voice and life outside marriage and then found with a woman as complex as he a marriage of unusual happiness. No man in my study better understood the psychology of war or found a more compelling voice to resist it. We need a better understanding of the thought and psychology that enabled such remarkable insights.

As a result of my work with Gilligan, I have approached this work by combining biographic and literary analysis. I explore the development and impact of experiments in voice as they unfolded in the lives of these men, and I sometimes clarify my argument about voice in terms of relevant novels of Hawthorne, James Baldwin, Richard Wright, and Joseph Conrad. Moreover, the study of Tolstoy's novels was indispensable in exploring his psychic shifts and struggles. David Lodge has argued, in this connection, that the art of the novel offers an invaluable road into the complexities of human consciousness, one that students of human consciousness ignore at their peril (2002, 42–61). Gilligan's use of classical and postcolonial literature and my use of seminal works of fiction exploit the power of Lodge's insight.

RESISTANCE AND RELATIONSHIP

Having shown in *Disarming Manhood* that the psychology of resistance in men often arises from relationships to nonpatriarchal women, I turned in *The Case for Gay Rights* to the implications of this psychology for my own life. The book examines the post-World War II struggle for gay rights and its impact on American constitutional law and focuses on two cases, *Bowers v. Hardwick*[2] in 1986 (denying the protection of constitutional privacy to gays and lesbians) and *Lawrence v. Texas*[3] in 2003 (overruling *Bowers* on this point).

The Case for Gay Rights tells this history by combining the personal and political from my perspective as a constitutional scholar and a gay man whose arguments over a period of thirty years influenced these constitutional developments. Collaborative work with Gilligan enabled me to understand my own personal and political psychology of resistance. I found that my resisting voice as an advocate of gay rights was a way of making psychologically possible a long-term, loving relationship with another man of now some thirty years. Resistance and relationship are psychologically linked, an important truth in my own life that explains why working with Gilligan so riveted me. Gilligan gave me a psychology which made sense of this truth and grounded it in my relationship to my mother and father, who lived in a remarkably egalitarian, sexually loving relationship. Developing constitutional arguments for recognition of gay rights enabled me and others to find a truthful voice that resisted injustice. This voice carried appeals to philosophy, interpretive history, constitutional law, psychology, and literature, as a new voice required new methods and perspectives. As Gilligan's work shows, *Roe v. Wade*[4] gave resonance to resisting voices of women. In the same way, legal, political, and scholarly discourse about gay rights—and the Supreme Court's acceptance in 2003 of many of the arguments supporting the human rights of gay and lesbian people—gave resonance to my voice and made new relationships possible.

CONCLUSION

In all of my work with Gilligan, our working hypothesis has been that a free voice of resistance to patriarchal conceptions of gender arises in women and in the men who stay in loving relationship with such women. What I call "Gilligan's Law" is the principle that the inclusion of unjustly marginalized or suppressed voices into any discussion must change not only the discussion but also the frame of discussion. If we take free and equal voice seriously as a requirement of democracy, we must open our hearts and minds to new experiments in voice that better meet this demand. Working with Gilligan has led me not only to write in new ways but also to teach collaboratively in new ways, ways that have been remark-ably creative both for myself and for Gilligan and for our students. Our relationship is itself remarkable—between a long-married woman with three sons and a gay man in a long-term, loving relationship. We have found, through our rather miraculous love for one another, a common ground in the value we both place on free and equal, loving relationships as the center of what dignifies and gives enduring pleasure to a human life. It has been a great and continuing joy for me to recognize, through Gilligan's presence in my life as a close friend and collaborator, something I had never experienced before as a law professor: that collaborative law teaching may, through love, become and be a pleasure.

Notes

1 For Carol Gilligan's interpretation, see Gilligan (2002, 131–5).

2 478 U.S. 186 (1986).

3 539 U.S. 558 (2003).

4 410 U.S. 113 (1973).

References

BRAUDE, Leo. 2003. *From Chivalry to Terrorism*: *War and the Changing Nature of Masculinity*. New York: Alfred A. Knopf.

GILLIGAN, Carol. 2002. *The Birth of Pleasure*: *A New Map of Love*. New York: Alfred A. Knopf.

———, and David A. J. Richards. 2008. *The Deepening Darkness*: *Patriarchy, Resistance, and Democracy's Future*. Cambridge: Cambridge University Press.

HAWTHORNE, Nathaniel. 1850. *The Scarlet Letter*. Boston: Ticknor, Reed & Fields.

JACOBS, Harriet. 1861. *Incidents in the Life of a Slave Girl Written by Herself*. Boston: Published for the Author.

LODGE, David. 2002. *Consciousness and the Novel*: *Connected Essays*. Cambridge, MA: Harvard University Press.

RICHARDS, David A. J. 1998. *Women, Gays, and the Constitution*: *The Grounds for Feminism and Gay Rights in Culture and Law*. Chicago: University of Chicago Press.

———. 2004. *Tragic Manhood and Democracy*: *Verdi's Voice and the Power of Musical Art*. Portland, OR: Sussex Academic Press.

———.2005a. *The Case for Gay Rights*: *From* Bowers *to* Lawrence *and Beyond*. Lawrence, KS: University Press of Kansas.

———. 2005b. *Disarming Manhood*: *Roots of Ethical Resistance*. Athens, OH: Swallow Press.

The Fear of Reckless Pleasure

However constraining it may be—however bound to tragedy it may be—patriarchal order carries certain comforts, not the least of which is that it promises to control the passion we associate with love's pleasure. Uncontrolled passion seems a fearsome thing. It is therefore no surprise that when The Birth of Pleasure (2002) *champions pleasure and resistance to patriarchal order, it arouses anxiety. Ruby Blondell is the first contributor to confront the fearsomeness of Carol Gilligan's embrace of pleasure. Appropriately enough, she does so in an interpretation of the raging, fratricidal, infanticidal Medea as antipatriarch.*

Carol Gilligan has a longstanding interest in ancient Greek tragedy, as evidenced by her discussion of Euripides's Iphigeneia in *The Birth of Pleasure: A New Map of Love*. But a vastly different Euripidean heroine came constantly to my mind while I was reading her book: Medea, who plays the whore to Iphigeneia's Madonna with a vengeance. We certainly cannot expect of Euripides's Medea the same *kind* of affirmation of love and pleasure that Gilligan finds in the story of Psyche, if only because tragedy has a way of being, well, tragic. The reappropriation of this character and this play in the cause of "love and liberation" will therefore have a rather different coloring.

The myth of Medea is deeply implicated in the patriarchal script that Gilligan urges us to challenge. Medea is a sorceress from beyond the boundaries of the Greek world, a "barbarian," in Greek terms (Blondell et al. 1999, 220)[1] with supernatural family connections[2] who falls passionately in love with Jason, a Greek adventurer who has come to steal her father's precious Golden Fleece. She defies her father to run away with Jason, killing a number of people in the process, including her own brother (whom she chops into pieces and scatters in the sea) and Jason's wicked uncle (whom she arranges to have boiled alive by his daughters). After they reach safety, Jason dumps Medea in order to make a politically advantageous marriage with the (unnamed) daughter of the king of Corinth. Medea punishes him by murdering not only the king and princess but also their own two young sons. If ever there was a story where love led to loss, where pleasure was "Act 1 in a play that ends badly" (Gilligan 2002, 114), this is surely it.

Yet, Medea also embodies a triumphant repudiation of female silencing. Like Hester Prynne in Nathaniel Hawthorne's *The Scarlet Letter* (1850), she frees her sexuality and thus places herself "outside the iron framework" of her culture. She transgresses Athenian marriage norms by defying her father to follow her own desire, choosing her own husband, providing her own "dowry"—in the form of the Golden Fleece, which she helps Jason to steal from her father—and giving herself in marriage instead of being transferred by her father to a man he has chosen for her. According to classical Athenian norms, a woman belongs inside the house, silent and unseen. In Euripides's play, Medea's first words on stage are, "I have come out of the house."[3] She goes on to denounce in public, at passionate length, the subordinate place of women in marriage, including the sexual double standard that prohibits women, but not men, from acting on their own desire. However different she may seem—and be—from Psyche, she too "breaks taboos on seeing and speaking, . . . insists on having a voice and not becoming an object" (Gilligan 2002, 209). Medea's emphatic acknowledgment and assertion of her own identity remain a persistent feature of her story as retold by later authors and later tradition.[4]

On page after page of *The Birth of Pleasure*, as Gilligan identified the symptoms of dissociation, my reaction was, "But not Medea!" Those symptoms include "loss of voice, difficulty in seeing or saying what one knows, dizziness, a sense of dislocation or . . . not really living one's life" (2002, 161). Not Medea! She never loses touch with either her love for her children or her grief, with the passion she felt for Jason in the past or the hatred she feels for him now that he has betrayed her, or with her loss of joy (see Euripedes, *Medea*, line 227); in sum, she never loses touch with her sense of herself as a thinking, feeling agent (see Blondell et al. 1999, 152).[5] The act of child murder is so shocking that the *reader* or *audience* is often drawn to a dissociative interpretation of Medea's character that would make her actions easier to bear, or at least to comprehend. Thus my students often claim that Medea does not "really" love her children. But the text does not admit this interpretation. She dwells poignantly upon her love of, and pleasure in, her children, at the very moment when she is about to kill them with her own hands. Unlike Zoe, a painfully dissociated interview subject from Gilligan's study of marriages in crisis (2002, 205), Medea has not put her feelings of lost joy "into a box" but keeps them in the forefront of her awareness. Even at the end of the play, when the children are dead and the grief-stricken Jason protests, "it's your pain as well" (Euripedes, *Medea*, line 1361), she fully acknowledges that pain and embraces it because it has brought her revenge (ibid., lines 1361–62).

The contrast with Euripides's Iphigeneia is suggestive. When Iphigeneia first finds out that she is to be killed in her father's pre-battle offering to the gods, she is horrified and begs poignantly to be spared this dreadful fate; shortly afterwards, however, in a startling about-face, she decides to embrace her role as a sacrificial victim. According to Gilligan's analysis, Iphigeneia undergoes this change because she has now internalized the patriarchal script at the expense of her own instinctive desires. Medea, by contrast, deplores the status quo. But she is brilliant at *faking* the kind of dissociation that Gilligan sees dramatized in *Iphigeneia at Aulis*—at *performing* the "double consciousness" of women under patriarchy with absolute clarity, full knowledge, and purposefulness. When she confronts Jason for a second time she *pretends*—for her own nefarious purposes—that she too has internalized the patriarchal script. She begs his pardon for her earlier anger at his remarriage and chastises herself for her willfulness (Euripedes, *Medea*, lines 876–7), declaring, with delicious irony,

> So now I praise you and I think you're sensible
> to add this family tie. It's I who am the fool.
> I should have helped you make these plans. I should have helped
> fulfill them, and then stood beside the marriage-bed
> to tend your bride with pleasure. . . .
> (Ibid., lines 884–8.)

> So I give way, admitting my wrong-headedness
> back then; but now I've planned things in a better way.
> (Ibid., lines 892–3.)

Jason patronizingly accepts all this: he says he does not blame her for her previous anger, since women are naturally emotional creatures (ibid., lines 908–10), and he praises her for having now become "sensible" (ibid., line 913). You would think he would know better by now. But the power of the patriarchal script is such that he is duped with amazing ease.

As Jason's gullibility might suggest, dissociation, in this play, is *his* province and that of his new bride, the nameless princess. His marriage to Medea casts Jason as an unmanly man, one who has rejected conventional gender norms to take direction from a woman. Tragedy ensues when he thinks better of this transgressive arrangement and decides to settle down with the princess, the very embodiment of the "suitable" woman under patriarchy: young, beautiful, and submissive, a daddy's girl who is easily distracted by pretty clothing and who suppresses her own feelings at the admonition of her future husband (ibid., lines 1147–57)— a suppression that results directly in her own death. Jason too is dissociated from his feelings. He belittles the power and significance of erotic passion, which he views, disparagingly, as a female concern (ibid., lines 568–73). And he is strikingly dissociated from his own pleasure in his children, showing no personal distress at the thought of losing them to exile. It is only when he actually does lose them—to death, not exile—that he gives voice to his delight in them, dwelling especially on the lost pleasures of physical intimacy (ibid., lines 1399–1403).

It is Medea who forces upon Jason this recognition of his own pleasure in his children by the somewhat desperate expedient of killing them— which in his case seems to be what it takes. She also murders those who compose the conventional family structure to which he aspires—the princess and her father—and leaves him deprived of personal ties of any kind. Medea too is alone at the play's end. She has asserted her autonomy and freedom in the most monstrous fashion, at the cost of all her intimate relationships: with parents, siblings, husband, and children. Yet, she has already identified a new sexual partner in Aegeus and found a new home at Athens. And she remains the mistress of her own destiny. She is one of the very few transgressive characters in Greek myth who receives no external punishment for her deeds. In contrast with poor Iphigeneia, this woman, who remains connected to herself and her feelings, no matter how horrifying that self and those feelings may be, is a survivor.

Medea thus represents the terrible threat to patriarchy of the non-dissociated woman, triumphant in her power. Needless to say, however, the patriarchal script reasserts itself in no uncertain terms. Medea's defiance of patriarchy is destructive of herself as well as others. Gilligan describes Hamlet, Othello, Macbeth, and Lear as heroes "who resist patriarchy; their heroism lies in their resistance, the tragedy is that they are chewed up in the process" (2002, 215). Medea's tragedy is that when deprived of her relationship with Jason, she herself destroys the most intimate relationship left to her, the principal source of her own remaining pleasure. By doing so she also destroys, at least in Greek terms, her very identity as a woman (see Foley 2002, Section III, Part 5).[6] The price of female autonomy, self-awareness, and effective agency is, apparently, monstrosity.

Medea as monster is patriarchy's security blanket, its reassurance of the wisdom, and, indeed, the necessity of suppressing female self-expression and autonomous choice. I need only cite the immortal words of Pat Robertson, for whom feminism is "a socialist, anti-family political movement that encourages women to leave their husbands, kill their children, practice witchcraft, and become lesbians" (quoted in Cooper and Schwartz 1992).[7] This is the Medea of modern popular culture, invoked as an archetype whenever a real woman kills her children. The two most notorious of such killers in the United States in recent years have been Susan Smith, who drowned her two small sons in a lake, inside a car, in 1994 in Union, South Carolina, and Andrea Yates, who drowned her five children in a bathtub in Houston, Texas, in 2001, while suffering from postpartum psychosis. Both women—but Smith more frequently[8]—were repeatedly likened to Medea in news stories and popular accounts (Peyser 1995).[9] Although the mass media did not focus on specifics, Smith's story does offer some interesting points of comparison with Medea's. Like Medea, she was an accomplished liar, claiming that her children had been abducted and performing femininity in her efforts to escape arrest[10]; like Medea, her motivation involved a sexual partner (she was trying to snare a new boyfriend who was not so keen on children) (ibid., Chapter 3); even the impromptu shrine to the children that grew up around the place of their death eerily echoed Medea's myth.[11]

But the analogy also obscures crucial differences. Those whom Smith deceived included Smith herself, to judge from her repeated insistence that she killed her children for their own good—a mode of rationalization common in women who kill their children (Resnick 1969, 325–41; Peyser 1995, 172–3; Meyer and Oberman 2001, 26–7). Like Yates, Smith was a pitiful, powerless, and deluded criminal very different in character from Euripides's equally criminal but strong-willed, clear-sighted, and powerful protagonist. Such modern child-killers are typically seen as emotionally disturbed, and public debate centers on their mental competence (Meyer and Oberman 2001, 68–72). The mental state of Euripides's Medea has also been of great interest to scholars. She is by no means insane, however, but fully and consciously responsible for her actions. As she famously declares at the conclusion of the long monologue in which she finally decides to kill her children, "I understand the evil I'm about to do" (Euripedes, *Medea*, line 1078). She makes a purposeful, reasoned choice and acts on it (see Foley 2002, Section III, Part 5).[12]

Unlike Smith or Yates, however, Medea has no need of an insanity plea. She has a different kind of defense available to her—the defense made famous by Jessica Rabbit when she protested, "I'm not really bad: I'm just drawn that way!"[13] John Fisher, director of the huge hit *Medea: The Musical* (1994), is quoted as saying, "People love this woman killing kids. They get a big kick out of it. It's weird. Killing kids is not okay! Killing kids is never okay—but for some reason it's okay for Medea. It's an interesting audience phenomenon" (in Wren 2002, 24). Fisher is, of course, exaggerating in the context of his own treatment of Medea, a musical comedy that centers on the interpretation of Euripides's tragedy as a "gay-empowerment play" (see Foley 2004, 25, 108–10). In most productions, obviously, the infanticide is staged so as to shock and horrify the audience. Nevertheless, it is remarkable that Medea's story can succeed as comedy at all.[14] It is hard to imagine such a treatment of Smith arousing anything other than disgust.

The availability of Medea's infanticide for humorous treatment presumably has something to do with the fact that no real children were harmed in the making of this story. Audiences can focus on Medea as a figure of power and appreciate and celebrate her affirmation of her own identity without facing the grisly reality of a documentary record. Her mythic stature depends in part on a lack of specificity in her circumstances, an absence of connection to known events, a cultural distance that leaves her open to appropriation in innumerable ways. Since she is "just drawn that way," she can be redrawn, over and over again, without being measured against historically or culturally specific "facts," news reports, or court records. Medea's malleability emerges powerfully from a fictitious theater review which treats Smith's murder as an updated interpretation of Euripides's play:

> Clearly this Medea is one to whom American women can relate— self-deprecating, devoted, and loving, with a secret sadistic underside capable of unspeakable horrors. . . . The staging is also thoroughly updated. . . . The dragon-pulled chariot in which she escapes in the end to a "foreign land" is here replaced by the black-and-white squad car, shielding her from an avenging audience at an "undisclosed location."[15]

To report on a news story as if it were a theatrical performance is to underline the essential fact that theater places us in a different relationship with reality from any story that purports to be a straightforward report of "true facts." However pitiful Smith may have been, her behavior is under *no* circumstances "okay."

This does not mean, of course, that *Medea* may not serve to give voice to pressing contemporary concerns. Directors of the play often use real-life resonances to add point to their productions—and vice versa.[16] In the theater, as Gilligan puts it, "we can stay in the presence of emotions and thoughts that are otherwise unbearable. . . . [T]he power of the tragedies, their greatness, lies in allowing us to see the tragedy and also to see *beyond* it" (2002, 216; emphasis added). The theater allows the unspeakable to be spoken, and among the most unspeakable of modern taboos is the ambivalence of many mothers, and the rage and hostility of a few, toward their children—a rage engendered in the matrix of the patriarchal family far more often than society at large is willing to admit (Resnick 1969; Corti 1998, Chapter 1; Meyer and Oberman 2001). Medea has given an extraordinarily powerful voice to women's anger under patriarchy. Burlesque versions of her story foreshadowed the late Victorian New Woman (Macintosh 2000b), and Euripides's tragedy served as "one of the founding dramas" for the suffragists of the early twentieth century (Hall 1999, 44). Since the start of "second-wave" feminism, productions of this play—along with other Greek tragedies featuring powerful female protagonists—have proliferated and show no sign of abating. It is not, presumably, as a mere homily against child murder that *Medea* has become, at the dawn of the twenty-first century, the most frequently produced of all ancient Greek dramas.[17]

This is the second face of Medea in the modern world. Countless productions in recent years have used her story to comment on the victimization of women. And since she is not only female but also a foreigner and "barbarian," she can also stand for oppressed racial minorities and other victimized groups. As a female "barbarian" victim of aristocratic Greek male betrayal, she is the quintessential outsider (see Blondell et al. 1999, 152–4). As such, she has become a figure of the Other, an emblem of the disenfranchised and dispossessed, a vehicle for protest and self-assertion on behalf not only of women but also of all victims who have the misfortune to lack her supernatural powers and divine family connections. The productions and versions of Euripides's play that have mushroomed since the 1980s reflect the rise not only of contemporary feminism but of resistance to colonialism, racism, and homophobia (see Hall et al. 2000).[18]

Medea's availability as a figure of resistance gains a further dimension from the fact that she is perhaps the most "performative" of ancient female roles (Macintosh 2000a; Reynolds 2000). "She allows us, if only for the length of her performance, the freedom to perform ourselves—or rather the selves that we should be, if we were not bound by convention, by law, by order and decree" (Reynolds 2000, 140). Her self-conscious enactment of femininity has made her particularly appealing to drag performers.[19] In a period of just a few years in the 1990s, I attended no fewer than three drag productions of *Medea* in Seattle alone (Frederickson 2000).[20] The first and most memorable of these was put on by a Greek Active, a Seattle theater group specializing in subversive performances of classic dramas (Blondell et al. 1999, 154, 168).[21] Their show was enhanced by an exceptionally transgressive script involving BDSM, incest, and bondage purveyed in a campy and intentionally outrageous style, as well as a chorus of lip-synching drag queens performing disco numbers like "Don't Leave Me This Way." The drag performer adopts the notional "clothing" of masculinity and femininity and takes it at its word, using it to challenge the very hierarchies that engendered it (Gilligan 2002, 18; Garber 1992).[22] As overtly affirmative of patriarchal gender norms as Medea's story may appear on the Robertson reading, this production allowed Euripides's play to serve instead as a vehicle for the celebration of transgressive sexual minorities in a show that was simultaneously shocking, erotic, and hilarious.

Such stigmatized groups self-consciously appropriate the trappings of patriarchal hierarchies in order to enact and promote modes of pleasure, relationships, and erotic practices that are subversive of contemporary patriarchal structures. Similarly, Euripides's script may be appropriated by modern performers in ways that work to subvert the patriarchal matrix in which it was first written and produced. Such productions give new meaning to Medea's freeing of the erotic self and its violent consequences. In a very different way from Gilligan's psychotherapy clients, the Greek Active performers went "into the heart of tragedy in order to find a path that leads back to pleasure" (2002, 56). And pleasure of a different kind becomes a further instrument for their subversions: the pleasures of performance. The theater opens doors to modes of pleasure, as well as thought and imagination, to which the real life of Smith cannot give us access.

The famous opening words of Euripides's play—which are, in essence, "If only none of this had ever happened!"—frame it as a "what if" story in which, in Gilligan's words, "the tragedy. . . lies precisely in the vision . . . of how the story might have gone differently" (ibid., 125). As a drama of patriarchy, *Medea* presents its heroine as a problem to be prevented or contained. But we are not told how. It is in part because no single answer is given to this question that Medea remains open to constant (re)appropriation. If a woman must kill her children in order to affirm her autonomy and freedom, this may be read as an indictment not of female desires for freedom (the Robertson interpretation) but of a system that, in Gilligan's terms, pits freedom against love instead of conditioning the one upon the other. The degree to which Euripides's play, from the perspective of its own time and place, mounts a challenge to patriarchal structures is heavily contested by scholars (Blondell et al. 1999, 156–8). But it remains extraordinarily available to appropriation by those who would now mount such resistance.

The ancient Greek storytelling tradition is one of use, reuse, and (re)appropriation, usually with little, if any, regard for the context of previous tellings. We therefore honor that tradition when we, in our turn, transform their stories for our own ends. Accordingly, I would like to conclude with my own vision for a production of Euripides's play. This is *Medea! The Musical.* I am not talking about John Fisher's hit show. My version is quite different. The opening number would be the song alluded to in my title: "How do you solve a problem like Medea?" In the course of the play, Jason would take a trip down memory lane with the rhapsodic solo, "I just met a girl named Medea!" The play would conclude, as in Euripides's, with Medea taking off in the magic chariot bestowed upon her by her divine grandfather, the god Helios. But in my version, the assembled cast and chorus, and perhaps the audience as well, would join in singing an "Ave Medea." I like to think that this production would challenge us in a whole new way to come to terms with the bifurcated image of the whore and the Madonna.

Notes

1   The Greek word translated as "barbarian" (*barbaros*) denotes someone whose native language is not Greek. Unlike "barbarian," it does not

conjure up images of a crude cultural or material existence. The Greeks nonetheless viewed such foreigners as inferior to themselves (see Blondell et al. 1999, 22–3).

2 Her grandfather is the sun god Helios, and Circe, the famous sorceress of the Odyssey, is her aunt.

3 All translations of *Medea* are my own, from *Women on the Edge: Four Plays* (Blondell et al. 1999).

4 Famous example is the line, "*Medea fiam!*" ("I shall become Medea!") in Seneca's play (*Medea*, line 171).

5 She touches briefly on the idea that killing her children is for their own good (Euripedes, *Medea*, lines 1060–3). In her case, however, it has considerable justification, since it would be quite reasonable to expect the Corinthians to kill her children in revenge for the king and princess—as they in fact did, in other versions of the myth (see Blondell et al. 1999, 152).

6 In classical Greek cultural terms, motherhood was a woman's intrinsic purpose. Medea's decision to kill her children may be seen as a victory for "masculine" aspects of her character over "feminine" aspects (see Foley 2002).

7 This oft-cited quotation derives from an undated letter, signed by Pat Robertson, sent to Christian coalition members in Iowa in opposition to a proposed State Constitutional Amendment that would extend constitutional protections to women.

8 Suzanne O'Malley (2004) uses an epigraph purporting to be a quotation from Euripides's play.

9 An Internet search links Susan Smith with Medea 14,500 times to Andrea Yates's 397. (By way of comparison, a search for Smith alone yields 149,000 hits, whereas Andrea Yates alone yields 110,000.) (Searches were conducted on January 27, 2005.)

10 "Susan's eyes gazed downward during her first press conference. Wispy hair pinned into a childish ponytail, sleep-deprived eyes shielded by prescription glasses[,] . . . [s]he looked so young. So forlorn" (Peyser 1995, 52–3).

11 For the cult of Medea's children, see Sarah Iles Johnston (1997). For John D. Long Lake—where Smith killed her children—as a "shrine to the dead," see Andrea Peyser (1995, 180–3).

12 Both decisions and the monologue have been much discussed and variously interpreted. For my own view of the contested lines 1078–80, see Blondell et al. (1999, 428n130). I agree with Helene P. Foley on the essential point that the infanticide is driven by rational judgment as well as emotion (see Foley 2002).

13 This remark, from the 1988 film *Who Framed Roger Rabbit?* gains its points from the fact that the film involves cartoon characters interacting with live actors.

14 For other comic versions, see Lillian Corti (1998).

15 *The Stranger*, 15 November, 1994 (a spoof item in the Theater section).

16 For productions of Euripides's play inspired by Smith and Yates, see Alan Dye (2002). In a play produced in Seattle in 2004 (*Dubya 2000: A Political Horror*), Smith's story was "retold as Medea and transplanted from South Carolina to Georgia so that it could take place in Athens" (Fetzer 2004).

17 The number of productions worldwide since the Renaissance of the five most frequently performed ancient Greek tragedies are: *Medea*, 777; *Agamemnon*, 761; *Antigone*, 742; *Oedipus the King*, 670; *Trojan Women*, 337. These figures, derived from Oxford University's Archive of Performances of Greek and Roman Drama (2010), are current as of January 2005 but, of course, are constantly changing as new evidence is discovered.

18 For twentieth-century productions and versions of *Medea*, many of which concern themselves with Medea as Other, see Hall et al. (2000). For more details on specific productions, see McDonald (1997), Corti (1998, Chapter 6), Hazel (1999, 259–77), McDonagh (2002), Smethurst (2002), Wetmore (2002), and Wren (2002, 22–6, 60–1)

19 Cross-dressing in theater can take various forms, not all of which are to be categorized as drag (for example, the original Greek performance by male actors). For various kinds of cross-dressed Medea, see Corti (1998, 187–9), Hall (1999, 58–60), Macintosh (2000b, 83–4), and Foley (2004, 89–103).

20 *Medea: the Musical* (which has drag elements) opened June 16, 2000. By sheer coincidence, another remarkably similar show opened in Seattle on the same day (Frederickson 2000).

21 Medea was played by Mark Mitchell. The show was directed by Keenan Hollahan (Dan Savage). It is reviewed by Sue-Ellen Case in *Theater Journal* (1993). For further details, see Blondell et al. (1999, 154, 168).

22 On cross-dressing, see Marjorie Garber (1992).

References

BLONDELL Ruby, Mary-Kay Gamel, Nancy Sorkin Rabinowitz, and Bella Vivante (eds and trans.). 1999. *Women on the Edge: Four Plays By Euripedes*. New York: Routledge.

CASE, Sue-Ellen. 1993. "Medea. By Euripides." *Theatre Journal* 45: 246–9.

CORTI, Lillian. 1998. *The Myth of Medea and the Murder of Children*. Westport, CT: Greenwood Press.

COOPER, Kenneth J., and Marless Schwartz. 1992. "Equal Rights Initiative in Iowa Attacked." *Washington Post*. 23 August.

DYE, Alan. 2002. "CSUH Director Brings Modern Vision to 'Medea.'" *The Pioneer*. 10 October.

FETZER, Bret. 2004. "On Stage," *The Stranger*, 14 October. Available at: www.thestranger.com/seattle/on-stage/Content?oid=19588 (last accessed on October 13, 2010).

FOLEY, Helene P. 2002. *Female Acts in Greek Tragedy*. Princeton, NJ: Princeton University Press.

———. 2004. "Bad Women: Gender Politics in Twentieth-Century Performance and Revision of Greek Tragedy." In Edith Hall, Fiona Macintosh, and Amanda Wrigley (eds), *Dionysus Since 69: Greek Tragedy at the Dawn of the Third Millennium*. New York: Oxford University Press, pp. 77–111.

FREDERICKSON, Eric. 2000. "The Gay Medea Challenge," *The Stranger*, 20 April. Available at: www.thestranger.com/2000-0420/culture_war.html (last accessed on January 3, 2006).

GARBER, Marjorie. 1992. *Vested Interests: Cross-Dressing and Cultural Anxiety*. New York: Routledge.

GILLIGAN, Carol. 2002. *The Birth of Pleasure: A New Map of Love*. New York: Alfred A. Knopf.

HALL, Edith. 1999. "Medea and British Legislation Before the First World War." *Greece and Rome* 46: 42–77.

———, Fiona Macintosh, and Oliver Taplin (eds), 2000. *Medea in Performance 1500–2000*. Oxford: Legenda.

HAWTHORNE, Nathaniel. 1850. *The Scarlet Letter*. Boston: Ticknor, Reed & Fields.

HAZEL, Ruth. 1999. "Unsuitable for Women and Children? Greek Tragedies in Modern British Theaters." In Eric Csapo, John Porter, C. W. Marshall, and Robert C. Ketterer (eds), *Crossing the Stages: The Production and Reception of Greek Theater*. Iowa City: Iowa University Press, pp. 259–77.

JOHNSTON, Sarah Iles. 1997. "Corinthian Medea and the Cult of Hera Akraia." In James J. Clauss and Sarah Iles Johnston (eds), *Medea: Essays on Medea in Myth, Literature, Philosophy and Art*. Princeton, NJ: Princeton University Press, pp. 44–70.

MACINTOSH, Fiona. 2000a. "Introduction: The Performer in Performance." In Edith Hall, Fiona Macintosh, and Oliver Taplin (eds), *Medea in Performance 1500–2000*. Oxford: Legenda, pp. 1–31.

————. 2000b. "Medea Transposed: Burlesque and Gender on the Mid-Victorian Stage." In Edith Hall, Fiona Macintosh, and Oliver Taplin (eds), *Medea in Performance 1500–2000*. Oxford: Legenda, pp. 75–99.

McDONAGH, John. 2002. "Is Medea's Crime Medea's Glory? Euripides in Dublin." In Marianne McDonald and J. Michael Walton (eds), *Amid Our Troubles: Irish Versions of Greek Tragedy*. London: Methuen, pp. 213–31.

McDONALD, Marianne. 1997. "Medea as Politician and Diva: Riding the Dragon into the Future." In James J. Clauss and Sarah Iles Johnston (eds), *Medea: Essays on Medea in Myth, Literature, Philosophy and Art*. Princeton, NJ: Princeton University Press, pp. 297–323.

MEYER, Cheryl L. and Michelle Oberman. 2001. *Mothers Who Kill Their Children: Understanding the Acts of Moms from Susan Smith to the "Prom Mom."* New York: New York University Press.

O'MALLEY, Suzanne. 2004. *Are You There Alone? The Unspeakable Crime of Andrea Yates*. New York: Simon and Schuster.

OXFORD UNIVERSITY, Archive of Performances of Greek and Roman Drama. 2010. "Database." Last modified January 10, 2010. Available at: www.apgrd.ox.ac.uk/database.htm

PEYSER, Andrea. 1995. *Mother Love, Deadly Love: The Susan Smith Murders*. New York: Harper Collins.

RESNICK, Phillip J. 1969. "Child Murder by Parents: A Psychiatric Review of Filicide." *American Journal of Psychiatry* 126: 325–34.

REYNOLDS, Margaret. 2000. "Performing Medea or, Why is Medea a Woman?" In Edith Hall, Fiona Macintosh, and Oliver Taplin (eds), *Medea in Performance 1500–2000*. Oxford: Legenda, pp. 119–43.

SMETHURST, Mae. 2002. "Ninagawa's Production of Euripides." *Medea American Journal of Philology* 123: 1–34.

WETMORE, Kevin J. Jr. 2002. *The Athenian Sun in an African Sky*. Jefferson, NC: McFarland.

WREN, Celia. 2002. "In Medea Res: An Ancient Greek Femme Fatale is the American Theatre's Passion of the Moment." *American Theatre* 19 (April): 22–6, 60–1.

Carol Gilligan suggests in The Birth of Pleasure *(2002) that the expression of authentic desire will have positive relational and therapeutic effects. In response, Simon Goldhill revives the ancient Greek warnings: the search for authenticity is doomed to end in self-deception, and desire is a signal of danger.*

Tragedy and Pleasure[1]
SIMON GOLDHILL

Ancient tragedy, as Aristotle would have us believe, provides cautionary lessons for the citizen faced by the perils of practical reasoning, and it is part of the philosopher's wonderment at the genre that its narratives of desire and dark consequences can bring "some sort of pleasure." Tragedy frames the space of Carol Gilligan's study in *The Birth of Pleasure*: *A New Map of Love*, and, like the didactic tragedies of antiquity, Gilligan's work bears a dark lesson that needs to be heard.

It would, of course, be impossible to tell the story of the psyche without taking a tragic turn. For Sigmund Freud, Oedipus is *the* tragic narrative that lurks inside every human being, and Freud himself, obsessed with Oedipus, seems to have constantly nagged away at Nietzsche's worry in *Beyond Good and Evil* (1967): "Which of us is Oedipus here? Who the Sphinx? It is a rendezvous, it seems, of questions and question marks."[2]

It has also seemed impossible to tell stories of love without tragedy. The long line of ancient Greek and Latin love stories, which Gilligan examines in *The Birth of Pleasure*, is everywhere veined with recollections of the great cultural edifice of fifth-century Athenian tragedy. When Jason seduces the young Medea in Apollonius's *Argonautica*—the text that was in turn the paradigm for Virgil's Dido and Aeneas—the grim joke is that we are inevitably watching him seduce his way into the tragedy of (Euripides's) *Medea*.[3] Love is inexpressible in Greek without loss. Love poetry is the anatomy of failure and hope, humiliation, and fantasy.[4] When the lovers of the Greek novel finally come together for bliss, the narrative has to end.[5] Our amusement and pleasure at the sexy and sophisticated love story can never lose its black undertow.

It is that undertow that I want to discuss, and if it seems ungracious to recall despair and misery and destruction in response to so whole-hearted a commitment to *The Birth of Pleasure*, it seems to me that both the story of Psyche and the "Regions of Light"—the signs of resistance that Gilligan finds in her research, in literature, and in her own past—do turn to face the shadows and darkness on which they are grounded. The reason given by the Talmud for why you smash a glass at a Jewish wedding is that you *should* always remember destruction at the moment of joy. This seems a particularly apt symbol for an author who explores marital crisis and the possibility of its resolution in a therapeutic process. To maintain joy in marriage, we have to face tragedy—to see what marriage must smash and what smashes from the start.

The story of Sonya and Phil, one of the couples for whom Gilligan served as co-therapist in the course of her research for *The Birth of Pleasure*, stands as an embodiment of the contemporary love story, both in its leaning toward tragic destruction and in its hope for the courage to open one's heart and express love despite the strictures of patriarchy. Indeed, Gilligan concludes her story of Sonya and Phil with these words: "Perhaps it is necessary to go into the heart of tragedy in order to find a path that leads back to pleasure" (2002, 54). But to see what lies in the heart of tragedy is surely to doubt one's ability to seize and hold pleasure.

Gilligan does not shrink from the notion that the path to pleasure can be found at the heart of tragedy. The muse of tragedy is present at *The Birth of Pleasure* in three ways: in the speaking of desire, in the quest for knowledge and control, and in the race against time.

THE DANGER OF SPEAKING DESIRE

It is one of the themes of Gilligan's work that the failure to express desire and the silencing of love form a self-destructive strategy, which can be rectified by self-knowledge through therapy. Much of the work in Phil and Sonya's therapy sessions has been taken up with questions and recriminations about Sonya's relationship with another man. Yet, when Phil finally gets to articulate what his ultimate nightmare is, it is "to never have the opportunity to show her how I really feel and to be a family man, to open my heart and to love her."[6] Gilligan comments, "The simplicity of this moment is exquisite. Phil's open-hearted expression of desire. And for a moment, history falls away." As the investigation proceeds, Phil is reduced to tears by the pressing of the therapist: " 'I think the real question is, will you leave me?' Phil begins to cry." And so out of his pain the choice is constructed for Phil: Will he fight to "defend his honor" (and thus lose his wife)? Or will he have "the courage to open his heart and express his desire"? It is clear which is the advisable route.

Reading the story of Phil and Sonya, I was immediately drawn to think of Deianeira in Sophocles's *Women of Trachis*. She is the wife of Heracles. She is sitting at home while he is off doing the labor and being a hero. He visits her, she says, like a farmer does his outlying fields—to sow and to reap. This normatively laden image of a man's role is precisely prophetic, as impregnating and destroying are what Heracles is best at.

Deianeira would like to be Penelope waiting for Odysseus: the faithful wife whose fame is established by virtue of her maintenance of her house against the threats of external and internal lures of transgression. And so she is. So she is until it is reported that Heracles is coming home with a fresh, young girl to be his bedmate. Deianeira desires her husband and wants to win him back, needs to express her love, and so she sends him a robe smeared with a love philter. Unfortunately, the love philter turns out to be a terrible poison, and Heracles dies in agonizing pain. Deianeira kills herself by stabbing—penetrating—herself on the wedding bed. Deianeira and Heracles never meet in the play: the image of marriage is of two figures who have no contact except through the sending of false gifts and misleading messages across the gap of their distance, linked only by their self-destructive misunderstandings. However nobly intended, it is the expression of desire that stimulates destruction and tragedy.

Desire is imaged as a violent, destructive, painful, and profoundly antisocial force. The play opposes the wild world of the beasts and monsters, where Heracles is the heroic and triumphant figure, to the domestic and feminine world, where Deianeira is waiting. But desire runs through both. Desire is the beast within, the inevitable presence of anti-civilization *within* civilization. And it is the very articulation of desire which releases what the chorus calls "the terrible power of Aphrodite."[7]

Phaedra in Euripides's *Hippolytus* is tugged into the depths by the utterance of a mere syllable. When she is wracked by desire for her own stepson, she decides to remain silent and starve herself to death. Her nurse, desperate to save her, prompts and goads but cannot find the root of her problem. It is only when the nurse mentions the name "Hippolytus" that Phaedra breaks. "Oh," she says (*oimoi*), merely. "That touches you?" asks the nurse, and from this point onward the descent into violence, mutual accusation, and the play's horrific conclusion is made to seem inevitable. The play is obsessed with speech and silence: whether you speak up or remain silent or struggle to intimate through the veils of language, each strategy has its own exquisite pattern of disaster. To speak desire in this world is to open a vista of pain and impending doom.[8]

Now, Freud and a century of feminism have made it painfully clear that the repression or misrecognition of female desire is a constant and damaging injunction of patriarchy. And feminist-inspired classical scholarship has analyzed how the ancient Greek city constructs desire in a particular, culturally specific way, a way which works to silence or stigmatize any expression of specifically female desire.[9] As in Victorian society, the ancient Greek "good woman" does not express sexual desire, and the woman who does express sexual desire is a danger or a corruption or both. The threat of Deianeira or Phaedra speaking out is certainly to be construed within those parameters, what Gilligan calls "traps of the old forms of womanhood" (2002, 153).

So "What's Deianeira to us?" might seem like a fair question. But what Deianeira's or Phaedra's stories tell us is not just a historical curiosity in the ongoing struggle against the strictures of the patriarchal system. Rather, these stories provoke a double question, a double question from tragedy to therapy: what would it be like to imagine that speaking desire *could* come without the veils and misreadings of self-expression? And what would it be like to imagine that speaking desire *could* come without destructiveness? Or to put the tragic question most bluntly, can we imagine desire without a measure of civilizing discontent? "The unalloyed voice is a contradiction in terms," writes Adam Phillips (1994, 137), and this is nowhere more true than when desire is being voiced.

In the analysis of Oedipus in *The Birth of Pleasure*, as in the work of Jonathan Lear, "knowingness" appears as a bar to "feeling." Yet "knowingness," the insider trading of knowledge, is also part and parcel of the self-aware exploration of the desiring self, unless we hypostatize in a rather worrying way. To say "it's how I feel" in tragedy is always the prelude to the enactment of desire's destructiveness. Self-awareness requires an admixture of knowingness as well as knowledge—unless we think love stories can and should be told without irony, jokes, or self-observation. Unless we believe in the "unalloyed voice." "Learning to speak one's desire" or "to express one's love," as an aim, needs to recognize both the destructiveness of desire and the irony and knowingness of self-expression if it is not to lose the "heart of tragedy" which grounds the search for the region of light. When Gilligan writes, "the simplicity of this moment is exquisite. Phil's open-hearted expression of desire," we must be very careful not to imagine that the moment is actually less than a highly complex, layered, and painful event. When she writes, "[a]nd for a moment, history falls away," tragedy, we should remember, shows again and again how hard it is for history ever to fall away: the dark undertow of the past is always pulling its victims into a hidden narrative.

The first provocation from tragedy, then, is the insistent recognition that speaking out is quite as dangerous for the self and for society as having an ox on your tongue.[10]

THE IMPOSSIBILITY OF KNOWLEDGE AND CONTROL

The second stimulus of tragedy concerns control—narrative control. The heady mixture of novels, poems, case histories, and life story that Gilligan so wonderfully puts together revolves around the lure of narrative and getting control over narrative. Of being mistress of your own story. Of having the therapist help find out how to retell the story. But tragedy again and again exposes this control as a besotting human fantasy. *Oedipus the King* ends with an extraordinary scene: The first words of the play are Oedipus's address to the citizens: "My children. . . ." The last words he speaks are to Creon, the new regent whom he had accused of treachery: "Do not take my children from me." The play traces not just the loss of his children but also the loss of the very possibility of such simple familial vocabulary, as incest undoes the categories of self-definition. But Creon does take away the children of Oedipus and offers these final lines of the play: "Do not seek control in all things. For the things you controlled did not follow you in life." At one level, this is brilliantly apt. As king, father, riddle-solver, Oedipus has been a figure of apparent control, whose every move has turned out to be overdetermined and multidetermined. When he solves the riddle of the Sphinx and thus saves the city, he is also self-destructively heading into his mother's bed and polluting the city. When he hears the oracle at Delphi, every step he takes to avoid the oracle's prophecy fulfills it. The play explicitly etymologizes the name "Oedipus" (*Oidipous*) as "Swollen Foot" (*oid-pous*), but the text also offers the punning etymology *oida pou*, "I know where"—and the one thing Oedipus never knows—but always signifies—is where he is from and where he is going.[11]

At another level, Creon's remark is even more telling, however. For, Creon is himself, at this moment, taking control. He wants to have the last word. He is the regent who is taking charge of the city and organizing things. *His* control—as he talks of Oedipus's lack of control—is being set up, framed as destined for a fall. And the story of Antigone to come signals all too clearly what a fantasy his sense of control is.

I don't know any reader of the *Oedipus the King* who has not wondered, as Gilligan does, why the hyper-intelligent Oedipus does not appear to notice the "coincidence" that Jocasta was given an oracle that predicted her son would marry her, and that he was given an oracle that predicted he would marry his mother—and put two and two together. How come he doesn't ask why his feet were maimed? Why doesn't he just look down? Why, after an oracle like that, didn't he just avoid killing anyone or sleeping with anyone older than himself? It is easy enough to ask those questions of Oedipus. What the play shows, however, is how hard it is for anyone to ask the right questions in their *own* lives. When you think you have solved the riddle, is it leading you to disaster? When you reach the crossroads, do you know which road you are following?

The most shocking drama in the Oedipus saga is not that we have to watch a man come to the recognition that he has killed his father and slept with his mother, brutal and painful though that must be. What is most shocking is the play's insistent and disturbing claim that it is exactly at the moment that you think you know where you come from and who you are that you are most open to a tragedy of self-deception.

The narrative of therapy is a narrative of a journey toward fulfillment, toward a story of control. Oedipus should stall every reader with a recognition that it is exactly when you think you are in place on the road and know where you are going that you are least likely to be in control of your own narrative. That is the humbling terror of tragedy. The undertow that drags you. As Aeschylus's Athena puts it:

> The person who suffers the Furies' onslaught
> Does not know where the blows of life come from,
> The transgressions of the family past drag him,
> And silent doom wastes him in hating anger,
> However loud he shouts

(Aeschylus, *Eumenides*, lines 932–7).

That is Aeschylus's tragic vision of man's lot in what is the *most* celebratory conclusion of a tragedy. It is a vision of each of us, ignorant of where the disasters of life come from, dragged into the depths by a family past and, for all our protestations and talking, wasted by a doom that explains nothing. It is an image profoundly at odds with the enlightenment ideals of modern therapeutic disciplines.

The talking cure may have a root in tragedy, but tragedy keeps posing it a question. "We know the way" are the last words of Gilligan's book: we could translate that as *oid' hodous*, another pun on the name of *Oidipous* culled from the text of *Oedipus the King* (Goldhill 1986, 218), the play which says that "knowing the way" is always leading you somewhere else.

THE TRAP OF TIME

Coming to knowledge is a central element of tragedy and of the therapeutic model. It is a connection that Freud made explicitly when he took Oedipus as a privileged model for psychoanalysis. The keynote of this theme in Sophoclean tragedy is the phrase—again from the *Women of Trachis*—*opse ekdidachtheis*: "I learnt in full all too late" (Sophocles, line 934). In tragedy, it is only after the event that knowledge gradually becomes clear—and it is always too late. Creon can only run to the tomb to find his son over the dead body of Antigone. And even then, even after the revelation, as Oedipus shows, knowledge can be blinding.

The consequences of knowing continue. Hegel strove to catch something of this with his shocking phrase *der Frevel des Wissens*, "the crime, the transgression of knowing." One of the questions Gilligan asks of Zoe, a patient who actually studies knowing, is how she knows she is in love with Sam and that he is in love with her. "In the way that you are absolutely certain about things. I knew," she replies. I find this a fully tragic response. It is tragic because, as Cassandra dramatizes, absolute certainty does not give the desired control over things at all, even though lack of knowing produces a lack of control. It is tragic because, as every human being in tragedy who presumes certain knowledge shows, misery is a consequence of acting on what is all too often misplaced certainty. But most of all, it is tragic because of what it says about the *moment* of knowledge. The moment of knowledge is always still part of an ongoing narrative and has consequence—it has *moment*, moment in the sense of weight, impact. There is a tension between knowledge as unending process—knowing— and knowledge as instant of recognition and possession. The space of that tension is where the wild things play: self-deception, risk, folly, self-interest, misrecognition—*der Frevel des Wissens*. That this is an inevitable part of the human is one legacy from tragedy to psychoanalysis.

Tragedy's black undertow threatens always to drag the optimism of therapy back into the shadows of misery. Tragedy's narratives show the danger of speaking desire, the failure of control over narrative, and the self-deceptions of the moment of recognition. And suggest that they are inevitable. Yet I do not wish to end this piece on such a note, which would be to miss the impact and responsibility of Carol Gilligan's work. While I was reading *The Birth of Pleasure*, a student of mine came to show me a piece of work that she was only just beginning to appreciate with pleasure. It was a school project she had written when she was seven, and now, after our study together on women's voices, which included Carol Gilligan's work, she wanted to share it with me. Her task had been to tell the story of Odysseus and the Cyclops and how Odysseus, blocked in the monster's cave, uses the false name "Noman" to trick his way out. My student, Jessie, at seven, wasn't wholly sure of her letters, and one letter had gotten turned round a bit. So when her fierce Cyclops demanded, "Stranger, tell me your name," Odysseus replied not "Noman," but "Woman". You can play through the rest of the epic for yourself. It works rather well. The whole story, though, for me was telling of how much I had benefited from Carol Gilligan's work and how much teaching about voice was also learning from her. I am not sure that the exchange would have happened, or that either my student or I would have understood and laughed quite so pleasurably without Gilligan's inspiration. Despite tragedy and all those lives in (Greek) ruins, perhaps there is hope . . .

Notes

1　This paper was written to be delivered at the conference to mark the launch of *The Birth of Pleasure*. I have regretfully removed most of the jokes in a probably foolish attempt to preserve the dignities of academic publication. Thanks are due, however, for the invitation and especially to Carol Gilligan for what was an occasion full of smiles.

2　On Sigmund Freud and Oedipus, see Peter L. Rudnytsky (1987).

3　For Apollonius's seduction scene, see Simon Goldhill (1991, 284–333, especially 301–06).

4　See Anne Carson (1986) and any of her poetry, and more prosaically Charles Calame (1999).

5　On the erotic novel in this light, see Goldhill (1995) and the more optimistic David Konstan (1994).

6　The following quotations from this case study are taken from Gilligan (2002, 51–4).

7　On the *Women of Trachis* (Trachiniae), see Charles Segal (1981, 60–108).

8　On Hippolytus, see Bernard Knox (1952, 1–31), Goldhill (1986, 117–37), and Barbara Goff (1990).

9　For a selective but exemplary sample, see Page du Bois (1988), Froma I. Zeitlin (1996), Victoria Wohl (1997), Helen King (1998), and Helene P. Foley (2001).

10　From the Latin *Bovem in lingua habet*, having an "ox on one's tongue" refers to speech that is either suppressed or false due to bribery. Ancient Greek coins frequently donned the image of an ox.

11　For these puns, see Goldhill (1986, 199–221).

References

CALAME, Charles. 1999. *The Poetics of Eros in Ancient Greece*. Translated by Janet Lloyd. Princeton, NJ: Princeton University Press.

CARSON, Anne. 1986. *Eros the Bittersweet*. Princeton, NJ: Princeton University Press.

DU BOIS, Page. 1988. *Sowing the Body: Psychoanalysis and Ancient Representations of Women*. Chicago: University of Chicago Press.

FOLEY, Helene P. 2001. *Female Acts in Greek Tragedy*. Princeton, NJ: Princeton University Press.

GILLIGAN, Carol. 2002. *The Birth of Pleasure: A New Map of Love*. New York: Alfred A. Knopf.

GOFF, Barbara. 1990. *The Noose of Words: Readings of Desire, Violence and Language in Euripides' Hippolytus*. Cambridge: Cambridge University Press.

GOLDHILL, Simon. 1986. *Reading Greek Tragedy*. Cambridge: Cambridge University Press.

———. 1991. *The Poet's Voice*. Cambridge: Cambridge University Press.

———. 1995. *Foucault's Virginity: Ancient Erotic Fiction and the History of Sexuality*. Cambridge: Cambridge University Press.

KING, Helen. 1998. *Hippocrates' Woman: Reading the Female Body in Ancient Greece*. London: Routledge.

KNOX, Bernard. 1952. "The Hippolytus of Euripides." *Yale Classical Studies* 13: 3–31.

KONSTAN, David. 1994. *Sexual Symmetry: Love in the Ancient Novel and Related Genres*. Princeton, NJ: Princeton University Press.

NIETZSCHE, Friedrich. 1967. *Beyond Good and Evil*. Translated by Helen Zimmern. London: Allen and Unwin.

PHILLIPS, Adam. 1994. *On Flirtation*. Cambridge, MA: Harvard University Press.

RUDNYTSKY, Peter L. 1987. *Freud and Oedipus*. New York: Columbia University Press.

SEGAL, Charles. 1981. *Tragedy and Civilization*. Cambridge, MA: Harvard University Press.

WOHL, Victoria. 1997. *Intimate Commerce*. Austin: University of Texas Press.

ZEITLIN, Froma I. 1996. *Playing the Other: Gender and Society in Classical Greek Literature*. Chicago: University of Chicago Press.

Odes to Pleasure

In The Birth of Pleasure (2002), *Carol Gilligan mines literary texts for clues about the psyche. Great writers, she argues, are keen observers of the psychic world. Great literature reveals a culture's coming-of-age stories, the ruts in its developmental paths. And great literature reveals human resistance to a culture's settled stories. Sophocles chronicles a life of fear and blindness that speaks resoundingly of maturation as repression and fearful restraint. Apuleius tells a love story propelled by open-eyed determination—a refusal to close one's eyes to desire.*

Just as Gilligan turned to literary texts for keys to the psyche, some of our contributors used literary forms to express the resonance of her message of resistance. In this spirit, Patricia Foster spins an autobiographical narrative of the progression from fear to desire.

Legacy
PATRICIA FOSTER

1

The wind howls, screeches in our ears as my husband and I load his baggage into the trunk and begin the journey to the airport in Marseille. We've been given directions, but the night—cloaked in blackness, shrouded in mist—is certain to trick us, trapping us in our ignorance. Strangeness looms inside the car as well as out. It shadows us as we drive in silence from our fishing village of Carnon, both of us worried about what the next five months will bring. In twenty years of marriage we've never lived apart, and now my husband will return to his job and our house in America while I teach at Paul Valéry University in Montpellier, France.

As we speed out of Carnon, past the broken phone booth and empty boulangerie, I watch the surf pitch against the rocks, ruffles of foam leaping wildly in the air. For the first time in twelve days such beauty seems foreboding, lonely. What, I wonder, will happen to me here? How, really, will I cope? But beneath that is a deeper, darker question: What will happen to love?

As we drive, I glance at my husband's profile, noticing his furrowed brow, his tense posture, but also the drift of his hand as he occasionally pats my thigh. For most of our lives, we've seen ourselves as orphans, outcasts, two people living outside the frame of our families' lives. In our early life together we believed we'd create ritual and meaning through art-making and writing, believed that art—sacred, glorious—would be a religion of rescue and escape. We were, in many ways, each other's mirror: rebellious, insecure, playful, and idealistic, believing, as most couples do, that we'd never repeat the mistakes of our pasts, never abandon either art or love. Now I'm the defector, the adventurer, the one pulling away. I've arranged to teach in France, and though we originally planned to be here together, our finances sabotaged that tidy tale. Still, I persisted. Some part of me wanted independence. And now I'd have it, wouldn't I?

Despite getting lost on Highway A-9 and feeling inadequate (to our embarrassment, neither of us speaks very much French), we find the airport in Marseille in time for my husband's flight. When I turn the car toward the parking lot, my husband surprises me by saying, "Don't come in with me. *Please.* I want to watch you go." I nod, and for a long moment we hold each other close, breathing in our mingled smells.

I'm glad for the distraction of the drive back to Montpellier, for the worry that I'll make the wrong turn off from A-9 and get lost in some small French town, missing my 10 a.m. class. Instead, I stay on course. And yet once I arrive at the university, all my feelings of guilt and fear come crashing in: I've sent my husband away. I've claimed time alone. Now I'm afraid. Afraid of losing my husband. Afraid of keeping him. Afraid of loneliness. Afraid of failing even at survival.

Sitting in the university coffee shop, I pull out *Fierce Attachments*, the book I'll be teaching in my Contemporary American Autobiography class, and I read the words of Vivian Gornick's feisty mother: "If you want to go sledding, you have to be prepared to carry the sled."

I stare into the gray winter sky, watching the rain drip through the poplars and splatter the window, smear the glass. I read the passage again and suddenly hear that tough, peasant woman speaking directly to me. "Yeah, *you*. Who did you think I was talking to?" I laugh out loud, understanding in a single instant what I've hidden from myself. I've always been afraid of carrying the sled, of setting the agenda and suffering the consequences, both the certain disasters and the sudden thrills. I was afraid, I knew, of my own desires; fearful of the dark, rainy night. I've come to France, where I can't speak the language to uncover this very thing: a voice that says, "I want."

That evening I watch the rough push of two surfers swimming in the sea. They seem wildly carefree, adventurous, though I see how closely they watch the waves, how nimble and practiced they are as they hug their boards, then rise in one fluid motion, black-suited gods riding the angry sea. When I walk out onto the jetty, I stand alone on the rocks, the wind tearing at my clothes and hair, sending a fine spray of water toward my face. Impulsively, I open my arms to the sea. A silly gesture, but why not?

2

But what have I told you? What am I getting at?

You may think I wrote only to elicit a difficult moment in marriage, a conflict with ambition and the coming to voice in the middle of my life. Though it's true I did, what provoked me was also a concern about sequence, the belief that emotion is conveyed through sequence and that sequence is the primary building block of narrative. The sequence I wanted to explore was the familiar story of separation and change, a progression from fear to desire, from "I'm afraid" to "I want." Or as Carol

Gilligan in *The Birth of Pleasure*: *A New Map of Love* might have articulated this in an "I poem"

I wondered what would happen to love
I persisted.
I stayed on course
Now I was afraid
I read.
I laughed.
I understood what I'd hidden from myself.
"I want."
I opened my arms.

I wrote this sequence immediately after reading *The Birth of Pleasure*, writing the first part quickly, unselfconsciously, a journal entry meant only for myself. Later, after I'd met Carol Gilligan in New York, I wanted to write about narrative pleasure, how *The Birth of Pleasure* is an aesthetic experience, a garland of stories woven together in rhythmic sequence. And yet once I began writing, what pulled me close was this: the instinctive belief that this book had acted as a conversion narrative: for a single instance, I saw clearly the story I had lived.

Could I, as a reader, use *The Birth of Pleasure* to understand the fundamental changes in my life during a five-month period in France? If the main focus of this complex book is an understanding of the cultural taboo against seeing and speaking what one intuitively knows and the dissociation that often results from such an injunction, why not apply what I'd learned to myself? Why not reveal the goods, tell the tale, delve into what the book implies: the threshold of memory is both sinkhole and salvation, where you alone must take the temperature of that underground water.

3

Two days after my husband leaves Marseille, I lie sprawled across the lumpy, low-slung bed, reading a book. I pull at thin, flimsy sheets and then snatch up the blankets, never once losing my place in the book. It's as if I'm floating on an island in a protective bubble, the wind roaring, waves crashing against the jetty, the sun fleeting and warm. I get up only to go to the bathroom, to make toast and tea, to stand for long minutes at the wide windows, mesmerized by the sea before I sink back into bed, into my book. I don't want to be anywhere else, to do anything else, to be anyone else.

The next evening I walk by the sea, watching the white-foamed waves slap against the rocks, waiting for the lights to blink on in Le Grande

Motte (the Big Clump, I call it) ten miles away. Above me, the sky is oyster white. It looks wrapped in gauze. Sand covers my ankles, coats between my toes. Gulls spiral overhead. "Hellloooo," I yell to my husband as if he might hear me across the ocean, and simultaneously my body relaxes, becomes elemental, vital. I stare at the rolling motion of the sea, flooded with a sudden happiness that I am here.

The moment comes unbidden. Why must pleasure be so ephemeral?

As I climb out onto one of the jetties, fitting my feet into the dry pockets between rocks, I remember reading in Isaiah Berlin that members of the pietist movement in eighteenth-century Germany believed that if you couldn't obtain from the world what you truly desired, then you had to teach yourself not to have those desires.

Teach yourself.

Not to want.

I stand absolutely still.

4

That evening, opening the doors of my apartment to let the sea breeze flood my room, I remember the first time my husband took me camping, how we woke on a beach in northern California and I ran into that pulsing surf. I was twenty-nine years old and had never been camping, had grown up believing it was "slumming." And yet I loved it. Every bit of it: the coziness of the tent, the simplicity of cooking everything in one pot, the sense of lingering, loafing, losing the day to watching the leaves shiver in the aspens or reading William Goyen while waiting for my bathing suit to dry. I felt as if I'd been liberated from a protocol I hadn't even known I'd subscribed to. And yet my delight was one more defection; the break in relationship with my family was a class break, a rupture over how I'd situate myself in terms of money and power. On this issue, my husband's break with his family was mysterious to me still—foster families, an alcoholic stepfather, a depressed mother, a past he refused to talk much about.

During girlhood, I'd felt enmeshed in my family's desire for power, our giddy need to propel ourselves up the economic ladder, to rush, rush, rush into significance, a doorway to beauty. And yet secretly, I was afraid. I didn't know if I could.

Then in my late twenties, I turned haughtily away, living with my husband in neither an apartment nor a studio, but in raw space—the shock of gray cement walls and concrete floors, bare bulbs dangling from twenty-foot ceilings, rectangular work tables dividing the room—attached to a real estate office. It was perfect for us, complete with shower stall, refrigerator, hotplate, and then a bathroom to be shared with the realtor and his wife as daytime neighbors. Two doors to lock before you pee.

Almost every evening, the realtor, Carl, knocked on our door, then poked his head in, cocktail in hand. "What are you two *playing* at today?" he'd ask, mocking this frivolous need to "discover yourself" in art and writing while the business of America was so clearly money and success and ownership, revving up the GNP. I might be on the floor with dyes and paints or hot wax and an iron, working designs into cloth or sitting at a table writing a poem that would be reassembled into a collage.

"Don't bitch, Carl. We're giving you credibility," my husband would say. "Every time you cheat all those Hispanics, you can think of us and know someone's doing something worthwhile."

"Right," Carl winked.

One night when Carl had gone home, we put David Bowie on the stereo and climbed ladders to hang a trapeze from the ceiling, a single shiny bar that glittered in the darkness, sleek, silver, seductive, our secret transport to another world. While "Ground Control to Major Tooooommmm," swelled in the background, we turned off the lights and threw open the double garage doors, letting the summer air float in, the smell of jasmine and lentil, eucalyptus and garlic, the shiver of wind in the palms, the rattle of engines in the distance. In the sky, stars receded into that blanket of blackness, the moon hung low, full, and ripe. At midnight, I climbed up on the trapeze and began my first flight to nowhere, my body swinging wide, then wider, swinging from the back of the studio, up and up, and out into darkness, the velvet thrill of flying.

Of course, we cobbled together jobs to pay the rent, working odd hours in offices and in the studio, which left most nights free to write or draw or paint. And because our lives were dedicated to creative work, the loss of time and sleep seemed a necessary sacrifice, the scattered meals and broken engagements an inevitable compromise. Some days we ate greasy fried chicken and mashed potatoes at 11 p.m. from The Lion's Den, cooked vegetables and rice on a hotplate for lunch. Or, at least, one of us did. Often, we ate alone, slept alone, one person working all night to finish a project. For a long time we were happy in the cocoon of ourselves, and yet as the years piled up, we traded the sensual relief of hours snatched free from art, hours of languor, silliness, romance for the inevitable need to produce more and more. Art, it turned out, was hungry, demanding, an insatiable monster. And yet we kept at it, dutiful, diligent, feeding the beast.

It never occurred to me to complain. How could I when I'd believed so ardently in the strategy?

When I drape clean, wet socks over the balcony railing to dry in the hot Mediterranean sun, I see how pleasant this simple task is. I love the sun on my hands, the wind in my hair, the sly usefulness of a task. Below me I watch a mother and two daughters walking toward the jetty, all three holding hands, the older daughter tightening her rust-colored sweater around her thin body, the younger darting off to find shells and bottle caps in the sand, then coming back and grabbing hold, fitting herself back into the female chain. Watching them, I long to be one of those girls walking on the beach. And it comes to me in a great gust of sadness that what I most resented in adolescence wasn't the climb up the economic and social ladder but the loss of intimacy such a climb required: my daddy working late at the hospital, my brother training for athletics, my mother, sister, and I rushing along the empty highways to a city for music lessons, dancing lessons, writing lessons, eating hamburgers in the back seat of the car.

And yet as I stare out into the blue-green sea, I'm stunned by the revelation that my husband and I unconsciously repeated this legacy, only changing the form. I remember nights when I felt sensual, tired, but not yet exhausted, my body ready to break all the rules. "Come to bed!" I'd call to my husband in the next room even though I knew he'd just started a painting. He didn't answer, and when I came to get him, he seemed distracted, contained, a smudge of yellow on his arm. He didn't even glance at my pouting face. I knew the rules: King Art trumps everything else. It was just as likely that I was the unavailable one, staying too long at dinner with a friend, critiquing an essay or a story or a collage, and missing the movie I'd promised him we'd watch.

I always thought writing and art-making would be enough, but little by little, creative work began to embody the duty-bound ambition of my family. It became a day job as well as a night job, full of deadlines and doubts and blurred loyalties. Oh, there were still nights of immersion, days of pleasure in the refinement of color and line and the quiet wonder of syntax. And yet, in time, something inside me felt empty. Hollow. And then one morning in late summer I stood in the back garden, unable to write, a clutch of lilacs in my hand. I knew I should go back inside and force myself to work, but my body said no. No to work over pleasure. No to duty and demands. Who cared about creativity if it starved the muscles of the soul? It was intimacy I wanted. A hot bolt of pleasure.

Now I sink to the floor of the balcony, the wind tossing my hair. I came to France to tell myself this: I am lonely. A simple, uncomplicated statement. *Lonely*.

5

And what is loneliness but a retreat, a distortion of desire? What was my loneliness but a new self hungry for pleasure? And what is pleasure? a little girl asks her mother. And how do you know what to want?

6

That night I sit at the kitchen table with my notebook. It's a dark, windless night, a night when the sound of a spoon dropping, clattering to the floor, echoes through the building. I write these words: *THINGS NOT TO WANT*: *Power*, *Money*, *Pleasure*. For twenty years such thinking held me in its grasp.

Art and writing were the only ways I knew to gain mastery, to achieve self-respect. And yet respect slipped and swayed, bounced and swirled, sometimes embracing me with flippant pride, sometimes swinging far beyond my reach. God knows respect can't be hammered into place, can't be grabbed and clasped, the marrow sucked from its bones. Like the moon, respect waxes and wanes.

I leave the table and step out into the chilly night air. The sea sleeps, a stillness interrupted only by an occasional restless wave turning over against the rocks. As I look into that blackness, I know that respect is necessary, and yet I also know it's not enough. Even as I think this, I knock three socks off the railing and watch as they drift—stiff little scraps of white—to the ground.

7

And what is pleasure? the little girl asks her mother.

> The story beneath the story is always messy, a dark, disorderly ride.
> The story beneath the story is full of switchbacks, detours, diversions.

The story beneath the story rolls back to my mother, a woman who (because of her own difficult childhood) believed a contradiction so spectacular I envied Sisyphus his push up the hill. More than anything my mother believed two things: you *must* succeed, and you *must* sacrifice everything for others—ambition and denial, the twin engines of your life. "There's no reason to be a failure," she whispered to me in the hall one afternoon as we carried stacks of clean towels toward the bathrooms. I had been worrying about a new and demanding job I'd just accepted.

From my knowledge of my mother's history in a small mining town in northern Alabama, I learned late in life that her dreams of success were tied to rage and the wild hope for immunity, a yearning for affirmation and reprieve on a grand scale. But the story that lies behind that yearning is terrifying, anguished, a fatal seed of destruction: a young girl trapped, raped by a brother, left bewildered, frightened, inconsolable, silent. Silent about rape. Silent about terror. And in the end, it's the silence that destroys, a silence that lifts its blunt head and instills terror of the body, of pleasure, of ever, ever letting down your guard. If you relax, you might invite harm, defilement, loss of control, and when pleasure beckons, your mind cramps, flinches, turns quickly away. *You must not!* For what is pleasure but the body released, unrehearsed, unburdened? *You must not!* You must not listen to the body, for the body might soar with rage, revenge, desire, pleasure at the touch of skin against skin. *You must not* . . . and you learn not to want, not to listen, not to follow instincts, clues, intuitions, visions. You look only outward for signs of approval and dismissal, for the nod, the slap, the beckoning hand.

Trauma held my mother's hand. Terror slipped its arm around her waist.

And then she forgot that they were there.

She went to sleep. I slept alongside her, nestled close.

And like little girls lost in the forest, we forgot that the way out must be invented, created. The birds have eaten the bread crumbs. Night is cold. Even the trees can lie.

And so it begins anew with each generation: A forest. A lost girl. Her decision to find her way out. To survive.

8

It's late April, and the Mediterranean is cold. The slap of waves makes my nipples hard, my arms chill-bumpy, my knees shaky. A shiver runs through me, and then I dive beneath the waves and lie submerged, safe. I grew up eight miles from the Gulf of Mexico, where I learned to be careful, to be afraid of sharks, barracuda, eels, and stinging jellyfish. Here, I feel brave. When I break the surface and begin to swim beneath a midday sun, there's a loud thrill of joy. Two boys swim far out past the jetty, racing each other, their heads tucked into the water, their arms moving in long, graceful strokes. Little kids splash in the shallow water. I do a surface dive, spreading out like a starfish on the bottom of the sea, arms fluttering, legs splayed, hair swirling in one tangled mass. I stay there as long as I can, then shoot up into the air for breath. There is no reason to ever leave. I swim out toward the jetty, feeling bold and beautiful.

9

In my small village of Carnon, I like sleeping alone, my body curled into the pillows, the windows open, a rapture of ocean wind. I push the table back, hide the ugly purple lamp with its ugly cone shade, then dance wildly to Imani Coppola in my living room. I go to anti-war marches and protests against the American invasion of Iraq because I'm against this war, but I also go because I need to be consoled, to be part of something larger than myself, some passion that speaks its name. I spend hours in the pale light of afternoon talking to female students about writing, to colleagues about the distortion of American–French relations, and some nights on the phone to my husband, who has been sitting in peace vigils in snowbound Iowa. We talk easily as long as the conversation circles around politics and dissent.

And then suddenly it's late April, and he's coming for a visit. I buy plants, a new tablecloth, sheets, a sexy tank top. I'm nervous about what will happen. I don't know what I'll feel, though I sense that I've changed, become more self-reliant, more playful, more attuned to solitude. At first we're careful, falling into the groove of habit: making dinner together, laughing about the horrors of his flight, telling stories about our lives in different continents. I think about what I want: intimate talk, sex, laughter, not work, ambition, deadlines. It's the body that directs me now, the body that says, "I'm alive," and to my delight, we make love with a passion that's supple and new, though there's a lingering shyness, a cautious rib of restraint.

One morning during our first week together, my husband sleeps late while I'm on the phone to the travel agent, trying to find a solution to complications in an upcoming trip to the United Kingdom. As I talk I'm aware that I've become more demanding, more inquisitive, that my voice in France is firm, insistent, and when my husband comes into the room, I feel stripped clean of caution, no longer afraid of rejection. Though often sexually shy, I drop the phone and push him toward the balcony where the sun sends down its warm mercy. How dizzying to make love outside and then to lie lazy and naked in the sun.

And this is what it means to want.

A week later something else begins to change, some collapsing of the old boundaries between us. It's late at night, and we've just returned from a trip to London and Paris. Now we're curled around each other, entangled like seaweed. The sea wind roars through the open doors, and we hold each other close as we talk quietly about our childhoods, the secret life of growing up. "Don't forget you're sleeping next to one of the great frog hunters," my husband whispers. "I used to stop by the pond before school and squat down just to check on the bullfrogs. Twenty minutes later, I was knee deep in water, and—what the hell—it was pointless to go to school."

"Already a delinquent," I tease, snuggling closer.

"Yeah, but I had my duties to the frogs in Sturbridge Village. I was living with John and Adeline."

"Your foster parents?" I know bits and pieces about this foster family, who, ironically, have the same first names as my parents. Often when I've asked about his early childhood, he's turned away, closing that door.

"Yeah, I don't even know how long I lived with them," he says, "which seems strange, but I think I lived somewhere else first, with another family, as a little kid. Then my mother came to get me when I was eight."

A gust of wind billows the curtains, and in our silence I listen to the pounding of the waves. I think about how little I know about his past, how I've assumed his mother was a kind of octopus-mother, cloying and demanding, reaching out to grab little parts of him. Back in Iowa I sometimes felt he wanted to grab little parts of me. But he also stood aside when I wanted to come to France even though he believed I was leaving him. Feeling his arms around me now, I know it took courage for him to come here, thinking as he did that I might be vanishing from his life.

"In Sturbridge I always had my secret place in the woods," he continues, and for the first time I hear something like yearning in his voice, "little ponds where the ice formed on the water, but I could see movement beneath the ice, fish swimming in slow, darting zigzags."

"I used to go out on this old rotting pier in Magnolia Springs," I tell him. "I could sit at the edge and stare into the deepest part of the river where the water was dark, almost blue-black. We called it 'Devil's Hole.'"

We talk about solitude, and I tell him about the thrill of walking out onto the jetties, the waves smashing the rocks, the beach empty, just me standing there as if I'm the only person in the world.

"I loved being alone in the woods around Sturbridge," he says, "but then my mother married and came to get me, taking me back to the city."

My mind slows. His mother retrieved him at age eight, the very age I felt abandoned by my mother. Until I was eight, I'd been my mother's shadow, a demanding child who insisted on a purple cowgirl suit, a red taffeta slip with ruffles around the hem, a child who wanted a place right next to my mother, close to her skin. Then when I turned eight, everything shifted: we moved to a new town; my mother went back to work; my father started drinking.

"I remember being so excited to be with my real mother," he whispers, and I'm surprised he's telling me this. "She took me back to Worcester, but there was something not quite right. I didn't understand it as a kid. She was, I see now, ambivalent about me. . . . I mean, I was the kid she wasn't supposed to have, so . . . well, I acted out and so did she."

An ambivalent mother. A mind-changing phrase.

As I listen tonight the symmetry between us falls quietly into place: two eight-year-old kids who drifted out to sea; two adults scrambling to find their way back to shore.

10

"But where's the Eighth Wonder of the World?" my husband asks the day before he leaves for America.

I laugh. He's referring to the large purple lamp with its ugly three-foot cone shade that once sat proudly on an end table and dominated the room. Surely purchased by the previous owner during an acid trip. "Yeah. I messed up. I had to put that away."

I open the closet so he can witness the Eighth Wonder of the World, which now takes up an entire side of that walk-in space.

"You gotta be careful what you throw away," he says, giving me a sideways glance.

"I'm a careful girl," I say and squeeze his hand.

In many ways, the plot ends here: a woman pulls away, leaps across an ocean to take her own measure, to listen to her instincts and hungers; only then can she circle back, understanding that pleasure is an attitude, a perspective, a new way of seeing the self in the story.

11

But of course the story and the plot are never quite the same.

I press my body against the story—a girl turning away from the gods of her family—and what I feel isn't freedom but a terrible loss, a stone weight in my chest, the emptiness of scattered leaves. In the story there is no final goodbye, no epiphany of release, no girl standing at the prow of a boat waving to those on shore, but a slow, anxious shift in another direction. In the story, doubt folds into the pleats of every decision. *How do I know what I know?* the body asks. *What voice inside me is really speaking?* The body knows there are many voices, ventriloquists competing for performance, scoundrels, beggars, victims, voyeurs, heroes, heroines, saints, sadists. The body knows that listening is a complex act. If only there was an elevator to get me *fast* down to the bottom of myself. Instead, I take the stairs slowly, one by one, from the sixth floor.

12

From my window, I watch the storm purge the land. Waves flirt with the rocks, white tongues of foam feeding the air. The wind moans. Shutters bang against the windows. Seagulls fly diagonally, so close to the windows I believe I could touch their white breasts if I tried. I sit cross-legged in front of all that energy and watch. I'd like to tell my husband about the single figure I see, hunched over, bent into the wind, walking down the beach, but my husband won't call for another six hours. For now, I'm alone again. Watching. Though it is near dark, I will put on extra clothes and a slicker and scramble onto the jetty.

I open the door and listen to the shout of the sea. And then I run down the stairs.

Singing the voice erotic, a world-renowned voice teacher lays bare the basic instincts—an anatomy—of theatrical performance as a verbal art. Here, as in the essays by Toni Morrison, Carmen Gillespie, and Robin D. G. Kelley, suppression of voice is associated with suppression of sexual desire. And here, as in the essays by Tomasello and Edward Tronick, the body is understood to be wired for relationship and pleasure. Most importantly, here is a full-throated cry of joy.

Vox Erotica[1]

KRISTIN LINKLATER[2]

The voice is inherently an erotic organ. The sensation of voice is part of the totalized, suspended Eros of childhood—what Sigmund Freud referred to as the polymorphous perverse world of childhood, on whose delights we slam the door as adults. Children, the object of their own love, explore indiscriminately the erotic potential of the whole body, and that erotic potential extends to the inner organs of the body and is in no way limited to the genitals. As adulthood teaches us to draw our energies up out of our bodies and to concentrate them in reasonable and rational thinking in the brain (which lives in the head), the pleasure principle is subdued to the reality principle, and polymorphous perversity becomes buried libido. Thought and speech become the servants of reason and fact, and the voice that expresses such thoughts loses, in adulthood, its map of the neuro-physiological circuitry that connects the voice with the sensuality of the body. When the connecting door between voice and auto-eroticism is shuttered, communication through mere language becomes dry, hollow, authoritatively vociferous, or shrill to the point where a larger erotic possibility shrivels and dies. Deliberately misused, the human voice could well be developed as a tool in aversion therapy for sex addicts.

We often toy with the word "play" as a central element of theater, and we often devise games that will bring us back, as actors, to a childlike state where the imagination has no critic to restrain it, where instinct and intuition are uncontaminated by the fear of judgment. Creativity grows best in the garden of innocence; we have to invent the means to give us back the freedom we lost when we left childhood behind. The voice must also be offered liberation from the prohibitions of society: "Learn to speak nicely"; "Don't shout at me"; "You're too loud, too noisy, too full of yourself and your ideas"; "Shut up!" If the actor is to be true to Oedipus, Medea, Cleopatra, Leontes, King Lear, or Queen Margaret, his or her voice must be unlimited by societal niceties, psychological inhibition, or emotional fear. The actor's voice must run, ripple, and pour through the sensory, sensual, emotional, and yes, erotic pathways of the body if it is to pick up and reveal the rush and nuance of a character's inner states of being.

On a daily basis in my classes, I tend to use the word "sensual" rather than "erotic" to describe the pleasure that may be experienced when the vibrations of the voice travel naturally through bone and cartilage and flesh. When these sound vibrations reach the appetite centers, it may be hard to draw distinctions between food, sex, and thrilling sound. There is, of course, currently a cultural conditioning that makes "sensuality" more acceptable than "eroticism" in pedagogical practice. Meanwhile, little differentiation is made these days between eroticism and sexuality, and sex has become a frightening subject except in advertising, stand-up comedy, and sitcoms. But Voice, Sex, and Pleasure are designed by Nature to be unified, so we, as actors, have to be intrepid vocal adventurers. We must confront Eros if we are to fulfill our creative destiny.

Here's the lovely and accurate anatomical picture I'd like you to entertain: the breathing musculature laces itself down the silky billowings of the diaphragm to be woven into the webbing of the pelvic floor along with the muscles and nerves of its genital neighbors. When the impulse to speak sparks, the interaction between breath and vocal folds creates vibrations of sound. Those vibrations are palpable throughout the body from the pelvis to the crown of the head (and can often be felt right down to the soles of the feet).

One must applaud Nature's innate sense of humor for giving both men and women vocal anatomy that is almost indistinguishable from female genitalia. Look at a video of the vocal folds in action, male and female—though, actually, I don't recommend looking at such a video unless you're pornographically inclined—and you might just as well be looking at the vagina. In other words, both men and women have tiny vaginas in their throats. Those humorous ancient Roman anatomists, doctors, or philosophers who gave Latin names to different parts of the human body labeled a certain area of the female genitalia *labia*, meaning "lips." I assume they saw a connection with speech. If we play fast and loose with etymology, we could conflate the Sanskrit *lingam* ("phallus") and the Latin *lingua* ("tongue") to speculate that women as well as men possess penises by virtue of having tongues.

As a voice teacher I allow myself an imaginative annual trip through the evolution of language. I look at the thousands of years of animal-roar communication that must have been necessary for survival among early humans (i.e., voice, before speech). A roar is rooted in appetite centers: a hunger for food and a hunger to propagate the species (though for many thousands of years, no connection was made between sexual activity and paternity). These appetite centers are both located deep down in the lower belly area. One can imagine undifferentiated roars signifying the desire for food or sex, causing chaos in early tribal communities over millennia until some quantum leap of consciousness articulated those roars into specifics: "Can we have saber-toothed tiger steak for dinner?" versus "How about a little nookie?" The instruments of speech that accomplished this astonishing evolutionary development—the lips, the tongue, the teeth—were originally deployed in appetite-related activities such as sucking, licking, biting, chewing, and early versions of kissing and were thus directly connected to the activities of the lower belly area. Speech, for contemporary, civilized, technologized humans, is more likely to be experienced as cerebral and utilitarian than erotic.

Autoeroticism is one of the great, unadvertised joys of voice work. By this I obviously mean autoeroticism of a polymorphous perverse nature, not limited by genital organization. Everyday speaking has the potential to be endlessly erotic. The organs of speech *could* be experientially connected with the sensuality of the body through the vibrations of the voice. Throughout the day we *could* be experiencing sexual titillation, if not sheer orgasmic delight, then just by dint of speaking. We could, by waving a psychophysical wand, become polymorphous perverse again in an instant.

We could blame the early Christians (for separating sex from the soul) or the Puritans (for forbidding the joy of secular singing except on Sundays in praise of God) or Descartes (for saying, "I think, therefore I am," rather than, "I am, therefore I think"); we could blame any one of them for denying us the erotic pleasures of the voice. But we are also left with some incontrovertible, anatomical facts that are ours to enjoy experientially and imaginatively if we choose. One of those facts is the internal weave that connects the solar plexus to the sacrum (the emotional center to the instinctive center) through breath. While this weave may be experienced vividly in the throes of sex, we seldom allow the same vivid connection in our daily chat. Of course, this excitement might not be appropriate for most of our verbal intercourse, but it is more appropriate, perhaps, than we might initially think.

What does this psychophysical situation imply for the actor? It implies that there is an enormous subliminal power available to arouse and disturb audiences on a bewildering level, and it occurs seismically, deep underneath the words being spoken. And it implies that the actor can gain access to erotic imagery only revealed to the ardent vocal explorer. Near the end of Cleopatra's story in William Shakespeare's *Antony and Cleopatra* (1623), for example, with Antony already dead and the inexorable humiliation of defeat looming, ready to die rather than submit, Cleopatra conjures up the image of Antony for Dolabella, the Roman who has been sent to guard her:

I dream'd there was an emperor Antony (5.2.93).[3]

Allow the imagery to travel down through the vibrations of vocal sound to the erotic–sensual centers of the body, and Antony becomes startlingly present:

His face was as the heavens; and therein stuck
A sun and moon, which kept their course, and lighted
The little O, the earth (5.2.97−9).

We know the double meaning of "O" to be "vagina"; we know that "the course" very often means sexual intercourse. The image that emerges is of Cleopatra and Antony making love—she is the earth, and he shines above her:

His legs bestrid the ocean [she is the ocean]: his rear'd arm [his erection]
Crested the world [Cleopatra]: his voice was propertied
As all the tuned spheres [the eroticism of voice], and that to friends [when he was being gentle];
But when he meant to quail and shake the orb [rouse Cleopatra to orgasmic excitement]
He was as rattling thunder. For his bounty
There was no winter in't; an autumn 'twas
That grew the more by reaping [They could make love all night, and each time he climaxed, he was ready for more]: his delights
Were dolphin-like [Dolphins are known for their polymorphous and ceaseless sexual proclivities]; they showed his back above
The element they liv'd in [What an enchanting description of love-making! She is his essential "element"] (5.2.102−09).

Only program notes or horrendously bad acting would explicate this to the audience. This is secret knowledge for the actor, not to be explicated. What do these secrets give the actor? Among a number of possibilities, there is the idea that, as Cleopatra arouses in herself the visceral, sensual, erotic memory of making love with Antony, she is making a last, desperate attempt to save her life through the seduction of Dolabella. This is not so much interpretation as divination, to be given weight or discarded as the demands of character, concept, and directorial choice dictate.

My point is that we evade the power of Shakespeare if we take refuge in metaphor rather than plunge fearlessly into the erotic vortex of his imagery: "What I am and what I would are as secret ['sacred' in some editions] as maidenhead," says Viola to Olivia in *Twelfth Night*, "to your ears divinity, to any other's profanation" (1.5.199−201). Viola is disguised as a boy, using her wiles as a woman, whispering into Olivia's ear; this is irresistible! "Give us the place alone," says the love-starved Olivia (1.5.202).

And thus later, Viola, bearing messages of love from Orsino to Olivia, to whom she pours her heart out, is aroused to poetic heights by her own impossible passion for Orsino, saying that if *she* loved Olivia, she would

> Make me a willow [the sorrowful symbol of unrequited love]
> cabin at your gate [the entrance to love]
> And call upon my soul within the house [the soul of the lover lives
> in her body];
> Write loyal cantons of contemned love,
> And sing them loud even in the dead of night;
> Halloo your name to the reverberate hills,
> And make the babbling gossip of the air
> Cry out "Olivia." (1.5.251–7)

Olivia is lost: seduced by voice.

Shakespeare splits open the safe ground of our mental foundations to expose the tremors and quakes of ever-present and superpotent eroticism in his words: to survive, we actors must screw our voices to the sticking place and have the courage in our utterance to let fly the arrows of Eros to crack and remold the mirrors we hold up to the underbelly of today.

The *vox erotica* does not simply serve the god of love. Every major passion engages the deep musculature of the pelvic floor and the primal instinctual nerve endings surrounding the sacrum. Hate, murderous rage, jealousy, and grief are not separated by some *cordon sanitaire* from the erotic. There is erotic energy in such lines as "Cry 'Havoc' and let slip the dogs of war" (*Julius Caesar*, 3.1.293) and in "God for Harry, England and Saint George!" (*Henry V*, 3.1.31) and in "I will chop her into messes" (*Othello*, 4.1.214) and in "Were my wife's liver/Infected as her life she would not live/The running of one glass" (*The Winter's Tale*, 1.2.357−9) and in Constance's lamentation in *King John*, "Death, death. O amiable lovely death!/Thou odouriferous stench! Sound rottenness!" (3.4.26−7) and later, "Grief fills the room up of my absent child/Lies in his bed, walks up and down with me." (3.4.96−7).

Moreover, the erotic energy of the voice is not limited to the works in classical repertoire. Where does *vox erotica* live in today's theater? In a time when irony and the flat reportorial tone are fashionable, there may be scant exercise for these classical connections. But surely the actor who plays Weston in Sam Shepard's *Curse of the Starving Class* (1976) must be plugging deep into his autoerotic, childhood richness when he says,

> I'll kill him! If I have to, I'll kill myself along with him. I'll crash into him. I'll crash the Packard right into him. What's he look like? WHAT'S HE LOOK LIKE? I'll find him. Then I'll find that punk who sold me that phony desert land. I'll track them all down. Every last one of them. Your mother too. I'll track her down and shoot them in their bed. In their hotel bed. I'll splatter their brains all over the vibrating bed. I'll drag him into the lobby and slit his throat. I was in the war. I know how to kill. I was over there. I know how to do it I've done it before. It's no big deal. You just make an adjustment. You convince yourself it's all right. That's all. It's easy. You just slaughter them. Easy. HE'S WITH MY WIFE! THAT'S ILLEGAL! (38)

Here Eros surely grapples with Dionysus, the god of tragedy and comedy, "the chorus-master of the fire-breathing stars"—as the philosopher Martha C. Nussbaum describes Dionysus in *The Fragility of Goodness*—"who links risk with value" and brings healing in a harmony that "is not simplicity but the tension between distinct and separate beauties" (1986, 82). The *vox erotica* is the instrument that guides us to the larger Self that lurks inside us, yearning to break free from the shackles of conformity, correctness, and the judgment of an imagined, hostile world.

Notes

1 This article previously appeared as "Vox Eroticus" in *American Theatre Magazine* (April 2003).

2 The author would like to acknowledge poet Richard Howard for inspiration on the subject of polymorphous perversity in his Columbia University lectures on the origins of modernism.

3 References are to act, scene, and line.

References

NUSSBAUM, Martha C. 1986. *The Fragility of Goodness: Luck and Ethics in Greek Tragedy and Philosophy*. Cambridge: Cambridge University Press.

SHEPARD, Sam. 1976. *Curse of the Starving Class*. New York: Dramatist's Play Service.

Anthony G. Amsterdam is a Professor of Law at New York University. He is also a litigator and consultant in public-interest cases involving issues of constitutional, criminal, and civil rights law. His publications include *Minding the Law* with Jerome Bruner (2000).

Terri Apter is a Fellow and Senior Tutor at Newnham College, Cambridge. Her books include *The Sister Knot: Why We Fight, Why We're Jealous, and Why We'll Love Each Other No Matter What* (2007), *The Confident Child: Raising Children to Believe in Themselves* (1997) (winner of the Delta Kappa Gamma International Educator's Award), and *Altered Loves: Mothers and Daughters During Adolescence* (1990) (a New York Times notable book of the year).

Ruby Blondell is a Professor of Classics at the University of Washington, Seattle. She has published widely on Greek literature, philosophy, and the reception of myth in popular culture. Her books include *The Play of Character in Plato's Dialogues* (2002), *Women on the Edge: Four Plays by Euripides* (1999, translated), and *Helping Friends and Harming Enemies: A Study in Sophocles and Greek Ethics* (1989).

Eva Cantarella is a Professor of Roman Law and Ancient Greek Law in the Law School at the University of Milano, Italy. Among her works available in English are *Pandora's Daughters: The Role and Status of Women in Greek and Roman Antiquity* (1987), *Bisexuality in the Ancient World* (1992), "Gender, Sexuality, and Law" in *Cambridge Companion to Greek Law* (2005), and *Images of Greek Pederastry: Boys Were Their Gods* (2008) (with Andrew Lear).

Lizzy Cooper Davis is a doctoral candidate in African and African–American Studies at Harvard University with a focus on Anthropology. Her interests include the anthropology of race, black Atlantic performance and spiritual traditions, and the role of the arts in social movements.

Peggy Cooper Davis is the John S. R. Shad Professor of Lawyering and Ethics at the New York University School of Law and the author of *Neglected Stories: The Constitution and Family Values* (1997).

PATRICIA FOSTER is a Professor in the Masters of Fine Arts Program in Nonfiction at the University of Iowa. She is the author of *All the Lost Girls: Confessions of a Southern Daughter* (2000, a memoir) and *Just Beneath My Skin: Autobiography and Self-Discovery* (2004, essays) and editor of *Minding the Body: Women Writers on Body and Soul* (1994) and *Sister to Sister* (1996). Eight of her essays have been chosen as notable essays for the *Best American Essays* series (edited by Robert Atwan).

CARMEN R. GILLESPIE is a Professor of English and Creative Writing at Bucknell University. Her published books include *A Critical Companion to Toni Morrison* (2007), *A Critical Companion to Alice Walker* (2011), and a poetry chapbook, *Lining the Rails* (2008).

SIMON GOLDHILL is a Professor of Greek at Cambridge University, Fellow of King's College, and Director of the Cambridge Victorian Studies Group. His forthcoming book is on Victorian engagements with classical antiquity. His earlier publications include *Language, Sexuality, Narrative: The Oresteia* (2004), *Reading Greek Tragedy* (1986), *The Poet's Voice: Essays on Poetics and Greek Literature* (1990), and *Love, Sex & Tragedy: How the Ancient World Shapes Our Lives* (2005).

TOVA HARTMAN is a Professor of Gender Studies and Education at Bar Ilan University of Ramat Gan, as well as a founder of Shira Hadasha. Her published works include *Appropriately Subversive: Modern Mothers in Traditional Religions* (2003) and *Feminism Encounters Traditional Judaism: Resistance and Accommodation* (2008, winner of the National Jewish Book Award).

ROBIN D. G. KELLEY is a Professor of American Studies and Ethnicity at the University of Southern California. He is the author of *Hammer and Hoe: Alabama Communists During the Great Depression* (1990), *Race Rebels: Culture Politics and the Black Working Class* (1994), *Yo' Mama's DisFunktional!: Fighting the Culture Wars in Urban America* (1997), *Three Strikes: Miners, Musicians, Salesgirls* (2001), *The Fighting Spirit of Labor's Last Century* (2002, with Dana Frank and Howard Zinn); and *Freedom Dreams: The Black Radical Imagination* (2002).

KRISTIN LINKLATER is a Professor at Columbia University. She is the cofounder of Shakespeare & Company, with Tina Packer. She has received major grants from the Ford Foundation, the Rockefeller Foundation, the Mellon Foundation, and the National Endowment for the Arts. She is the author of *Freeing the Natural Voice: Imagery and Art in the Practice of Voice and Language* (2006) and *Freeing Shakespeare's Voice: The Actor's Guide to Talking the Text* (1993).

TONI MORRISON is the Pulitzer Prize-winning author of nine novels and six works of non-fiction. She is the Robert F. Goheen Professor in the Humanities, Emerita at Princeton University. In 1993, she was awarded the Nobel Prize for Literature.

TINA PACKER is the Artistic Director of Shakespeare & Company, which she cofounded with Kristin Linklater. She has directed forty-eight productions, including *Othello*, *King Lear*, *Macbeth*, the world premiere of *The Scarlet Letter* (by Carol Gilligan), *Coriolanus*, *Richard III*, *The Merchant of Venice*, *A Midsummer Night's Dream*, *Julius Caesar*, *The Merry Wives of Windsor*, *Henry IV* part I, the world premieres of *Summer* (adapted from Edith Wharton by Dennis Krausnick), and *The Fly-Bottle* (by David Egan). Her publications include *Power Plays*: *Shakespeares Lessons in Leadership & Management* (2000).

MIRIAM RAIDER-ROTH is an Associate Professor of Educational Studies at the University of Cinncinati. She is the author of *Trusting What You Know*: *The High Stakes of Classroom Relationships* (2005) and coeditor of *The Plough Woman*: *Records of the Pioneer Women of Palestine, A Critical Edition* (2002).

TERRENCE REAL is a senior faculty member of the Family Institute of Cambridge in Massachusetts. His works include *I Don't Want to Talk About It*: *Overcoming the Secret Legacy of Male Depression* (1998), *How Can I Get Through to You?*: *Reconnecting Men and Women* (2002), and most recently, *The New Rules of Marriage*: *What You Need to Make Love Work* (2007).

DAVID RICHARDS is the Edwin D. Webb Professor of Law at the New York University School of Law. His publications include *The Deepening Darkness*: *Patriarchy, Resistance, and Democracy's Future* (2009) (with Carol Gilligan); *The Sodomy Cases*: *Bowers v. Hardwick and Lawrence v. Texas* (2009), and *Women, Gays, and the Constitution*: *The Grounds for Feminism and Gay Rights in Culture and Law* (1998), and *Fundamentalism in American Religion and Law*: *Patriarchy as Threat to Democracy* (forthcoming).

WENDY STEINER is the Richard L. Fisher Professor of English, and Founding Director of the Penn Humanities Forum at the University of Pennsylvania. She is the author of various books on the contemporary arts, including *The Scandal of Pleasure*: *Art in an Age of Fundamentalism* (1995) and *Venus in Exile*: *The Rejection of Beauty in Twentieth-Century Art* (2001), and is librettist and producer of *The Loathly Lady*, an opera based on Chaucer's "Wife of Bath's Tale."

KENDALL THOMAS is the Nash Professor of Law at Columbia University Law School, as well as a cofounder and the Director of the Center for the Study of Law and Culture. His writings have appeared in several academic journals and volumes of collected essays. He is a coeditor of *Critical Race Theory: The Key Writings that Founded the Movement* (1996) and *What's Left of Theory?* (2000).

MICHAEL TOMASELLO is a codirector of the Max Planck Institute for Evolutionary Anthropology in Leipzig, Germany. His recent works include *Origins of Human Communication* (2008), *Constructing a Language: A Usage-Based Theory of Language Acquisition* (2003), and *Why We Cooperate* (2009).

EDWARD TRONICK is the Director of the Child Development Unit and an Associate Professor of Pediatrics and Psychiatry at the Boston Children's Hospital. He has coauthored and authored more than one hundred and fifty scientific papers and chapters. His most recent paper is entitled, "Why is Connection with Others so Critical? The Formation of Dyadic States of Consciousness: Coherence Governed Selection and the Co-creation of Meaning out of Messy Meaning-making."

NIOBE WAY is a Professor of Applied Psychology at New York University. Her work focuses on the intersections of culture, context, and human development, and she has written numerous books and articles on these topics. She is the author of *Deep Secrets: The Friendships of Adolescent Boys* (forthcoming).

KENJI YOSHINO is the inaugural Chief Justice Earl Warren Professor of Constitutional Law at the New York University School of Law. He is the author of *Covering: The Hidden Assault on our Civil Rights* (2006) and is currently working on a book tentatively titled *Justice In Shakespeare*.